PHILOSOPHY AND THE SCIENCES IN ANTIQUITY

There has been much discussion in scholarly literature of the applicability of the concept of 'science' as understood in contemporary English to ancient Greek thought, and of the influence of philosophy and the individual sciences on each other in antiquity. This book focuses on how the ancients themselves saw the issue of the relation between philosophy and the individual sciences. Contributions, from a distinguished international panel of scholars, cover the whole of antiquity from the beginnings of both philosophy and science to the later Roman Empire.

ASHGATE KEELING SERIES IN
ANCIENT PHILOSOPHY

The *Ashgate Keeling Series in Ancient Philosophy* presents edited collections of leading international research which illustrate and explore ways in which ancient and modern philosophy interact. Drawing on original papers presented at the S.V. Keeling Memorial Lectures and Colloquia at University College London, this series incorporates contributions from the Anglo-American philosophical tradition and from continental Europe, and brings together scholars internationally recognised for their work on ancient philosophy as well as those whose primary work in contemporary philosophy speaks of the importance of ancient philosophy in modern philosophical research and study. Each book in the series will appeal to upper-level and graduate students and academic researchers worldwide – both those who are interested in ancient philosophy and those who are working in the relevant areas of contemporary philosophy.

Philosophy and the Sciences in Antiquity

Edited by

R.W. SHARPLES
University College London, UK

Routledge
Taylor & Francis Group

LONDON AND NEW YORK

First published 2005 by Ashgate Publishing

Reissued 2019 by Routledge
2 Park Square, Milton Park, Abingdon, Oxon, OX14 4RN
52 Vanderbilt Avenue, New York, NY 10017

Routledge is an imprint of the Taylor & Francis Group, an informa business

Publisher's Note
The publisher has gone to great lengths to ensure the quality of this reprint but points out that some imperfections in the original copies may be apparent.

Disclaimer
The publisher has made every effort to trace copyright holders and welcomes correspondence from those they have been unable to contact.

A Library of Congress record exists under LC control number:

ISBN 13: 978-0-8153-9106-7 (hbk)
ISBN 13: 978-1-138-62016-2 (pbk)
ISBN 13: 978-1-351-15172-6 (ebk)

Contents

Preface

Stanley Victor Keeling was born in 1894 and was educated at University College London, Trinity College Cambridge, and the Universities of Toulouse and Montpellier. He was first Lecturer and then Reader in Philosophy at University College London; he retired in 1954 and lived in Paris until his death in 1979. His published works included an annotated edition of McTaggart's *Philosophical Studies* (London, 1934) and a book on *Descartes* (London, 1934; 2nd, revised ed., Oxford, 1968); in 1948 he gave the British Academy annual Master Mind lecture on Descartes (*Proceedings of the British Academy* 34 [1948] 57-80).[1]

Although Keeling's own published work was on more recent philosophy, he wrote of his desire to ensure that the study of Greek philosophy 'should assume in our university courses a position commensurate with its importance'. Accordingly, when in 1981 an annual Stanley Victor Keeling Memorial Lecture at University College London, on a topic from ancient Greek philosophy was founded by the generosity of an anonymous donor, it was felt appropriate that many, though not all, of the lectures should be given by scholars whose major published work has not been in this field, in order to show how study of the ancients related to their own work.[2]

The lectures were subsequently supplemented by a series of Colloquia funded by the same donor; here too one principle has been a concern with the relation to contemporary thought of ancient philosophy and its interpretation, and another has been the promotion of discussion between 'continental', especially French, and 'Anglo-Saxon' philosophical traditions on the common ground of ancient philosophical texts. The first colloquium, in 1994,[3] had as its theme the position of Aristotle in relation to contemporary debates concerning realism in ethics; the second, in 1998, interpretations of Aristotle from late antiquity to the nineteenth

---

[1] See the 'Biographical Sketch' by E. Senior, and the bibliography of Keeling's publications, in S.V. Keeling, *Time and Duration*, ed. G. Rochelle: Lewiston, Queenston and Lampeter, Edwin Mellon Press, 1992 (Problems in Contemporary Philosophy, vol.31).

[2] Nine of the first ten lectures have been published in R.W. Sharples, ed., *Modern Thinkers and Ancient Thinkers: The Stanley Victor Keeling Memorial Lectures 1981-1991*, London: UCL Press, 1993; and nine of the second ten in id., ed., *Perspectives on Greek Philosophy: S.V. Keeling Memorial Lectures in Ancient Philosophy 1992-2002*, Aldershot: Ashgate, 2003.

[3] Published in Robert Heinaman, ed., *Aristotle and Moral Realism*, London: UCL Press, 1995.

century;[4] the third, in 1999, was concerned with Descartes and ancient philosophy, and the fourth, in 2001, with the influence of Plato on the development of Aristotle's ethics.[5] The present volume contains the papers and one of the formal responses at the fifth colloquium, in 2003.

For assistance in organizing and running the Colloquium I would like to thank Amanda Cater and Alison Angel in the Department of Greek and Latin at UCL. For undertaking the publication of this volume and for assistance and advice in its preparation I would like to thank Paul Coulam and the other staff of Ashgate Publishing. Above all, however, thanks are due to the donor of the funds, without which this and the other Colloquia in the series would not have been possible.

Bob Sharples
Department of Greek and Latin,
University College London

---

[4] Published in R.W. Sharples, ed., *Whose Aristotle? Whose Aristotelianism?* Aldershot: Ashgate, 2001.

[5] Published in R. Heinaman, ed., *Plato and Aristotle's Ethics*, Aldershot: Ashgate, 2003.

List of Contributors

Philip J. van der Eijk is Professor of Greek in the University of Newcastle upon Tyne, England

R.J. Hankinson is Professor of Philosophy and Classics in the University of Texas at Austin, USA.

André Laks is Professor of Philosophy in the Université Charles-de-Gaulle, Lille III, France.

James G. Lennox is Professor and Director of the Center for Philosophy of Science, University of Pittsburgh, USA.

Sir Geoffrey Lloyd is Emeritus Professor of Ancient Philosophy and Science in the University of Cambridge, England.

Dominic J. O'Meara is Professor Ordinarius in the Department of Philosophy in the Université de Fribourg, Switzerland.

R.W. Sharples is Professor of Classics at University College London, England.

Anne Sheppard is Senior Lecturer in the Department of Classics, Royal Holloway, University of London, England.

Chapter One

Introduction: Philosophy and the Sciences in Antiquity

R.W. Sharples

The use of the modern English term 'science' in discussion of classical antiquity is problematic. That is so not only because of the problems in applying terms from one culture to another, especially when those cultures are separated by time as well as by space; it also reflects the fact that the modern term is itself problematic. It is used to denote both a particular type of intellectually rigorous enquiry – though philosophers of science disagree over exactly what this is – and also, in common usage, to denote certain areas of enquiry, on the basis that these are ones to which the scientific method is particularly appropriate. Some, indeed, have sought to argue that they are therefore the only areas of enquiry that are worth pursuing, or even the only ones about which meaningful assertions can be made; others, conversely, have extended the scope of the term 'science' by speaking, for example, of 'political science', an expression that may involve a certain degree of persuasive definition.

In other modern European languages the equivalents to 'science' have a wider use than they do in English: German can speak of theology as *Religionswissenschaft* and of the study of classical antiquity as *Altertumswissenschaft*, though in the latter case at least an element of persuasive definition in the advocating of a particular approach to antiquity cannot be ruled out; and British scholars evaluating research proposals in other countries will feel a slight jolt of unfamiliarity when asked about the 'scientific competence' of a specialist in, for example, Greek tragedy.

From the point of view of ancient Greek culture too it is the English usage that is the exception – though it needs to be emphasized at the outset both that negotiations within a culture on how terms are to be used are dynamic processes, like the development of that culture itself (see André Laks' paper in this volume), and that in speaking just of the aspects of 'ancient Greek culture' considered in the present volume, we are concerned with a period lasting roughly one millennium. The ancient word which we most naturally render by 'science', and which can be used in the plural to refer to the study of different specialist subject-matters (*epistêmê*, in the plural *epistêmai*), comes to have as its basic meaning – developed particularly by Plato and Aristotle, but reflecting trends apparent in the culture even earlier[1] – knowledge for which justification can be given; that is, claims that can be justified by appeal to some agreed or self-evident basis, and therefore claims that form part of some informal or (increasingly) formal *system*.[2] The first three of a set of Stoic definitions will serve both to illustrate this and, by its references to *virtue*, to highlight an aspect of the ancient philosophical approach which modern English readers may find surprising:

> *Epistêmê* is a secure and unchangeable grasping by reason; a second [sense of] *epistêmê* is a system of *epistêmai* of this sort, for example the rational *epistêmê* of particulars which is present in the good man; and a third, a system of technical *epistêmai* which has stability in itself, as the virtues do.[3]

Such 'scientific knowledge' is contrasted with mere experience, which may be as much (or more!) use in practice,[4] but cannot in itself provide a reasoned justification for its claims – which is not to say that empiricist, i.e. experience-based,[5] epistemologies were not developed, or even that the question whether Aristotle himself is an empiricist is one that admits of an easy, or a simply negative, answer. Nor was such 'scientific knowledge' confined to what contemporary English would regard as the most obvious examples of 'the sciences'; for Aristotle the difference between ethics and (say) astronomy was one of degree in achievable rigour and precision, rather than a difference of kind.[6] This does not however mean that 'scientific' method was not more normally associated with some subjects than with others. Proclus' project, in his *Elements of Theology*, of making theology into a deductive system of the same sort as the geometry set out in Euclid's *Elements* was indeed nothing more than an attempt to put into practice what statements by Plato and Aristotle suggest should be possible; but it remains somewhat extreme even in the ancient context. And, while in philosophical circles *epistêmê* was

---

[1]   The crucial rôle in the development of ancient Greek philosophy and science of the demand for *justification* of positions in debate has been shown above all by Lloyd (1979).
[2]   On the whole question of the foundations of knowledge in ancient Greek philosophical thought see the outstanding discussion by Wardy (1996).
[3]   Stobaeus, *Ecl.* II.7.5ℓ p.73.19-74.1 Wachsmuth = *SVF* 3.112 = LS 41H.
[4]   For the contrast see for example Aristotle, *Posterior Analytics* 2.19 100a4-9, *Metaphysics* A 1 980b28-981a3 (both passages stressing, indeed, that experience *gives rise to* knowledge); for the greater practical use of experience, *Metaphysics* A 1 981a12-24, *Nicomachean Ethics* 6.7 1141b16-22.
[5]   *empeiria* = experience.
[6]   Aristotle takes *mathematics* as his point of contrast in this regard in *Nicomachean Ethics* 1.3 1094b11-27. That he does so is significant in the ancient context – see further below – but problematic for the present point in that pure mathematics is not an empirical science. Astronomy, which is indeed in part a branch of applied mathematics, is a part of the theoretical 'wisdom' contrasted with practical wisdom in *Nicomachean Ethics* 6.7; see especially 1141b1-2.

certainly regarded as a superior cognitive activity,[7] ancient culture was largely free from one particular factor that has prompted persuasive definitions of subjects as 'sciences' in modern times, namely the claim in some quarters that the *natural* sciences encompass all that is worth saying about human activity and experience.[8]

'Scientific knowledge' or *epistêmê* was a concept developed and refined by philosophers, who to a large extent took mathematics – a non-empirical subject – as their paradigm. The aim of the present volume, and of the colloquium from which it took its origin, is to examine the relation between philosophy and the individual sciences from the perspective of the ancients themselves, in so far as this is possible. How did they understand this relation, and how did they make use of it in argument and debate? Considering this will also throw light on the process by which, historically, specialist areas of study of the natural world – 'sciences' – became detached from philosophy and obtained an autonomy of their own. It may indeed, as pointed out in André Laks' paper in this volume, be more accurate to describe the process as one by which philosophy itself came to have a more clearly defined agenda.

Laks' paper advances this discussion by distinguishing between three processes that are often confused, professionalization, specialization and differentiation; the first, he argues, is anachronistic for the Presocratic period, and the third does not imply the second. The fact that a subject has developed into a specialized body of knowledge does not necessarily mean that it has to be the sole or major concern of everyone who practises it. In studying the differentiation of branches of knowledge our approach should emphasize activities and methods, rather than adopting a static analysis in terms of different subject-matters. Laks' distinction between his second and third processes reappears in a different form in Philip van der Eijk's paper (86) as a contrast between 'specialization of subjects' and 'the emergence of specialist practitioners'.

The theme of the relation between different branches of knowledge is continued in Jim Hankinson's paper on Aristotle's philosophy of science. Aristotle's requirement that scientific demonstration should be from *per se* premises creates problems both for the analysis of subordinate sciences and for the use of common principles shared by more than one science. Hankinson's solution (46-7) is that the proper principles of a specific science, though derived from common principles or from the principles of a higher science, are none the less primitive and underived *in the context of the specific science*. This analysis can, he shows, accommodate even the use of geometry in medicine to explain why circular wounds heal more slowly; but this will be at the cost of a drastic reduction of the number of cases which will actually be proper targets of Aristotle's objection to using a principle from one

---

[7]   I put the point this way to avoid complications concerning, for example, the distinctions drawn by some in antiquity between discursive and non-discursive reasoning.

[8]   On this issue in general see Stone and Wolff (2000), and as it relates to Greco-Roman antiquity in particular Sharples (2000).

science to prove something within another. Hankinson concludes by noting that Aristotle sees as problematic precisely the procedure that is characteristic of modern science, that of finding the most general laws possible that apply to a number of different domains.

James G. Lennox develops the theme by examining, from the evidence of references and programmatic statements in the texts themselves, where Aristotle located zoology among the natural sciences. Striking among his conclusions are the recognition that Aristotle sees the study of living things as setting standards for *all* natural science (62-3) and the conclusion – echoing, indeed, Aristotle's own remarks – that the place of the *De Anima* in Aristotle's study of nature and living things is problematic (70). Section four of Lennox' paper considers Aristotle's view of the relation between the *phusikos*, or natural scientist, and the physician, as we confusingly today name the doctor. He shows that while a distinction between the study of facts and the study of reasons is for Aristotle found both within zoology and between medicine and zoology, it is in the latter case rather than the former that the notion of a subordinate science examined in Hankinson's paper is appropriate; medicine is not (for Aristotle) itself concerned with the causes of disease (68).

The relation between medicine and philosophy is a central theme of Philip van der Eijk's survey of medicine in the fourth century BC and of modern scholarship on this period (see especially 82-3). The period is, as he shows, both an important one in the history of the discipline, and a relatively obscure one; the medical literature of this period was already the product of a distant past as far as the majority of our surviving ancient sources were concerned, but did not share in the classic status that Galen in particular established for the Hippocratic writings. Both for ancient sources and for modern scholarship, the tendency for the canonical status of Plato and Aristotle to obscure the other intellectual currents of their time may play a part too. Van der Eijk shows in his paper how medicine in this period developed in a way that was influenced by the epistemological preoccupations of Plato and Aristotle: classification, the drawing of precise distinctions, the establishing of consistent terminology, inference from appearances and the limits of causal explanation all constitute points of contact between medicine and philosophy. Even in the subject-matter studied there continued to be a considerable overlap between the interests of doctors and those of philosophers.

Geoffrey Lloyd examines the way in which Galen appeals to mathematics as an example of rigorous intellectual method and an answer to scepticism. He notes that the latter point – the *certainty* achievable by mathematical reasoning – was at least as important for Galen as was the former. However, he shows that not only Galen's discussion of how mathematical method can be applied to medicine, but also his mathematical examples themselves, fail to distinguish clearly between *a priori* and *a posteriori* reasoning; for all that Galen stresses how unpopular mathematics was among many people in his day (*plus ça change!*), his examples are sometimes elementary and, in the case of the geometry of the optic nerve, fail to do justice to the complexities of the anatomical situation as Galen himself describes them.

Dominic O'Meara shows how the mathematical study of music formed part of an increasing emphasis on mathematics in the philosophy of late antiquity, and how music was seen as being valuable both in moral and in theoretical terms; significantly, the former relate not just to the direct psychological effects of music, but to the ways in which the mathematical structure of music was seen as having implications for the discussion of ethics – the relation, moreover, not being a fortuitous one but reflecting the place of mathematics in the Neoplatonist account of the soul. O'Meara ends his discussion by suggesting that there is scope for a similar enquiry concerning not only the ethical, but also the physical theories of late antiquity. In her response to O'Meara's paper Anne Sheppard explores further the way in which the Neoplatonists distinguished between the mathematical and the therapeutic aspects of music, while drawing on traditional ideas about the latter; she also shows how Porphyry and Iamblichus disagreed on the way in which the therapeutic effects were to be explained in terms of a mathematical structure of the universe and of the human soul.

To attempt to draw a single conclusion from these papers risks obscuring the diversity of their subjects and of the points that they make. One theme that emerges is the importance of mathematics in the history both of ancient Greek philosophy and of ancient Greek science. Mathematics provided philosophers – above all Plato and Aristotle, but through them all those influenced by them – with a model of proof and of derivation from first principles which seemed to provide answers that could be relied upon and would resist every challenge. That the influence of mathematics is to be explained by its answering this need is suggested by the way in which even theories of knowledge which were not greatly influenced by mathematics – such as the empiricist theories of the Stoics and Epicureans – sought to base knowledge on indisputable and incontrovertible foundations. The aspects of Greek philosophy that were to be important for ancient Greek science cannot indeed be explained in terms of the influence of mathematics alone; the concern of Plato's Socrates with definitions, and of the Sophist Prodicus with terminological distinctions, do not show specifically mathematical influences. Nevertheless, precision was certainly at home in the conception of knowledge derived from mathematics too. The exact chronological relationship between advances in the later fifth and fourth centuries BC in philosophy on the one hand, and mathematics on the other – the question of who was influencing whom – is one on which more work still needs to be done.

Through philosophy, mathematics gave to the sciences a particular conception of what a system of knowledge should be like. That conception included a requirement for order and system. At times indeed this may have been *too* influential. The disregarding of minor irregularities in the observed phenomena was a necessary condition for Greek astronomy, in particular, to advance in the way it did; but disregarding minor irregularities could also involve dismissing what might have been highly informative. Similar processes were at work in other sciences too.[9] There were those who explicitly recognized the limits of enquiry –

---

[9] See Lloyd (1987) 285-336.

Theophrastus[10] and Diocles,[11] for example; but the notion of a limit can be negative as well as positive. It can be seen as a frontier which one should seek to advance, but it can also be seen as an invitation to remain on the safe and well-defined territory that one already occupies. The treatment of all branches of knowledge as essentially similar could also lead to the application of models of enquiry that were not those best suited to the study of the natural world. The influence of ancient philosophy on ancient science thus had both positive and negative aspects.

What, finally, of the influence of ancient science generally (and not just of mathematics) on ancient philosophy? Much of the activity of ancient philosophers is in what we would now classify as 'science' rather than as 'philosophy', and it would hardly be appropriate to speak of *influence* where 'science' is what is actually being practised.[12] Concern with natural philosophy was particularly characteristic of the Peripatetic school; Posidonius, the Stoic who was said to be like a Peripatetic because of his interest in a wide range of topics in nature,[13] is simply the exception who proves the rule. But Plato in the *Timaeus*, Epicurus in his consideration of astronomical and meteorological phenomena,[14] and Seneca in the *Natural Questions*[15] all consider the natural world, with a view indeed to an overriding agenda which is philosophical in a narrower sense; even the Neoplatonists, too often regarded as a by-word for unworldliness, were concerned with natural philosophy – and the influence of their approach on subsequent thought should not be underestimated.[16]

Consequently, if we are to consider the influence of science on ancient philosophy, it seems more useful to do so taking 'philosophy' in a narrower sense; are there instances of specifically philosophical theories that were influenced by the sciences of the time? One example is the influence of new anatomical discoveries on Peripatetic accounts of the soul (below, p.83), already apparent in Strato. Another is the Stoic conception of cause, the ancestor of the modern concept.[17] How far the elaborate distinctions between types of cause recorded in our sources are Stoic, how far some of them are purely medical, and how far those that *are* Stoic

---

[10] Theophrastus, *Metaphysics* 8 9b1-24, and fragments 158-9 FHS&G; and for limits in a 'downwards' rather than an 'upwards' direction – in the analysis of individual phenomena rather than in the search for first principles – the discussion of Vallance (1988).

[11] See van der Eijk, 99-101.

[12] Nor is this simply a matter of a difference between ancient and modern uses of the term 'philosophy'; Aristotle's view of where the boundary between philosophy and medicine lies is not one that his medical contemporaries would have been happy with (4) – though their complaint would have been not that he extended philosophy too widely, but that he confined medicine too narrowly.

[13] Strabo 2.3.8: 'There is in him (Posidonius) much investigation of causes and Aristotelizing.'

[14] Epicurus, *Letter to Pythocles*; see also Lucretius, books 5-6.

[15] See Sharples (2000) 14-16.

[16] See for example Pines (1961); Siorvanes (1996) 207-316.

[17] See Frede (1980).

originated in medicine and were taken over by philosophers is unclear;[18] but it is significant that Clement of Alexandria, who is one of our principal sources for these distinctions, collected the material with a view to philosophical discussion.[19] At an earlier period, it is medicine that Plato makes Socrates cite as an example of methodical understanding – even though, characteristically, he couples this immediately with a warning of the dangers of relying on authority.[20] Even though philosophers regarded philosophy as a higher activity than the sciences, this does not mean that the sciences did not influence philosophy.

References

FHS&G = W.W. Fortenbaugh, P.M. Huby, R.W. Sharples, and D. Gutas (1992), *Theophrastus of Eresus: Sources for his Life, Writings, Thought and Influence*, Brill, Leiden.
LS = A.A. Long and D.N. Sedley (1987), *The Hellenistic Philosophers*, Cambridge University Press, Cambridge.
SVF = H. von Arnim (1903-1924), *Stoicorum Veterum Fragmenta*, Teubner, Leipzig.

Duhot, J.J. (1989), La conception stoïcienne de la causalité, Vrin, Paris.
Frede, M. (1980), 'The Original Notion of Cause', in M. Schofield, M.F. Burnyeat and J. Barnes (eds), *Doubt and Dogmatism*, Clarendon Press, Oxford, 217-49.
Lloyd, G.E.R. (1980), *Magic, Reason and Experience*, Cambridge University Press, Cambridge.
Lloyd, G.E.R. (1987), *The Revolutions of Wisdom*, University of California Press, Berkeley.
Pines, S. (1961), '*Omne quod movetur necesse est ab aliquo moveri*: a refutation of Galen by Alexander of Aphrodisias and the theory of motion', *Isis* 52 21-54; reprinted in S. Pines, *Studies in Arabic versions of Greek texts and in medieval science*, Magnes Press, Jerusalem and Brill, Leiden, 1986, 218-51.
Pohlenz, M. (1940), *Grundfragen der Stoischen Philosophie*, *Abh.Göttingen*, phil.-hist. Kl. 3.26.
Pohlenz, M. (1967), *La Stoa: storia di un movimento spirituale*, revised by V.E. Alfieri et al., La Nuova Italia, Florence.
Sharples, R.W. (2000), 'Science, Philosophy and Human Life in the Ancient World', in Stone and Wolf (2000),7-27.
Siorvanes, L. (1996), *Proclus: Neo-Platonic Philosophy and Science*, Edinburgh University Press, Edinburgh.
Vallance, J. (1988), 'Theophrastus and the Study of the Intractable: Scientific Method in *De lapidibus* and *De igne*', in W.W. Fortenbaugh and R.W. Sharples (eds), *Theophrastean Studies*, Transaction, New Brunswick (Rutgers University Studies in Classical Humanities, 3) 25-40.
Wardy, R. (1996), 'Ancient Greek Philosophy', in N. Bunnin and E.P. Tsui-James (eds), *The Blackwell Companion to Philosophy*, Blackwell, Oxford, 482-99.
Wolff, J. and Stone, M. (2000) (eds.), *The Proper Ambition of Science*, Routledge, London.

---

[18] See Pohlenz (1940) 108ff., (1967) I.209; Frede (1980) 241-2; Duhot (1989) 190.
[19] Clement of Alexandria, *Stromateis* 8.9.
[20] Plato, *Phaedrus* 270bd; cf. *Gorgias* 464-5, 500e-501a.

Chapter Two

Remarks on the Differentiation of Early Greek Philosophy

André Laks

Dans l'état primitif de nos connaissances il n'existe aucune division régulière parmi nos travaux intellectuels; toutes les sciences sont cultivées simultanément par les mêmes esprits. Ce mode d'organisation des études humaines, d'abord inévitable et même indispensable ... change peu à peu, à mesure que les divers ordres de conceptions se développent. Par une loi dont la nécessité est évidente, chaque branche du système scientifique se sépare insensiblement du tronc, lorsqu'elle a pris assez d'accroissement pour comporter une culture isolée, c'est-à-dire quand elle est parvenue à ce point de pouvoir occuper à elle seule l'activité permanente de quelques intelligences. (Auguste Comte).[1]

I

Here is what L. Zhmud writes in an 1994 article about the early relationship between Greek science and philosophy: 'The specialization of science and philosophy happens in Greece astonishingly early. Already at the end of the 6th century and the beginning of the 5th century, we find the figures of "pure" scientists (*Gelehrter*), such as Cleostratos of Tenedos or Hecataeus of Miletus, and "pure" philosophers, such as Heraclitus or Zeno of Elea. In the course of the fifth century, this specialization deepens, especially as far as science is concerned (*in der Wissenschaft*). Outstanding mathematicians such as Hippocrates of Chios, Theodorus of Cyrene and Theaetetus have not left any trace of philosophical studies; this is also true for the astronomers Oinopides of Chios, Meton, and Euctemon of Athens, and many treatises of the Hippocratic Corpus bear also on purely professional medical questions. At the same time, philosophy maintains an interest for scientific knowledge, although with Socrates and many Socratics a completely new brand of philosophy develops.'[2]

G.E.R. Lloyd has repeatedly argued against this kind of position (although not against Zhmud's particular assertion, as we shall see in a moment), most recently and

---

[1]   Comte (1975), 31.
[2]   Zhmud (1994), 4 (my translation).

systematically in a piece in French entitled 'Le pluralisme de la vie intellectuelle avant Platon'.[3] There he argues that neither the terms used by the Ancients, and especially the participants themselves, such as *philosophia, sophia, sophistes, historia, phusis, mathematike,* nor our own classificatory terms, refer to a special kind of scientific activity or field such as is supposed by a differentiated state of affairs. Just to take up the case which might seem the most favourable to a 'Zhmudian' view: there is little doubt that Hippocrates of Chios was a specialist dedicated to mathematical problems.[4] But there is a question about what we are to conclude from this. Lloyd insists that it is artificial to put him in a sequence with Euctemon and Meton to conjure up a category of early 'mathematicians' (which Zhmud does not strictly speaking do, since he classifies the latter as astronomers; this raises the question, obviously, of what 'mathematicians' means, for *mathematikoi* has a broader scope than our 'mathematics'), and this for two sets of reasons: one negative, which is that we do not really know anything about Euctemon, the second positive, which is that according to the depiction of him in Aristophanes' *Birds,* 992-1020, Meton looks like 'another Thales' rather than a specialist.[5] Moreover, and more importantly, there were some non-mathematicians around, or not specialized mathematicians, who were doing extremely serious, 'professional' mathematical work, such as Antiphon, Bryson, and Democritus.[6] And if we turn to medicine, we will see that what is supposed to be a medical corpus displays a variety of interests which are hardly captured by a specialized view of what medicine is, for some medical authors are pointedly interested in cosmological, other in linguistic or ethnological matters (Zhmud also has a restriction: *'many* treatises...' [my emphasis]).[7] All this, and much more, leads Lloyd to stress what he calls the 'complexity of the cartography of intellectual activities in the fifth and the fourth centuries and the difficulties of assigning various individuals to neatly defined categories, whether these are theirs or ours. The borders here remain both contested and fluid.'[8]

I have no special wish to reconcile the two positions just mentioned. But I think that one can raise some questions and make some conceptual distinctions that complicate somewhat the either/or picture which seems to emerge from their confrontation. This is the topic of the following observations, which do not aim at being more than observations.

---

[3] Lloyd (2002).

[4] Still, I would like to suggest that the remark in Aristotle, *Eudemian Ethics* 1247a16-20 according to which Hippocrates was rather bad in business matters, although he was a geometer, might not so much be a testimony of his narrow specialization as a special point about the relationship between theory and practice.

[5] See 1009 (cf. 1000-1001, for a reference to a 'physical' doctrine).

[6] Lloyd (2002), 48f.

[7] *Ibid.* 44f.

[8] *Ibid.* 53. Note that Lloyd's reflection extends beyond the fifth century.

We may start from the very cautiousness of Lloyd's conclusion: 'the reaction to the situation I described should not be to give up all hope of giving meaning to different paradigms of intellectual enterprise in competition ... but cautiousness is in order.'[9] I cannot agree more that we should be cautious. But we should also ask what the hope of distinguishing 'the paradigms in competition' can be founded on, if we concentrate exclusively on the fluidity of the situation. The beginning of an answer to this, I think, lies in the fact that even assuming that we are not dealing with specialized knowledge in the Preplatonic area, we must nevertheless reckon with some *process* of specialization. Moreover, one might ask whether fluidity of the borders and reconfiguration of the discipline are not phenomena that are going on constantly (though maybe at a different speed) in any discipline even after its disciplinary status has been established – which would of course relativize the conclusions we may draw from the argument about fluidity in the Preplatonic period. For reasons that will appear in a moment, this is probably even more true of philosophy than of any other discipline. In any case, we should not oppose specialization as a static category to fluidity or complexity, which is just such another static category, but rather work towards understanding the dynamics of specialization. It should be immediately added that this process of specialization is heterogeneous, first because every discipline has its own prehistory, condition and pace of development and ways of interaction with other branches of knowledge, but also because philosophy seems to represent, among ancient disciplines, a special case anyway. There are physicians in Homer, and for that matter in any civilization; there had been Babylonian astronomers and mathematicians. There might be drastic changes between Homeric and Hippocratic medicine, between Babylonian and Greek astronomy. But it seems difficult to deny that both are directed, at some level, to an identifiable object (wounds and illness; astronomical data). Philosophy, on the other hand, is another matter, for in its case, a totally new object, or perhaps better set of problems, had to be conceived of, and not just a new take on an already identifiable subject matter. Thus the relationship between *sophos* and *philosophos* is not the same as that between proto-astronomers and astronomers.

The question of philosophy's specificity is especially important, because of the flourishing of a certain trend in scholarly literature, which is well represented by the following quotation taken from Nightingale (1995): 'The discipline emerged at a certain moment in history. It was not born, like a natural organism. Rather, it was an artificial construct that had to be invented and legitimized as a new and unique cultural practice. This took place in Athens in the fourth century BCE, when Plato appropriated the term "philosophy" for a new and specialized discipline – a discipline that was constructed in opposition to the many varieties of *sophia* or "wisdom" recognized by Plato's predecessors and contemporaries.'[10] Nobody would deny that Plato, or for that matter Socrates, reshaped philosophy in depth, nor that in some

---

[9]   *Ibid.* 52.
[10]   Nightingale (1995), 14.

derived sense, he may be considered as its 'inventor'. But we should resist the temptation of abusing the language of artificiality and invention. Even if little is known about the early life of the word 'philosophy', we know enough to say that it was already used in a quasi-technical sense before Plato, and I think it is important to be allowed to describe as 'philosophical' some brand of intellectual activity that antedates the appearance of the word itself.

A remark about the dynamics of terminological shifts is in order here. One can argue in a general way, I think, that language, although it may be inventive, also possesses its specific kind of inertia. Neologisms are always possible, but it might also take some time before language reflects a given change of practice. New wine is poured into old bottles. One could speak, in this respect, of a principle of linguistic or terminological 'delay'. The word 'philosophy' is a case in point. Although C. Riedweg recently suggested in his book on Pythagoras that the story of Pythagoras' inventing the term 'philosophy' might be true (which would bring us back to the end of the sixth century),[11] most scholars agree that the term, in its specialized sense, is a relatively late coining.[12] As a matter of fact, the evidence, which is sparse but significant enough, points to the 430s as the period in which philosophy came to refer to a rather special kind of activity – 'rather special' not necessarily meaning that it specialized in the study of a definite *subject-matter*. One would think, of course, that Socrates was by that time already making a distinctive use of the term; but apart from Socrates, there is a set of three interesting texts testifying that this is the period where the term came to the fore.

There is, first, the famous chapter 20 of *Ancient Medicine*, in a difficult passage which contains the first known occurrence of the abstract term *philosophia*:

> Now some, physicians as well as knowledgeable men, claim that it is not possible to know medicine if one does not know what man is ... . But the talk of these people concerns philosophy, as Empedocles or other authors on nature have written going back to the origins telling what man is, how he was first born, and how he was put together. But I think that all of this kind that has been said or written on nature by some knowledgeable man or physician has less to do with the medical art than with painting. And I think that in order to have some precise knowledge of nature, there is no other source than medicine.[13]

---

[11] Riedweg (2002), 120-8. The famous anecdote features in Cicero, *Tusc.* 5.8 = Heraclides Ponticus, fr. 88 Wehrli.

[12] Most recently Mansfeld (2003), 165 in his review of Riedweg. The classical discussion on the topic is Burkert (1960).

[13] λέγουσι δέ τινες καὶ ἰητροὶ καὶ σοφισταὶ ὡς οὐκ ἔνι δυνατὸν ἰητρικὴν εἰδέναι ὅστις μὴ οἶδεν ὅ τί ἐστιν ἄνθρωπος· ... τείνει δὲ αὐτέοισιν ὁ λόγος ἐς φιλοσοφίην, καθάπερ Ἐμπεδοκλῆς ἢ ἄλλοι οἳ περὶ φύσιος γεγράφασιν ἐξ ἀρχῆς ὅ τί ἐστιν ἄνθρωπος, καὶ ὅπως ἐγένετο πρῶτον καὶ ὅπως ξυνεπάγη. ἐγὼ δὲ τουτέων μὲν ὅσα τινὶ εἴρηται σοφιστῇ ἢ ἰητρῷ, ἢ γέγραπται περὶ φύσιος, ἧσσον νομίζω τῇ ἰητρικῇ τέχνῃ προσήκειν ἢ τῇ γραφικῇ. νομίζω δὲ περὶ φύσιος γνῶναί τι σαφὲς οὐδαμόθεν ἄλλοθεν εἶναι ἢ ἐξ ἰητρικῆς.

There has been an ongoing debate what the word *graphikê* in this passage, to which philosophy is disparagingly compared from the point of view of the kind of medicine the author advocates, should be taken to refer to: 'painting', or rather 'art of writing' (sometimes 'literature')? I have been convinced by J. Jouanna's defence of 'painting' in his 1990 edition of the treatise, where he notes that, while the verb *graphein* can of course refer both to writing and painting, the substantive *graphikê* in the fourth century is only attested in the sense of 'painting', and that there is no reason to think that things were different in the fifth century.[14] But I do not think that the word is suggested by the mention of Empedocles, as is further suggested by Jouanna, in order to explain the surprising comparison. The fact that Empedocles' Aphrodite in fr. 31 B 23 (= 64 Bollack) brings about the infinite variety of generated forms by mixing together the four roots, as the painter mixes the four basic colours on his palette, is far too little to justify a parallel between philosophy and painting, first because philosophy is not practised by the Empedoclean Aphrodite, second because the medical author does not aim at attacking Empedocles in his own right, but as a representative of a genetic kind of approach (going back to the first origins), which he associates with 'philosophy'. It seems to me that since the treatise as a whole is directed against a kind of speculative medicine which operates on the ground of unwarranted assumptions,[15] painting might well be taken as a paradigmatic instance of an art that does not aim at changing the state of the world, and hence is purely theoretical.[16] The reproach, which is aimed at philosophical approaches in general, would have been the more cruel to Empedocles that he alone, among the 'first philosophers', stressed (and stressed in the most emphatic way) the efficacy of knowledge, illustrated by the thaumaturgic power, among others, of 'bringing back from Hades the strength of a dead man'.[17] Whatever interpretation we opt for, the passage from *Ancient Medicine* not only illustrates an early 'disciplinary' conflict (within medicine, and between medicine and philosophy), but also clearly points to a use of 'philosophy' whereby the term refers to the activity of those who study 'nature',[18] and who do that, in the opinion of this particular medical author, in a speculative way.

The second text which is relevant in this context is §13 of Gorgias' *Encomium of Helen*, which, in the section devoted to the power of discourse, presents us with a threefold division of discursive activities. Gorgias lists first the arguments of

---

[14]   Jouanna (1990), 208, n.8. The translation is also adopted by Vegetti (1998). For previous discussion, see Festugière (1948), 60f. n.71; Müller (1965). Schiefsky (forthcoming) adopts the latter's 'art of writing' in the sense of composing written works. But is not the author himself writing?

[15]   Chap. I, 1-3; 13; 15-16.

[16]   Other explanations have been put forward on the same lines. Pohlenz (1918), for example, thinks that painting belongs, along with philosophy, to the category of secondary, non-necessary arts (cf. the view reported by Plato, *Laws* X, 889d).

[17]   Fr. 111 Diels-Kranz = 12 Bollack. On the status of this fragment, see Laks (2003).

[18]   This will of course be taken up in Plato's *Phaedo*, 96a6-8.

those who are called *meteorologists* (οἱ τῶν μετεωρολόγων λόγοι), then the fights of those who are engaged in *judicial arguments* (τοὺς ... διὰ λόγων ἀγῶνας) and finally the competitions related to *philosophical arguments* (φιλοσόφων λόγων ἀμίλλας). Given that meteorology refers to the study of the sky and meteorological phenomena, that is of the whole cosmos, it seems clear that the category of those whom Gorgias here calls meteorologists overlaps to a great extent, or may even coincide, with those whom the author of *Ancient Medicine* sees as indulging in philosophy. Gorgias himself uses the term philosophy for something else, namely some kind of argumentative 'competition'. Competition is certainly not incompatible with meteorology,[19] but I submit that what Gorgias here has in mind is the kind of dialectical interchanges, Socratic or not, that we are familiar with from Plato's dialogues and Aristotle's *Topics*, the object of which is not the world and its natural processes, but *any* subject which might point to semantic and logical problems.

The third text to which I would like to draw attention is Prodicus' definition of the term *sophistes* as reproduced in Plato's *Euthydemus*. According to Plato's Prodicus, whom we have no reason to think of as not corresponding to the historical Prodicus, the *sophistes* constitutes a figure on the border between the *philosopher* and the *politician* (305c6), at the point of articulation, that is, between the two great orientations of human activity, namely theory (represented here by philosophy) and action (represented here by politics). This is not only interesting because we learn that Prodicus, whom we classify as a sophist, viewed the 'sophist' in a new, and already quasi Platonic perspective, but also because we have here an explicit reference in the original text to a 'border' (*methoria* is the term used to refer to the *sophistes* as being 'between the lines').

On the basis of this evidence, to which that provided by the Socratic material should be added, one can probably conclude that by the time these views were produced (that is, again, around the last third of the fifth century), philosophy had become an activity recognizable as such. This does not mean, however, that the object of philosophical activities would have been rigidly set (this is the point, of course). Philosophy refers, in one case, to study of nature (*Ancient Medicine*), in another, to dialectical contest (Gorgias), thirdly to theoretical activity (Prodicus), and finally, taking Socrates into account, to man's happiness. What are we to do with this variety of characterizations? One fact whose force should probably not be underestimated despite its apparent triviality, and which I take to be relevant, is that philosophy is by nature a discipline whose borders are open or, to be precise, more widely open than others, so that there are special difficulties in claiming that it bears on a specific object. This remains true *even if* we are talking about beginnings and recognize that we are still moving in a world where intellectual activities were not already undifferentiated. There are, further, quasi-sociological reasons that explain philosophy's unique plasticity. Even in a context where philosophy is vilified,

---

[19] If a reference is needed, Parmenides, fr. 8.60, uses athletic terminology ('overtake', παρέλαυνειν) to assert that no mortal rival will ever overcome his own cosmology.

and conceived of as a ridiculous and useless game just good for idle minds, its repute remains such that many want to be called philosophers, and tend to deny the title to others:[20] the situation was apparently not different then than it is now. Seen in this perspective, the fact that various texts do not give the same reference to the term may simply reflect the process by which the term was appropriated, or for that matter rejected, by various groups. But all this should not prevent us from asking, from a more objective perspective, whether we cannot detect some common features in philosophical activity that explain why it came to be felt as an independent discipline. I think that the answer to this question should be positive, which does not mean that it should not be nuanced or cautious.

First, from a commonsensical or practical point of view, all these activities involve something theoretical, and are not linked to any practical use. *Philosophia* might well capture this, as is suggested (if I am right) by the strange comparison between *philosophia* and *graphike* in the *Ancient Medicine* passage. But to this negative determination, some positive ones can be added. Of course, it is impossible, nor is it really desirable, to define once for ever what philosophy is, or for that matter has once been. But it does not seem unreasonable to see philosophy emerging in Greece at the crossing of three intellectual trends. First, early philosophy develops a kind of discourse which bears on 'everything', or on all things, and in this respect has a claim to universality, whatever is the manner in which this universality is conceived – whether it is cosmic, or linguistic.[21] (This would be, in A. Comte's scheme, the metaphysical counterpart of the need, at the end of the process of differentiation, to compensate scientific specialization by some specialists in scientific *generalities*).[22] Second, there is no doubt that the 'secularization' of causal explanation plays a tremendous role in the emergence of philosophy, as well as in the birth of new scientific approaches, in that the recourse to old divinities in the explanation of how the cosmos came about is replaced by natural entities.[23] Finally, there is the development of rational argumentation as such. None of these criteria is straightforward, and each of them raises specific difficulties. One such difficulty, concerning the last one, would be that rational argumentation is not necessarily explicit, so that we have to work with the difficult concept of *implicit* rational argumentation as well.[24] Another one would be that secularization certainly does not mean setting aside theological discourse. More generally, we are talking about ideal types, whose instantiations display more than

---

[20]   See Plato, *Republic* 6 495d.
[21]   The two passages adduced above from *Ancient Medicine* and *Encomium of Helen* illustrate the point. On this criterion of totality, cf. Long (1999), 12.
[22]   Comte (1975), 34.
[23]   For the use of the concept of secularization in this context, see for example Vernant (1996), 202; Burkert (1994/95), 186. The term raises a series of interesting problems that will be tackled elsewhere.
[24]   This is not considered, for example, in Schofield's picture of Anaxagoras as a non-argumentative thinker (Schofield, 1980).

one irregularity. In spite of all these problems, each of which would need a long elaboration, the criteria just mentioned, taken together, yield a reasonable picture of the origins of early Greek philosophy, whereas by stressing too much the (indubitable) flexibility of disciplinary borders, we might become incapable of properly understanding the complex synergy that resulted in the emergence of the new brand of intellectual activity. I would personally argue that in order to reconstruct this story one cannot use as basis only what authors 'are' or even on what they 'write', but also, and even more, how they *read* and *react*. The way in which modern physics was born in the 18th century might provide us with some indications about the way new disciplines emerge, before any talk of professionalization.[25]

II

It is useful, I think, to distinguish in this perspective between professionalization and specialization on the one hand, and differentiation on the other.

Although they are themselves closely related, professionalization and specialization are not wholly equivalent. The first term is an essentially institutional notion, it implies the existence of corporations, rules for belonging, schools and schooling. We should therefore avoid the term when talking about the archaic period, if we think (as I do) that there were no schools around, or at any rate not in the rather restricted sense that Diels gave to the word *Schule* in his famous 1887 article, where, reacting against Wilamowitz and Usener, who had recently drawn attention to the Platonic and post-Platonic schools, he claimed that Presocratic thinkers were also dependent on school organization.[26] Moreover, professionalization also implies dedication of an individual to a single activity, at least for some significant part of the day. In spite of its literal meaning, and the fact that Plato's principle according to which an individual should devote himself to only one kind of activity ('to do one's own', τὰ ἑαυτοῦ πράττειν)[27] is often called the 'principle of specialization', the word may be taken otherwise, if you consider not the individual, but his skill. A specialist is somebody who possesses a certain field of competence (or claims this to be the case), which might or might not go with his engaging in a single activity, and which in any case does not imply the existence of an institutional, professional infrastructure. The distinction might be helpful in understanding how not only Empedocles or Diogenes of Apollonia, but even Parmenides himself, for example, might well have been 'physicians' as well as 'philosophers', in some sense of the word 'physician', and how they may have combined different 'specializations' (of course, Empedocles, who has explicit

---

[25] On this, see Stichweh (1984).
[26] Diels (1887); Wilamowitz (1881); Usener (1884). On this topic, cf. Laks (forthcoming).
[27] Plato, *Republic* 2 369e-370a.

pretensions to healing, would not be the same kind of physician as Diogenes, if he was one, nor for that matter Parmenides).[28]

On this view, specialization, although closely related to professionalization, can be construed as holding a middle place between professionalization and differentiation. For differentiation does not relate in the first place to the individual, but rather to a certain 'field'. It is more on the objective side than on the personal and the institutional side, for it has to do with the theoretical gesture of defining a specified, and hence restricted domain of competence, whatever competence you exercise beyond that. Of course, there is, again, a link between differentiation of a field on the one hand, specialization and professionalization of the individual on the other. Once a field of competence is defined, then it is natural to assume that this field of competence is best exercised if a given individual devotes herself entirely to it. This is, precisely, the point of the so called Platonic principle of 'specialization', which might already be the background of Heraclitus' attack against polymaths such as Hesiod, Pythagoras, Xenophanes and Hecateus.[29] Still, we can conceive of knowledge being differentiated, and not the persons. The so-called 'sophists', or at least some of them, are I think a case in point, for *sophistes* might well refer to a kind of individual who gathered in himself many branches of already existing, and hence differentiated, branches of knowledge, rather than to people who represented the undifferentiated state of the disciplines themselves. It is a pity that we do not know more about Diogenes of Apollonia's use of the term, by which he seems to have referred to *phusiologoi* like himself.[30] But Hippias, who explicitly claimed to engage in and teach arithmetic, astronomy, geometry and music, but also grammar and antiquities,[31] may also be more representative than we are prone to think, even if he (purposefully, no doubt) overdid it.[32]

I have already alluded above to one last and to my mind very important distinction, which concerns differentiation itself. This is the distinction between external differentiation (what the German calls *Ausdifferenzierung*) and internal differentiation (*Binnendifferenzierung*). The fact that a social group (or an organic part) differentiates itself from another does not mean in any way that it is homogeneous – quite the contrary. Self-assertion against the environment is regularly, and probably necessarily, accompanied by internal division, competition – in accordance with Hesiod's principle 'the potter hates the potter'[33] – and hence distinction, which means that transgression of existing borders paradoxically

---

[28]   An inscription dating from the first century published in 1962 taught us that Parmenides, who is referred to as *phusikos*, belonged to the *Ouliades*, a family which was dedicated to medicine (fr. 1 Mansfeld, 1987).

[29]   22 B 40 and 129 Diels-Kranz.

[30]   fr.2 Laks. I have translated the isolated word, of which I have made an independent fragment, 'hommes de science'.

[31]   Plato, *Protagoras*, 318d; *Hippias Minor*, 336c-368d; *Hippias Major*, 285c.

[32]   On Hippias, see Brunschwig (1984).

[33]   An effect of the second, good *Eris*: Hesiod, *Works and Days*, 17-26.

belongs to the process of setting them up. This, I reckon, must be especially true of philosophy, whose object, as I have already stressed, is less easily identified than that of the so-called 'special sciences'.

What is interesting and difficult in this respect is that philosophy, in accordance with its distinctive interest in totalities and generalities, has a vocation to encompass specialized disciplines at some level. Aristotle's *Metaphysics* Λ 8, a chapter which is the more interesting in that Aristotle ends up recognizing that the philosopher may not have the last word in astronomical matters (although he does not exclude this either) provides a good illustration of the tensions that result from this situation.[34] But Aristotle works in an environment where disciplines have already been differentiated, and in this sense specialized (professionalization remains, I think, another matter). Presocratic material is much more difficult to tackle, because it does not explicitly discuss the question of the relationship between philosophy and the other disciplines. An interesting case-study is provided by Diogenes of Apollonia and more precisely by his detailed description of man's venous (and for that matter arterial) system, extensively quoted by Aristotle in his *Historia Animalium*.[35] There is, first, the question of the setting of the passage in the original work. It is perfectly clear from indications in Simplicius, who, although he does not quote the text, obviously refers to it when he talks, in the summary he gives of Diogenes' thought, about the latter's 'detailed anatomical description of the ducts' (ἀνατομὴν ἀκριβῆ τῶν φλεβῶν),[36] that the passage comes from the first book of Diogenes' main treatise *On nature*. It is striking that some interpreters have nevertheless wanted the passage to stem either from the second book, which would have developed a physiology, or else from another such book that Diogenes may (or may not) have written, *On the nature of man* (Περὶ φύσεως ἀνθρώπου).[37] The question how many books Diogenes wrote, and what their titles were, is an obscure one.[38] But the important fact, in the context of the present argument, is that the discussion about the provenance of the fragment reflects some uneasiness about its status, 'philosophical' or 'physiological'. The fact that it is transmitted by Aristotle in a zoological work, in a chapter devoted to 'the most common anhomoeomerous part in the animal', namely blood, and 'the part in which blood is by nature contained', that is the blood-channels, is itself significant, because one might ask to what degree Aristotle's own treatise, that is the framework of the quotation of

---

[34] 'As to the actual number of these movements, we now – to give some notion of the subject – quote what some of the mathematicians say, that our thought may have some definite number to grasp; but, for the rest, we must partly investigate for ourselves, partly learn from other investigators, and if those who study this subject form an opinion contrary to what we have now stated, we must esteem both parties indeed, but follow the more accurate.' Aristotle, *Metaphysics* Λ 8, 1073b10-17.

[35] *Historia Animalium*, 3.2, 511b31-513b11.

[36] *In Physica*, 153f. Diels. φλέβες are not 'veins': see Laks (1983), 60.

[37] Cf. Laks, commentary on fr. 10 (= 6 Diels-Kranz), 61.

[38] On this see Laks (1983), 247-9.

Diogenes, is or is not philosophical in nature (assuming that the question makes sense).

The environment in which this quotation appears is also most interesting. Aristotle adduces Diogenes' description between that of a certain Syennesis, which is rather short, and that of Polybus. Polybus, Hippocrates' son in law, is much more famous than Syennesis, which may explain why Aristotle adds, when quoting the latter, 'the physician of Cyprus', while Polybus is referred just by name (the same is true of Diogenes, except that his origin is mentioned: the Diogenes in question is the one from Apollonia). In any case, it is clear that Aristotle quotes Diogenes in a sequence of professional physicians. Of course, the question arises as to whether Diogenes was also a professional physician, and this might have been the case, although it is mostly on the basis of this fragment (and more generally on the 'biological' outlook of Diogenes' thought) that people have speculated about his professional interests. But even if Diogenes was a professional physician, it is also fairly clear that there is a 'philosophical' reason for the care with which he describes the ducts in the way he does. Diogenes' basic thesis is that the principle, namely air, is 'intelligent',[39] and the way in which intelligence is enhanced or impeded in man constitutes an important part of the demonstration. This is why the existence of a network through which air and blood are distributed 'through the whole body'[40] (for Diogenes' ducts transport not only blood, but air as well; one might even say that they transport air in the first place) is so important; sensation and thought ('intelligence' in the encompassing sense in which Diogenes uses the term) depend on this distribution, which also explains further physiological functions such as digestion, reproduction, and sleep.[41] One could say that in Diogenes' case, doing philosophy implies doing medicine, in the same sense that in Aristotle's case, doing first philosophy implies doing astronomy – up to a certain point, perhaps.

III

A history of how philosophy differentiated must operate with some ideas of what is supposed to be differentiated, hence with some criteria of demarcation between science and philosophy. Now there is no simple answer to the question of demarcation – a question which has of course been the object of an epistemological and philosophical debate. One might take a strong or a milder view. Among the strongest views is, again, that of Zhmud, who distinguishes scientific problems

---

[39]   Simplicius, *in Phys.* 151.29f., cf. fr. 3 Laks.
[40]   Cf. Theophrastus, *On the Senses*, §§43-5.
[41]   For sleep, cf. T41 Laks (= A29 Diels-Kranz); reproduction, T15 (= A24); digestion, Theophrastus, *On the Senses*, §44 and Laks (1983), 151.

from philosophic ones in that the former can, whereas the later cannot, be solved.[42] This is on the one hand a somewhat harsh criterion, which some at least of the problems belonging to the history of science would not pass, and on the other hand not a decisive one, since there are many soluble problems which are not scientific problems. Among the weaker criteria that are mobilized in the discussion feature: proof, experimentation, use of the empirical evidence, rational argumentation, the secularized outlook of the procedure.

I do not wish to engage in a discussion about these criteria, nor consider whether other possibilities are available. I want to suggest, rather, that the question of the specific relationship between science and philosophy might receive some light if we consider their common relation to a third term, namely myth. For some of the problems at least that we face using or tracing the distinction between science and philosophy, that is two kinds of rational discourse, reproduce, on a smaller scale, those we encounter when we try to draw a line between myth on the one hand and rational thought (whether scientific or philosophical) on the other: does not some form of rationality operate at the mythical level, too? (On this, there should by now exist a fairly large consensus). Epicurus' remark in his *Letter to Pythocles*, §87, which is directed against those who stick to a single explanatory model, while sense-data allow for a multiplicity of explanations, is most illuminating in this respect: 'when one retains this, and rejects that, although it is as compatible as the other with what one sees, it is clear that one abandons the study of nature (*phusiologia*), and falls headlong into myth.' Whatever merits one wants to grant to Epicurus as a scientist, the notion, which is here implied, that myth is not a genre, but a function, is extremely appealing: if the unicity of explanation is to an Epicurean theory of multiple explanations what eschatological stories are to rational or scientific explanations, such as determinism for example, then it is legitimate to give it the same name as those, namely 'myth'. The same is true of the relationship between science and philosophy, which, in some cases at least, can serve as alternate and legitimate descriptions of the same kind of activity, depending on how you construe science and philosophy.

The debate initiated by G.S. Kirk's reaction to Popper's vindicating Presocratic thinkers as a paradigm for scientific debate in his celebrated 'Back to the Presocratics' can be read in this light,[43] but I would like to illustrate the point here by referring to J. Mansfeld's notion, defended in an article entitled 'Myth Science Philosophy, A question of origins',[44] that philosophy, in spite of Aristotle, does not begin with Thales, but with Parmenides. What we are confronted by in Thales, Anaximander and Anaximenes is the beginning of *scientific* thought. The interesting point in Mansfeld's argumentation is how he explains the difference of approach

---

[42] Zhmud (1997), 1.
[43] See Lloyd (1991), chapter 5 ('Popper versus Kirk: a controversy in the interpretation of Greek science').
[44] Mansfeld (1990).

between Aristotle and 'us'. The idea is that for Aristotle, natural science is naturally part of what philosophy is (it remained so until at least the 17th century: think of Descartes, Pascal, Leibniz), so Aristotle has no problem with considering the Milesians as philosophers. But for us, who do make a neat distinction between natural science and philosophy, they are not philosophers, there are just scientists. They are even, according to Mansfeld, the *first* scientists, because medical scientific practice is, according to him, derivative from cosmological science, in chronological as well as in conceptual terms.

The idea, which is interesting in itself, also serves well to illustrate the general point, whose triviality does not diminish its truth, that we (and not we alone) recognize something as philosophical only if it corresponds to what is at a certain moment called philosophical. But it is also interesting for two other reasons.

First, it should be noted that Mansfeld's reading of Aristotle does not square exactly with Aristotle's explicit argumentation for including Thales and Anaximenes among philosophers (which might or might not be the reason why Anaximander is, so strikingly for us, absent from Aristotle's considerations at that point). It is true that Thales is presented by Aristotle as the founder of *natural* philosophy. But the reason why this is so is not that he practises something which is a branch of philosophy, namely natural science. Rather, he is a natural *philosopher* because he for the first time elaborates a theory of substance, which at some point is referred to by the word *phusis*.[45] (Of course, we would probably by now all agree that this reflects Aristotle's own interpretation of what Thales does, not Thales' own enterprise, but this is a separate point). In other terms, the important fact is that natural philosophy is philosophy as such, not that scientific thinking is as such part of what philosophy is.

It remains true that Aristotle's concept of *phusis* overlaps only partly with that of substance. As I have suggested elsewhere,[46] Aristotle in fact operates in this chapter with two distinct concepts of *phusis*, the first that I have just mentioned, which might be called the *substantial* or strong one, and a second one, which I would call the *secularizing* one, and which is weaker. The idea is that nature is autonomous, and not dependent on the gods, at least on the traditional gods. Aristotle does not insist or even remark at that point that for the Milesians, and at least for Anaximander and Anaximenes, the principle is divine, but this would be no argument against working with a secularizing concept of nature. For according to at least one recognized use of the mechanism of secularization, secularization does not mean getting rid of the gods, but transferring their attributes to other, natural entities. In this perspective, Thales and the Milesians are natural philosophers not so much because they have a theory of substance, but because their principle is different in nature from that of the theologians. Now if that is the case, that is if we operate with a weaker concept of *phusis*, we might have good

---

[45]   Aristotle, *Metaphysics* A 3, 983b14.
[46]   Laks (2004).

reasons to include the Milesians among 'philosophers', independently of the fact that they study nature in Aristotle's philosophical sense. This does not mean, of course, that they could not also be described as 'scientists', from a certain point of view, even if what they practise is not scientific from another point of view (that of the mathematicians, for example), or even if it is 'mythic', from a certain perspective (for example, an Epicurean one).

There is a second, more general point, and this is that we have to ask whether the implicit parallel between the Greek complex philosophy/science and the 17th century situation is really illuminating. The point is that you can hardly compare a situation where the two domains of first and second philosophy are already clearly differentiated, with a situation where they are in the process of being differentiated.

In any case, it seems to me that many difficulties we have in dealing with the description of early Greek science and philosophy vanish as soon as we mobilize a functional concept of science and philosophy. This semantic approach, for sure, makes the problem less interesting than we might have hoped. But it might help us to concentrate on more substantial questions.

References

Brunschwig, J. (1984), 'Hippias d'Elis, Philosophe-Ambassadeur', in *The Sophistic Movement* (Proceedings of the 1st International Philosophy Symposium, Sept. 27-29, 1982), Athenian Library of Philosophy, Athens, 269-76.

Burkert, W. (1960), 'Plato oder Pythagoras. Zum Ursprung des Wortes Philosophie', *Hermes* 88, 159-77.

Burkert, W. (1994/95), 'Orientalische und Griechische Weltmodelle von Assur bis Anaximandros', *Wiener Studien* 107/108, 179-86.

Comte, A. (1975), *Philosophie première. Cours de Philosophie positive*, vol.1, Hermann, Paris.

Diels, H. (1887), 'Über die ältesten Philosophenschulen der Griechen', in *Philosophische Aufsätze Eduard Zeller gewidmet*, Fues, Leipzig, 239-60.

Festugière, A.J. (1948), *Hippocrate, L'Ancienne Médecine*, Klincksieck, Paris.

Jouanna, A. (1990), *Hippocrate, L'Ancienne Médecine*, Collection des Universités de France, Paris.

Laks, A. (2003), 'Phénomènes et références: Eléments pour une réflexion sur la rationalisation de l'irrationel', *Methodos* 3, 9-33.

Laks, A. (2004), 'Aristote, l'allégorie et les débuts de la philosophie', in B. Pérez-Jean and P. Eichel-Lojkine, (eds), *L'allégorie de l'Antiquité à la Renaissance*, Champion, Paris, 211-20.

Laks, A. (forthcoming), 'Die Entstehung einer (Fach)Disziplin: Der Fall der Vorsokratischen Philosophie', in G. Rechenauer (ed.) *Frühgriechisches Denken*, Vandenhoeck und Ruprecht, Göttingen.

Lloyd, G.E.R. (1991), *Methods and Problems in Greek Science*, Cambridge University Press, Cambridge.

Lloyd, G.E.R. (2002), 'Le pluralisme de la vie intellectuelle avant Platon', in A. Laks and C. Louguet (eds), *Qu'est-ce que la philosophie présocratique / What is Presocratic Philosophy?*, Presses Universitaires du Septentrion, Lille.

Long, A.A. (1999), 'The scope of Early Greek Philosophy' in A.A. Long (ed.), *The Cambridge Companion to early Greek philosophy*, Cambridge University Press, Cambridge, 1-21.

Mansfeld, J. (1987), *Die Vorsokratiker*, Philipp Reclam Jun., Stuttgart.

Mansfeld, J. (1990), 'Myth Science Philosophy, A question of origins', in J. Mansfeld, *Studies in the Historiography of Greek Philosophy*, van Gorcum, Assen, 1-21. (Originally in Italian, 'Mito Scienza Filosofia, una questione di origini', *Quaderni di Storia* 20 [1984] 45-67.)

Mansfeld, J. (2003), 'Book Notes: Presocratics', *Phronesis* 48, 164-73.

Müller, C.W. (1965), 'Schreibkunst oder Malerei?', *Sudhoffs Archiv* 49, 307-11.

Nightingale, A. (1995), *Genres in Dialogue: Plato and the Construct of Philosophy*, Cambridge University Press, Cambridge.

Pohlenz, M. (1918), 'Das zwanzigste Kapitel von Hippokrates *De prisca medicina*', *Hermes* 53, 396-421.

Riedweg, C. (2002), *Pythagoras. Leben, Lehre, Nachwirkung*, Beck, Munich.

Schiefsky, M.J. (forthcoming), *Hippocrates*, On Ancient Medicine, translated with introduction and commentary, Brill, Leiden.

Schofield, M. (1980), *An essay on Anaxagoras*, Cambridge University Press, Cambridge.

Stichweh, R. (1984), *Zur Entstehung des modernen Systems wissenschaftlicher Disziplinen. Physik in Deutschland 1740-1890*, Suhrkamp, Frankfurt am Main. (Partial French translation of this book by F. Blaise under the title *La Naissance de la physique moderne*, Lille, Presses Universitaires du Septentrion, 1991.)

Usener, H. (1884), 'Organisation der wissenschaftlichen Arbeit, Bilder aus der Geschichte der Wissenschaft. Bilder aus der Geschichte der Wissenschaft', *Preussische Jahrbücher* 53, 1-25. (Reprinted in: H. Usener, *Vorträge und Aufsätze*, ed. A. Dieterich, Teubner, Leipzig and Berlin, 1907, 67-102.)

Vegetti, M. (1998), 'Empedocle "Medico e sofista" (*Antica Medicina* 20)', in K.D. Fischer, D. Nickel, P. Potter (eds), *Text and tradition. Studies in Ancient Medicine and its transmission. Presented to Jutta Kollesch*, Leiden/Boston/Cologne, 289-99.

Vernant, J.-P. (1962), *Les origines de la pensée grecque*, Presses universitaires de France, Paris.

Vernant, J.-P. (1996), 'Ecriture et religion civique en Grèce', in J. Bottéro, C. Herrenschmidt, J.-P. Vernant (eds), *L'Orient ancien et nous. L'écriture, la raison, les dieux*, A. Michel, Paris, 189-223.

Wilamowitz -Moellendorff, U. von (1881), *Antigonos von Karystos*, Weidmann, Berlin. (Reprint by Weidmann, Berlin and Zurich, 1965.)

Zhmud, L. (1994), 'Die Beziehungen zwischen Philosophie und Wissenschaft in der Antike', *Sudhoffs Archiv* 78, 1-13.

Chapter Three

Aristotle on Kind-Crossing[1]

R.J. Hankinson

In a number of places, Aristotle seems to state unequivocally that no science can make use of the principles of any other science in its demonstrations. Elsewhere, however, he seems not only to countenance such borrowings, but on occasion to make them an essential feature of the construction of scientific explanations. And since science is, for Aristotle, fundamentally an explanatory enterprise, this is a particularly uncomfortable position to be in. In this paper, I seek to offer an interpretation of Aristotle's views on the issues that tries at least to minimize the tensions involved.

I

I will begin with a brief sketch of Aristotle's picture of demonstrative science, *epistêmê*.[2] Aristotelian sciences (as I will continue to call them) are organized bodies of knowledge in which facts of a particular domain are arranged in such a way as to exhibit the relations of dependence that hold between them. These dependences are causal and explanatory; and a properly-structured science is one which is laid out in such a way that the relations of deductive consequence that hold between the fundamental facts, or axioms, and the derivative facts, or theorems, is made patent by their being arranged in syllogistic form, paradigmatically in the universal affirmative mood Barbara ('A belongs to all B; B belongs to all C; so A belongs to all C': or in the standard notation, AaB, BaC ∴

---

[1] 'Kind-crossing' is the usual designation of the phenomenon in question, and I retain it since it is customary; however, as will become apparent, I would prefer to talk (albeit somewhat barbarously) of 'domain-crossing': see n. 15 below.

[2] Some cavil at describing Aristotle's *epistêmai* as sciences and his practice as scientific; such objections have some point to them insofar as they serve as a corrective to those too-sanguine accounts of Aristotle's achievements that seek to assimilate them more or less directly to those of modern science; but equally such concerns can be overdone, and we can be hyper-corrective about such things (the dangers of this were somewhat in evidence at the Colloquium).

AaC).[3] The axioms of a science Aristotle calls 'principles' (or 'sources' or 'origins': *arkhai*), and scientific understanding, or *epistêmê* in its dispositional sense, consists in seeing why the predicates hold of their subjects in the conclusions of the syllogisms.

Thus, in the schema above, we need to know why A holds of all C. To this end it is not enough simply validly to infer it from any set of premisses; nor is it even enough to infer it soundly from any set of true premisses; rather the requisite premiss-set must be such that the middle term ('B': the one which appears in each of the premisses but not in the conclusion) *explains why* A holds of C.

There are several ways in which a syllogism may truly conclude from true (and scientific) premisses, and yet not yield an explanation of the conclusion. First, consider a chain of deductions, in which each term in the sequence has a greater extension than its successor: (1) AaB, BaC ∴ AaC; (2) AaC, CaD ∴ AaD; (3) AaD, DaE ∴ AaE; evidently we may extract further syllogisms from this, e.g. (4) AaB, BaE ∴ AaE, or (5) AaC, CaE ∴ AaE. Suppose now we want to know which of (3)-(5) really explains the fact that A holds of E – how are we to determine this? Aristotle's answer is that we should seek the middle term (B, C, or D) *in virtue of which* the predicate holds of the subject; and he argues at *Posterior Analytics* 2.18, 99b7-14 that this should be the one 'nearest to that for which it is the explanation'. That formulation is ambiguous, since it could refer either to the subject or the predicate of the conclusion (and plainly these will yield opposing results); but the following sentence makes it plain that Aristotle means 'nearest to the subject-term', and hence he apparently opts for (3) as the appropriately explanatory deduction. But his reasons for so doing are hardly convincing: if all the intermediate links are also explanatory, then presumably all of them should be implicated in a full explanation of the conclusion.[4] Moreover, it is not easy to think of such a sequence (where each successive subject-class is a proper subset of the predicate-class), and where it is plausible to suppose that the middle-terms are genuinely explanatory. Consider A = 'American', B = 'Southerner', C = 'Texan', D = 'inhabitant of Travis County', E = 'Austinite'; it is easy enough to arrange those terms in a syllogistic hierarchy, but it is hard to think that an Austinite is an American *because* (for any genuine non-epistemic sense of 'because') he is a Southerner or an inhabitant of Travis County (or for that matter because he is a Texan).

But in any case, Aristotelian science typically involves sequences of deductions some at any rate of whose premisses reflect not class-inclusion but class-equivalence. At all events, Aristotle treats definitions as an important type of axiom; and definitions, by definition, convert, i.e. the definiens is co-extensive with

---

3   In the expression 'AaB', A is the predicate, B the subject, and so A has (potentially) the greater extension; a more natural way of expressing the proposition in ordinary English would be 'all Bs are As'.

4   See Barnes (1994), 257-8.

the definiendum (although they do not of course convert *as definitions*: if A defines B, then B cannot define A; the relation of being a definition is asymmetrical). And in general it seems that, for Aristotle, to explain why an attribute F holds universally of some kind K, we need to isolate the class of items C such that K is included in C and all and only members of C are F (i.e., at that level the universal generalization converts: in the technical jargon it is a 'commensurate universal').[5] Thus all humans are mammals, all mammals are animals, and all animals are mortal, but humans are mortal in virtue of their being animals and not in virtue of their being mammals (since mammals are themselves mortal in virtue of being animals); thus a syllogism linking humans to mortality by way of their animality will be explanatory, while one which does so in virtue of their being mammals (or any other class with a smaller extension than that of animals: 'primates' for instance) will not be.[6]

Finally, sound syllogisms may fail to be explanatory in another way when they make use of commensurate universals: where two properties F and G are co-extensive, but F is responsible for G-ness and not vice versa, if all As are Gs one may argue from that and the fact that all Gs are Fs that all As are Fs. But then the middle term will not be explanatory; one will not know *why* all As are Fs (and indeed there may be no independent reason why; As may be Fs primitively and immediately). Aristotle offers several illustrations of this in *Post. An.*, but one will suffice. Astronomers prove that the moon is spherical because of the phase-patterns it exhibits; hence one may argue that everything which exhibits phases of this type is spherical, while the moon exhibits phases of this type: and so it is spherical. But its phase-structure is not the cause of its sphericity – rather it is its sphericity which (along with certain other conditions) causes it to exhibit this phase-structure (*Post. An.* 1.13, 78b4-13; cf. 78a22-b4; 2.16, 98a35-b24). The upshot of this is, as Aristotle notes on several occasions, that it is not enough simply to deduce the fact. To be properly scientific, the syllogism must exhibit the reason why it is a fact.[7]

This is implied in a key passage from the beginning of *Post. An.*:

---

[5]   On commensurate universals and their role in demonstrations, see Barnes (1994), 258-9, for a deflationary account; see also Kullmann (1974), 183 and Inwood (1979); I am inclined to think that there is a special role in Aristotle's science played by them – but it is very difficult precisely to spell out, and beyond the scope of this paper.

[6]   'But surely the class of mortal living things is broader than animals, and includes plants?' In that case change the explanation; or, alternatively, suppose that there are two causally-distinct types of mortality, as Aristotle allows that human and avian longevity will be distinct properties if they derive from distinct causes (*Post. An.* 2.17, 99b4-7; cf. *de Longitudine Vitae* 1, 464b19-30; but cf. ibid. 5, 466a17-b4, where longevity in general is reduced to a single cause, namely the quantity and quality of the contained moisture). On the types of explanation in Aristotle, see Lennox (1987); see also Hankinson (1995a).

[7]   As a true definition must embody the reason why the thing defined is the thing that it is: *Post.An.* 2.10, 93b29-94a19 (and see n. 13 below); cf. *De Anima* 2.2, 413a13-20.

T1. Demonstrative science must proceed from premises which are true, primary, immediate, more intelligible than, prior to, and explanatory of the conclusion.... The premises must be (a) true, since what is false cannot be known, e.g. the commensurate diagonal. They must be (b) primary and (c) indemonstrable, since otherwise they will not be known without demonstration; for to know that of which there is a demonstration (other than incidentally) is to have that demonstration. They must be (d) explanatory, (e) more intelligible and (f) prior: explanatory since we only have scientific knowledge when we know the explanation; prior since they are explanatory; and already known not only in the sense that they are understood, but in that they are known to be true. (*Post. An.* 1 2, 71b20-33)

Condition (a) is trivial. (b) and (c) come to the same thing, for to be primary in this sense just is to be underivable from any prior and explanatory principles; to use another Aristotelian technicality, they are *immediate*: they are of the form AaB, and there is no middle term X such that AaX and XaB and X explains why B is A. Aristotle equally (and intelligibly) links (d) and (f), priority and explanatoriness; and finally they are 'more intelligible' than what they entail just in the sense that the cognitive security with which we understand the derivative truths depends upon, and is a function of, that with which we know the fundamental ones, even if as a matter of fact we first learn the facts, the derivatives, and only later the reasons why:[8] which is to say, again, that the fundamental premisses are explanatory of their theorems.[9]

One further feature of this picture needs to be put on the table: Aristotle believes that some at least of the axioms of a properly-constituted science must involve the predication of *per se* attributes of the fundamental items in the domain. Aristotle's account of *per se* attributes is obscure and difficult.[10] But crucial to his account is his distinction between two sorts of *per se* predication which he thinks figure in demonstrative syllogistic:

T2. *per se* are those which (a) belong in the essence, as for instance line belongs to triangle and point to line (for their essence derives from these things, and inheres in the formula which says what they are); and (b) if what it holds of itself inheres in the formula which makes clear what it is, as both straight and curved belong to line, and

---

[8]   See *Post. An.* 1.2, 72a5-6; *Nicomachean Ethics* 1.4, 1095b6-7.

[9]   Aristotle distinguishes in many places between things which are 'more intelligible in themselves' and things which are 'more intelligible to us' (e.g. *Post. An.* 1.2, 71b33-72a5; *Metaphysics* Z 3, 1029b1-12; *Nic. Eth.* 1.4, 1095a30-b4; *Prior Analytics* 2.23, 68b35-7; *Topics* 6.4; *Phys.* 1.1, 184a16-26; *De An.* 2.2 413a11-13); see Barnes (1994), 96-7.

[10] In *Post. An.* 1.4, he distinguishes four ways in which predicates may hold of their subjects *per se*; *Metaph.* Δ 18, 1022a24-36, on the other hand classifies five; and as Barnes (1994, 112) says, 'only one of these has a clear counterpart in our passage [i.e. *Post. An.* 1.4]'; although, as he notes, Kirwan (1971, 168-70) discerns more parallelisms between the texts.

odd and even, prime and compound, square and oblong to number: in each case there inheres in the formula which says what it is either line or number. (*Post. An.* 1.2, 73a34-b3)

Barnes (1994, 112-14) labels (a) and (b) 'I1' and 'I2-predications' respectively;[11] and, following Philoponus, formalizes them as follows:

(I1)   A holds of B in itself = $_{df.}$ A holds of B and A inheres in the definition of B;

and

(I2)   A holds of B in itself = $_{df.}$ A holds of B and B inheres in the definition of A.

Aristotle's illustrative examples of I2-predications in T2 are problematic (see Barnes for discussion; but see also n. 22 below); but again we may safely ignore the difficulties involved, since it is the I1 cases which are the more important. At least the following seems to be safely assertible: the axioms (some or all of them) of Aristotle's demonstrative sciences involve predications in which the predicate holds of the subject in a particularly strong, definitional or essential manner. And it should also be noted that it is not sufficient for such a predication merely that it be a necessary one, since for Aristotle there are predicates that hold necessarily of their subjects, and yet which are not part of the essence or definition of those subjects. Indeed, these express precisely the properties entailed by and explained by the essential properties. Thus, for Aristotle, the property of having an angle-sum of 2R is a necessary property of any triangle – but it is not part of the essence of triangularity, since it is itself derived from facts of that essence and further geometrical axioms (it is in fact a '*per se* incidental' property of triangles: see below, T5 and 30-32); put another way, it can be *proved* – but then by the strictures of T1 above, it cannot be a basic, axiomatic fact.[12]

To take another example, much beloved of the mediaevals: the capacity for laughter is proper to human beings (i.e. only humans are capable of it: hyenas aren't really laughing – or at any rate they aren't getting the joke): *Parts of Animals* 3.10, 673a8. Why should human beings not then be defined as 'mortal animals capable of laughter'? That formula will certainly accurately delimit the extension of

---

[11]   'I' abbreviating 'in itself', Barnes' preferred rendering of *kath' hauto*, or *per se*.

[12]   Couldn't we develop an alternative axiomatization of geometry in which the angle-sum theorem was axiomatic, and was used to prove other propositions as theorems, such as for example that the angle on a straight line is 2R? No doubt we could. But for Aristotle and his strongly realistic metaphysics, such an alternative axiomatization would not merely be cumbersome and inelegant (although no doubt it would) – it would also fail to exhibit the actual, objective, structural facts of the matter; on these issues, see Tiles (1983).

the class of humanity. The answer is that, for Aristotle, proper definitions, those which will feature in a properly-organized demonstrative science, are Lockean real definitions: that is, they make patent the essence of the kind in question.[13] And although Aristotle does not spell this out, it is surely plausible to suppose (and to suppose that he supposed) that our capacity for laughter, not just as a physiological reaction (such as that to tickling, or the so-called *risus sardonicus*) but as an expression of a certain type of psychological response, is itself dependent upon more general facts of our rationality: it is because we are rational that we see the joke; and rationality is a definitional feature of humanity. Hence, once again, although the capacity for laughter and (a certain type of) rationality are co-extensive, there is an asymmetric relation of explanatory (and ontological) dependence that holds between them; our rationality explains our capacity for laughter and not the other way round.

II

Let us now turn to the question of the independence of, and the possible inter-relations between, the sciences.

> T3. The majority of the principles concerned with each science are proper[14] to it; hence it is a matter for experience to provide us with the principles concerned with each domain (*genos*).[15] I mean for example that astronomical experience provides us with those of astronomical science. For once the phenomena[16] had been adequately grasped, then and in this way were astronomical demonstrations discovered; and the same thing holds for any other craft or science whatsoever. So once the attributes have been grasped in the case of each domain, it will immediately be within our power readily to exhibit the demonstrations. (*Pr. An.* 1.30, 46a17-24)

---

13 Aristotle certainly countenances nominal definitions, and they play a role in the process of constructing the sciences. But they form no part of their completed structure. See *Post. An.* 2.10; Barnes (1994), 222-3; Demoss and Devereux, (1988); Deslauriers, (1990).

14 *idion*: 'proper' in the traditional logical sense of belonging only to the domain in question, and belonging to it necessarily.

15 I translate '*genos*' as 'domain' here (the term is also used in this context in the English of Scholz, 1975) since I think that that is the closest to its general sense in this context – of course the word also means 'kind' and (more specifically and relative to *eidos*) 'genus' or 'superset', and 'genus' or 'kind' are the usual translations offered here (cf. Tredennick (1960), 61-3; Barnes (1994), 12-13) but the issue here has obviously a greater extension than that of simply natural kinds; and the connotations of 'genus' (at any rate if it implies being a superset of some proper subset) are also too restrictive.

16 On the notion of the *phainomena* as they relate to astronomy, see also 38-9 n. 49; it is significant that Aratus entitled his verse rendering of Eudoxus's astronomy *Phainomena*; but Euclid gave the same name to his axiomatized treatment of the science.

That passage among other things expresses Aristotle's commitment to empiricism: first you collect the appearances, and only then do you begin to essay their causal explanation, in the form of demonstrative organization, a position made explicit at *Part. An.* 1.1, 639b6-11 (cf. 640a9-15; 1.5, 645b1-14), which also refers to the *phainomena* of the astronomers, and their subsequent mathematical organization, although this text implies (as do others) that 'grasping the phenomena' amounts to more than merely accumulating a set of raw data.[17] But for our purposes what really matters is the first sentence of T3. Each science is a distinct body of demonstrative knowledge, with its own proper domain, the majority of whose principles (axioms) are peculiar to it. But that talk of the majority implies (conversationally at least)[18] that some at least of the principles of some sciences will not be proper to them but will (presumably) either range more broadly across a variety of sciences, or be borrowed from some suitable higher-order science.[19]

And indeed that is exactly what we seem to find:

> T4. Since in each domain it is the attributes which hold of it *per se* (*kath' hauta*), and *qua* the domain in question, which hold of it of necessity, it is clear that scientific demonstrations (*hai epistêmonikai apodeixeis*) are concerned with the *per se* attributes and are constructed out of them. For the incidental (*kata sumbebêkos*) attributes are not necessary,[20] so we do not necessarily know why the conclusion holds, not even if it holds always the case, as long as it does not hold *per se*, for example, [in the case of] inferences on the basis of signs: for we will not know *per se* something which is *per se*, nor [will we know] the reason why [it holds]. And to know the reason why is to know through an explanation. Therefore it is necessary that both the middle term hold of the third and the first of the middle *per se*. (*Post. An.* 1.6, 75a28-36; cf. 74b27-32)

---

[17] This introduces complex and controversial issues regarding Aristotle's views concerning the mechanisms and proper analysis of concept-formation: see *Post. An.* 2.19.

[18] And perhaps more strictly than that – it is certainly a feature of Aristotle's treatment of 'for the most part' propositions (as well as that of later Empiricist doctors: see Hankinson. 1987) that if As are Bs for the most part, then some As will fail to be Bs: see Hankinson (1995a), 113-15. On the interpretation of Aristotle's 'for the most part' propositions, see Judson (1991a); Barnes (1994), 192-3 (on *Post. An.* 1.30, 87b22-8).

[19] These two possibilities may come to the same thing: if two or more sciences share an axiom, that fact is unlikely to be accidental, and hence their sharing of it will itself be explained by their all standing in a suitable relation to the higher-order science of whose domain the axiom is a proper component; see further below, 43-7.

[20] This claim is too sweeping: for Aristotle, as we have seen (27) some incidental attributes are necessary (since they hold of their subjects *per se*: consider the case of the angle-sum property of triangles, 27; and cf. T5) – incidental in the sense that they do not belong to the essence of the thing in question, necessary in that they are ineluctable consequences of facts about that essence (indeed demonstrations will be largely, if not entirely, of *per se* incidentals). But this is a pardonable unclarity in this case, and Aristotle's point here is clear enough.

Unless you derive your conclusion by way of *per se* attributes, you won't really know the fact in question, in the full sense of having structural understanding of it. We may indeed have incidental knowledge (or rather knowledge on the basis of things incidentally true), but not proper understanding. It is worth underlining the fact that Aristotelian 'incidental knowledge' need not be deficient in any point of certainty or deductive soundness: 'inferences on the basis of signs' can yield perfectly good, exceptionless universal conclusions (although some such arguments are indeed defeasible).[21] An example of such a proof by signs is the following: any woman who is lactating has conceived; this woman is lactating; so this woman has conceived (*Pr. An.* 2.27, 70a13-16). But lactation is evidently a result of pregnancy, not a cause of it. The case is similar to that of inferring the moon's sphericity from its phase-structure discussed earlier (25), although in the latter case the attribute demonstrated (sphericity) may well be thought to be a *per se* attribute of the subject (the moon), while being actually pregnant evidently is not of any woman.[22]

This is the point of the sentence rather clumsily rendered 'for we will not know *per se* something which is *per se*, nor [will we know] the reason why [it holds]': we will have some sort of knowledge (knowledge *de re* if you like) of what is as a matter of fact a *per se* attribute, but not in a *per se* way; i.e., we will not have *epistêmê*, understanding, of it (cf. T1 above). On the other hand, the basic *per se* premisses are immediate, and hence for them there is no knowing the reason why, at any rate by way of a middle term (Aristotle sometimes suggests that in these cases A holds of B in virtue of itself, i.e. in virtue of its simply being B, and hence they supply their own reasons for being true: 1.24, 85b24-6; 1.31, 88a7-8; but whatever we might say about that, it is clear that we do not have *epistêmê* of them).[23]

Aristotle draws the following conclusion from the argument of T4:

T5. Thus it is not possible to prove something by crossing from another domain (*genos*), for example something geometrical by way of arithmetic. For there are three things involved in demonstrations: one is what is demonstrated, namely the conclusion (and this is what holds of some kind (*genos*)[24] *per se*); another is the axioms (and the axioms

---

[21]   Aristotle discusses their logic at *Pr. An.* 2.27: on this passage see Burnyeat (1982) and Hankinson (1997).

[22]   In fact, although being prègnant is clearly not a *per se* attribute of a woman (at any rate in the I1 sense – might it be in the I2 sense? Certainly 'being female' looks as though it should figure in any account of pregnancy), being capable of pregnancy may well be (at any rate for a suitably broad sense of 'capable', such that even an infertile woman is capable in this sense of conceiving); but these issues, interesting though they are, need trouble us no further.

[23]   At least when Aristotle is being self-consciously respectful of his own technical vocabulary; *nous* is of first principles, *epistêmê* of truths derivative from them: *Post. An.* 1.2, 71b16-17; 2.19, 99b20-26; b5-17.

[24]   It seems better here to sacrifice consistency of rendition for lucidity here: the attributes evidently hold not of the entire domain, but of its subject-matter.

are those things from which [the demonstration takes place]);[25] and the third is the underlying kind whose properties and *per se* incidentals the demonstration makes clear. So the items from which the demonstration takes place may be the same; but when the domain (*genos*) is different, as in the case of arithmetic and geometry, it is not possible to make an arithmetic demonstration apply to the attributes of magnitudes, unless magnitudes are numbers (however, how this can be done in certain cases will be described later).[26] (*Post. An.* 1.7, 75a38-b6)

Here for the first time we come upon the prohibition on kind-crossing; but it is as yet unclear what this prohibition amounts to, or how broad the ban is supposed to be. Aristotle's first example is that of the impossibility of proving anything in geometry by way of arithmetic – and geometry and arithmetic did indeed seem distinct to the Greeks, in spite of their habit of representing certain arithmetical features in geometrical terms (a practice which still echoes for us in our nomenclature of squares and cubes). Certainly the notion of something approximating to a Cartesian reduction of geometry to algebra would have seemed highly foreign to them. A proof in geometry, then, should proceed by way of *per se* truths about the fundamental items of the domain: points, lines, planes, figures, not by way of axioms of number-theory or whatever.[27]

But there is something else important about this passage. The prohibition on using the axioms of a sister science is commended by way of consideration of 'the three things involved in demonstrations'.[28] The first is the conclusion, or, strictly

---

[25] 'Axioms' here might refer to the particular principles of the science in question, but that seems unlikely in view of the use of the term *axiôma* elsewhere to refer to the 'common axioms' (1.10, 76b14; 1.11, 77a27: see below, 42-3), and particularly in view of the claim in the next sentence that 'the items from which the demonstration takes place may be the same', i.e. for different sciences. Ross (1949, 531) remarks: 'it is rather misleading of A. to describe them as *the ex hôn*; any science also needs ultimate premisses peculiar to itself.... but the axioms are in a peculiar sense the *ex hôn*, the most fundamental starting-points of all'. Ross writes this because he discerns a general distinction between proving from (*ek*) something and proving through (*dia*) it; but it seems clear at least that Aristotle does not observe any such distinction consistently, if he does so at all: cf. e.g. T18; see Barnes (1994), 139; and below, 40-42.

[26] At *Post. An.* 1.9, 76a9-15; 76a22-5; 1.13, 78b34-79a16.

[27] Even so, it is important to note that the expression of such proper principles need not eschew arithmetic notions – it is just that they cannot be the principles of arithmetic itself. Consider the 19th definition of Euclid: 'rectilineal figures are those contained by straight lines, trilaterals those contained by three, quadrilateral those contained by four, and multilateral those contained by more than four straight lines'; here a geometrical definition makes use of arithmetical concepts (numbers): but it does not deploy arithmetic axioms.

[28] Aristotle refers to a similar tripartition at 1.10, 76b11-16 (T15), but it is not clear whether these two classifications (and some others) are in fact parallel; see Barnes (1994), 143-4; and below, 41-2.

speaking, the predicate of the conclusion,[29] the second the axioms which drive the proof, and 'the third is the underlying kind whose properties and *per se* incidentals the demonstration makes clear'. The 'underlying kind' is presumably then the set of the fundamental items of the domain;[30] and some at least of the axioms will specify primitive *per se* attributes of those items. Aristotle allows in the next sentence that 'the items from which the demonstration takes place may be the same' – i.e. some of the linking principles may be common to more than one science – but the items themselves are not to be traded across domains. I may perhaps use the objects of one domain to illustrate facts in another (presenting numerical facts such as powers by way of geometric representations, for instance); but I cannot prove anything in the first domain by employing the members of the second (I cannot prove the commutativity of addition by swapping around finite *lengths*), because, as the last sentence suggests, numbers aren't magnitudes.

Thus one sense in which one science may *not* employ the axioms of another is now clear: no one science can legitimately make use of the particular *per se* principles of another co-ordinate science, since they are by definition concerned with the objects of a distinct domain. Thus if geometry and arithmetic really are separate sciences, the particular principles of one, concerned as they are with spelling out the *per se* attributes of the proprietary objects of that domain, cannot serve to ground any inference in the other, since the typical conclusions of such inferences will make reference only to the attributes of its particular denizens.

But what of the suggestion that some of the intermediate principles may be the property of more than one science? Aristotle continues:

T6. Arithmetical demonstration always sticks to the domain with which the demonstration is concerned, and the same goes for the other [sciences]. Consequently, the domain must either be the same without qualification, or at least in a way, if the demonstration is going to cross; and it is clear that it is impossible in any other way, since it is necessary that the extreme and the middle terms be from the same domain: for if they are not *per se*, they will be incidental. For this reason it is not possible to prove

---

[29]   See Barnes (1994), 130.

[30]   However, see n. 24. I talk here (and throughout) of a science's being delimited by its domain; in a fascinating, as yet unpublished paper, which he has been kind enough to let me see, Reviel Netz argues that the function of Aristotle's *qua*-operator (although he doesn't like the use of the term 'operator' in this context) is to specify *how* a science looks at objects (and this, rather than the identity of the objects themselves, determines the scope of the science). This may very well be right – but Netz's point is basically about the ontological status of the items of a science (must they have absolutely separate existence?); e.g., do geometrical lines and points *really* exist. And this question is distinct from that of whether (in a less ontologically-committing manner) the sciences do still have their own proper objects (lines, points, etc. for geometry).

by way of geometry that contraries belong to a single science,[31] and not even that two cubes make a cube.[32] (*Post. An.* 1.7, 75b7-14)

The argument of T6 may be expressed as follows. All demonstrations involve *per se* attributes; if F and G apply *per se* to A, then F and G belong to the same domain as A; hence no demonstration can make use of attributes derived from another domain. As it stands, that argument is too vague to be assessable – but it is at least clear that it only goes through (for any attributes F and G) if Aristotle is committed to the claim that all the attributions in a proper demonstration will be *per se*. Now obviously they cannot all be *per se* in the fundamental sense of I1;[33] but T5 explicitly asserts that the predicate-terms in the conclusions of demonstrations will hold in a sense *per se* of their subjects, while T4 affirms that demonstrative knowledge is *per se* knowledge of the conclusion. The relevant sense of *per se* is surely (at any rate in some cases) that of the *per se* incidentals, as T5 expressly indicates. Thus we may demonstrate the angle-sum theorem for triangles; and the property of having 2R is a *per se* incidental of triangles as such, 'incidental' only in the sense that it is not part of the essence of triangularity. Thus the apparent implication of T6 (and it is only a conversational implication) that '*per se*' and 'incidental' are exclusive categories ('if they are *per se*, they can't be incidental')

---

[31] The proof of this is a job for general metaphysics or logic: cf. *Metaph.* Δ 2, 1004a9-1005a18. That contraries belong to the same science is, as Barnes notes (1994, 131-2) an Aristotelian commonplace (cf. *Metaph.* E 10, 1018a26-31; *Top.* 2.7, 113a14-19, 4.3, 123b1-8, etc.), and applies to practical skills as well: if a doctor knows how to cure he knows *ipso facto* how not to (*Metaph.* Θ 2, 1046b5-24; cf. *De An.* 3.9, 433a4-6; compare Plato, *Republic* 1, 333e-334b).

[32] I.e., there is a z such that, for any x, y, $x^3.y^3 = z^3$ (Euclid, 9.4; cf. Heath, 1925, vol. 2, 46). In fact, as is obvious by elementary algebra, $x^3.y^3 = xy^3$ (i.e. z will equal the product of x and y).

[33] Unless definitions themselves contain derivative components; for if all the premisses of a demonstration are *per se* in the sense that the attribute expressed by the predicate must be part of the definition of the subject, but some of the propositions are derivative (i.e. they are conclusions from more basic premisses), then it must be possible for derivative properties to figure in Aristotelian definitions. Some definitional attributes may indeed in a sense be derivative; that is, it may be possible to explain why individuals of this sort have the property in question: if 'mortal' is partially definitional of humans, human mortality may itself be a consequence of the fact that humans are matter-form composites, and no such composite can last forever (cf. *Long. Vit.* 2-3, 465a13-b33). But in that case it looks as though the explanation will be taking place in another, superordinate science (that of material things); and I find it difficult to imagine how one might conclude from within a particular science to a partial definition of some member of its domain, while Aristotle explicitly argues in book II of *Post. An.* that there is no demonstration of definition, at least in the strict sense, although in a sense demonstrations can exhibit definitions: *Post. An.* 2.3-10, esp. 2.8, 93a15-b20.

must be rejected.[34] Thus the deductive consequences of *per se* attributes will themselves hold *per se*, albeit only derivatively.

And in general, in the sort of deficient kind-crossing proof Aristotle is considering, the conclusion will be a *per se* proposition but it will not have been shown to hold as such (and hence it will not be understood in the fullest Aristotelian sense). Take the quasi-proof ('q-proof') by way of geometry that the product of two cubes is a cube. In this case the conclusion itself is surely not incidental (at least in any strong sense incompatible with its being *per se*): it is after all a perfectly general and straightforward truth of arithmetic, and hence on Aristotle's account ought to be both necessary, and to follow from properly *per se* axioms (of arithmetic). But the point is that, in this case, although the conclusion does predicate a *per se* attribute of its subject, it does not so predicate it as such – in this sense, it is akin to the q-proof of human mortality on the grounds that all humans are mammals. The means by which the conclusion has been deduced – an excursus through geometry – cannot serve to ground an arithmetic theorem as such.[35] This is a case where what we know will be a *per se* attribute, but we will not know it as such: 'we will not know *per se* something which is *per se*' (29-30, T4).

This analysis seems to be confirmed by a passage from chapter 9:

T7. Since it is clear that it is not possible to demonstrate anything otherwise than from its principles[36] if what is to be proved holds of it *qua* that thing, scientific knowledge will not merely consist in proof from true, indemonstrable and immediate propositions. For it is possible to prove in this way in the manner of Bryson's squaring.[37] For arguments of this sort prove in regard to something common, which will also hold of something else; and for this reason the arguments apply to other things which are not of the same domain. Thus he knows, not *qua* the thing in question, but incidentally, or else

---

[34]   '*Per se*' is avowedly a term with multiple senses: Aristotle devotes a chapter of his 'Philosophical Lexicon' (*Metaph.* Δ 18) to elucidating their distinctions; see n. 10, and n. 20.

[35]   Perhaps it does not do so at all: suppose the 'proof' takes the form of considering a number of different cubes, and showing that they all conform to the theorem, and then inferring inductively that the theorem holds of all cubes; then it will presumably have the status of a conjecture such as that of Goldbach that every even number is the sum of two primes.

[36]   Does this mean that any demonstration must make use only of principles proper to domain as such? This seems to be the natural implication of Aristotle's language here. But if all the principles must be proper in this sense for there to be a demonstration *per se* of a *per se* attribute, then there can be no such thing as a subordinate science, or at least that there can be no *epistêmê* as such of the theorems in a subordinate science. The former consequence is clearly to be avoided if at all possible; but even the latter still makes a very strong claim, albeit one which Aristotle might possibly have been able to subscribe to in a certain sense: see 46-50.

[37]   Sc. of the circle.

the demonstration would not apply to another domain as well. (*Post. An.* 1.9, 75b37-76a3)

Squaring the circle (i.e. producing a square equal in area to the area of a given circle on the basis of geometrical reasoning) was a notorious problem in Greek mathematics; and Bryson's attempted solution has caused immense controversy.[38] But it apparently involved computing the areas of inscribed and circumscribed polygons of an ever-increasing number of sides, in order to push the difference between them towards zero by a method of exhaustion. If this is right, then it is probable that Aristotle is objecting to his use of some general principle of the form 'things greater than all the same things and less than all the same things are equal',[39] a principle which applies to numbers as well as to magnitudes (or in this case areas), and hence is not proper to geometry.

This suggests that Bryson's error is simply to make use of a principle whose scope is more general than that of geometry alone;[40] and that is also suggested by another example of the error in question, drawn from an earlier passage (*Post. An.* 1.5, 74a4-13). Aristotle notes that there are several ways to go wrong, and hence to fail to prove something 'primarily and universally': (a) we may fail to see that the item of which we are proving the attribute is a species of a higher genus all of whose members share it;[41] (b) there may be a more general middle-term which doesn't have a collective name;[42] or (c) the subject of which it is proved may be

---

[38] Cf. Heath (1925), 223-5, 2; (1948), 48-50; Mueller, (1982). Aristotle mentions Bryson's 'proof' on two occasions in *de Sophisticis Elenchis* (171b12-18, 172a2-7), where he describes it as 'eristic', in contrast with that from lunes, which 'applies only to geometry on account of its being derived from the proper principles'. Aristotle implies at *Categories* 7, 7b27-33 that no successful quadrature has yet been achieved; at *Eudemian Ethics* 2.10, 1226b28-30 he insinuates that it is impossible. At *Phys.* 1.2, 185b15-18, he distinguishes between 'proofs' which it is up to the geometer to refute, such as that 'by means of segments' with those which are not in the geometer's domain 'such as that of Antiphon', which presumably involved some sort of mechanical construction. Bryson's clearly falls into the first camp, as does the 'Eudoxan' solution found at Euclid, *Elements* 12.2.

[39] See Tredennick (1962), 64-5.

[40] This is not the only possibility; Aristotle might think that Bryson's method works for squaring in general (i.e. of other figures), and hence doesn't explain how the circle as such is squared; but if that were right, then the appropriate response would surely be that in that case there is no squaring of the circle as such at all, any more than there is proving the angle-sum theorem of an isosceles triangle as such: see n. 41 below; and in any case, the passages from *Soph. El.* (n. 38) tell strongly in favour it.

[41] The error is illustrated at 74a16-17: if you prove the angle-sum theorem using an isosceles triangle, and are unaware of any other triangles (or perhaps rather unaware that the theorem applies in virtue of the general class of triangles) then you will mistakenly think that it holds of the isosceles as such (cf. *Post. An.* 1.24, 85b4-15; and T9).

[42] I.e. suppose that although there are triangles, there is no general term for them: this is

part of a larger whole of which the attribute holds in general.[43] These are different sub-species of the same general class, one in which the attribute is proved as though it were peculiar to a particular subject, when in fact it is not. As an example of type (b) Aristotle instances the law of the alternation of proportionals:[44] one might think that the law applied *qua* number or *qua* line or *qua* solid or *qua* period of time, and indeed formerly it was proved separately in all these cases; but now it is proved universally, and properly, of the general case (74a17-25). This suggests that Aristotle is thinking of something like the following argument:

[A]   (1)   *a, b, c, d*, are proportional numbers
       (2)   proportional numbers alternate
so
       (3)   *a, b, c, d* alternate;

and that is inadequate, presumably because, since (2) is a special case of a more general truth of proportion which applies to any quantity, the middle term does not adequately explain the conclusion: it is not in virtue of their being proportional *numbers* that *a-d* alternate; it is in virtue of their more generally being *proportionals*.[45]

However, it is now easy to see that the case of [A] is not on all fours with that of Bryson; worse, they seem to yield results which turn out to be quite incompatible

---

the type illustrated by the case of the law of proportionals below.

[43] 'For although the demonstration will hold of those parts, and will do so in every case, still the demonstration will not be of it primarily and universally (by "of it primarily and universally" I mean of this thing primarily and *qua* itself)': *Post. An.* 1.5, 74a9-13.

[44] I.e. if a:b::c:d then a:c::b:d.

[45] Barnes writes: 'an argument of the sort Aristotle is objecting to might run:
       (1) All proportional numbers are *B*;
       (2) Everything *B* alternates;
       (3) All proportional numbers alternate' (1994, 134);
but this seems unlikely, partly because no hint is given as to the possible sense of '*B*' here (although I suppose a plausible interpretation might be 'proportional', in a general sense), but mainly in view of Barnes' subsequent objection to Aristotle's conclusion that (in his version) 'you do not understand the item as such' (which I render 'thus he knows, not *qua* the thing in question, but incidentally' – the verb is third, not second person in the Greek), which he takes to mean 'you will not know that A belongs to C as such', to which he objects 'in general, if AaC is concluded from AaB and BaC, then A will belong to C not as such but as *B*' (135); that is surely right – but irrelevant here. The 'thing in question' is the general truth, absent from my argument [A], that all proportionals alternate; the non-understander's knowledge is incidental because it depends on the derivative, regional truth (A2). This account gets exactly right, then, the required relationship between the appropriate choice of middle term (and major premiss) and knowledge of something as such and non-incidentally. Note that Euclid's celebrated discussion of proportion in *Elements* 5 talks in perfectly general terms about magnitudes.

with one another. Bryson supposedly goes wrong by employing a principle of too great generality, one which is not confined to geometry. On the other hand, [A] and its like go wrong because, although all the premisses are restricted to the domain in question, the predicate holds of the subject in the conclusion not as such but in virtue of some more general relation; and so [A] is not explanatory. The difficulty is now starkly apparent: there seems to be no way of constructing a genuine demonstration in such cases, since if the argument is explanatory, it cannot proceed via proper principles, and if it proceeds via proper principles, it cannot be explanatory. If this result holds, the whole project of demonstrative science (at any rate in regard to cases of sub- and super-ordination) is in deep trouble.

That painful result depends on the supposition that all of the principles of a proper Aristotelian science must be proper to it (see n. 36 above); and perhaps that supposition is mistaken:

> T8. Of the things which are used in the demonstrative sciences, some are proper to each science while others are common; but common in virtue of analogy, since they are useful only insofar as they belong to the domain which falls under the science. Proper [principles] are such as that a line or the straight is such and such, common, such as that if equals are subtracted from equals the remainders are equal. It is enough [to assume] each of these insofar as it is in the domain; for he will achieve the same result even if he does not assume it universally, but only as it applies to magnitudes (or, for the arithmetician, to numbers). (*Post. An.* 1.10, 76a37-b2)

The example of a common axiom here is one of Euclid's axioms of equality, one of his so-called 'common notions' (*Elements* cn. 3), 'common' presumably at least in part in Aristotle's sense: it is not a proper principle of either arithmetic or geometry, but functions equally in both.[46]

So it is evident that Aristotle does allow his sciences on occasion to range outside their proper domain in search of properly explanatory principles – the question is, how can they do this without compromising their integrity? After all, the sciences are supposed to deliver *per se*, non-incidental knowledge, and, as an earlier passage has it,

> T9. We know something non-incidentally whenever we know it in respect of the thing in virtue of which it holds, on the basis of the principles of that thing *qua* itself, as for instance when being equal to two right-angles holds of what it holds of *per se* and from

---

[46] But see Ross (1949), 56-7, who stresses that the '*koinai ennoiai*' are common in the sense that they are common property of mankind: compare *Metaph.* B 2, 996b27-9: 'by "demonstrative" I mean those common opinions from which everyone proves'; cf. 997a19-21: 'every demonstrative science studies, in the case of a particular subject-matter, the *per se* incidentals from the common opinions'; and compare the status of the (rather different) *koinai ennoiai* of the Stoics. Aristotle mentions this principle at *Pr. An.* 1.24, 41b13-22 and *Metaph.* Γ.3, 1005a23-6.

its principles.[47] Consequently if this too holds of what it holds of *per se*, necessarily the middle term will be in the same domain. (*Post. An.* 1.9, 76a4-9)

How, then, can we allow middle terms to be borrowed from other domains and still know something properly and non-incidentally on the basis of them? Aristotle immediately offers one answer:

> T10. If this is not the case, then it will be like [proving results in] harmonics by way of arithmetic. And such things are indeed proved in this way, but there is a difference: for the fact proved is of another science (since the underlying domain is different) while the reason why is of the higher [science], to which the attributes belong *per se*. Consequently it is clear from these things too that it is not possible to demonstrate anything in an unqualified way otherwise than from its principles; but in these cases, the principles have something in common. (*Post. An.* 1.9, 76a9-15)

Sciences can be subordinate to other sciences, and in various places in the *Analytics* Aristotle gives a variety of examples of such subordination: (a) harmonics is subordinate to arithmetic (75b16; 76a10, 24; 78b38; 87a34); (b) optics to geometry (75b16; 76a24; 78b37); (c) mechanics to geometry (stereometry) (76a24; 78b37); (d) empirical to mathematical harmonics (79a2);[48] (e) observational astronomy to mathematical astronomy (78b39; 79a1);[49] and finally, and perhaps

---

[47] I.e. of triangle as such: see n. 41 above.

[48] This is presumably not the same relation as that of (a); and it is tempting to take 'mathematical harmonics' here to be equivalent to 'harmonics' of (a), thus yielding a three-fold distinction of types; a similar triad can be generated by subordinating 'the study of the rainbow' (see T20 below) to optics and geometry. On these issues see Barnes (1994), 158-62; Lennox (1986), 44-9.

[49] Aristotle's two mentions of relations between different branches of astronomy in these two passages are puzzling; they are only three lines apart, so it seems natural to suppose that he is referring to the same relationship, and the same *relata*, in each case, particularly since he does not suggest otherwise; but the language he uses is strikingly different in each case, and he is, ostensibly, using the two examples to exemplify different facts about the language at any rate of subordination. Aristotle begins the paragraph with the claim that the science which studies the fact it not the same as that which supplies the reason, when the former is subordinate to the latter (78b34-7); he then gives a list of pairs of sciences related in this way: 'e.g. optics to geometry, mechanics to stereometry, harmonics to arithmetic, and *ta phainomena* to astronomy (*astrologia*: not of course its modern near-homonym, but explanatory astronomy)' (78b37-9). But then he says: 'some of the sciences are near-synonyms, such as mathematical and nautical astronomy, and mathematical and empirical harmonics' (78b39-79a2). Is 'nautical astronomy' equivalent to '*ta phainomena*'? On balance the likely answer seems to be 'yes'; but it is also possible that Aristotle here indicates the existence of another triadic system of studies (cf n. 48 above), although it is difficult to see how exactly such a triad could be constructed, and how the various aspects of astronomical theory and practice could be parcelled out among them. For this use of

most surprisingly, (f) medicine to geometry (79a14). We will return to that last case later (T20 below).

But these cases are not on all fours with those involving common principles such as the equals axiom. In all of (a)-(f), whatever may be the differences between them, one (superordinate) science provides some of the explanatory mechanism for another subordinate science (the subordinate science is not of course simply a branch or a sub-set of the other – it will involve its own particular axioms and postulates which introduce and specify some of the relations which hold between the items that form its particular subject-matter).[50] But in the latter case, the particular sciences (geometry, arithmetic) are co-ordinate – and each of them in a way makes use of more general principles which are common to both.[51] But, again, the question remains: how are they to do so, consistently with Aristotle's strictures on structure? In a number of places, Aristotle seems to say that only in the case of genuine subordination can one science make use of material derived from another:

> T11. Nor can something belonging to one science be proved by way of another, unless they stand in such a relation to one another that one is subordinate to the other, as are optics in relation to geometry and harmonics in relation to arithmetic. Nor indeed [can it be shown by geometry] whether something holds of lines but not *qua* lines and *qua* derived from the proper principles, as for instance whether the straight line is the most beautiful, or whether it is the contrary of the curved; for these things hold not *qua* their proper domain but *qua* something common.[52] (*Post. An.* 1.7, 75b14-20)

'*phainomena*', in the sense of an organized set of empirical data, see T3 above, and n. 16. On all of this, see Barnes (1994), 158-62; Lennox (1986), 43 n. 27, writes: 'Commentators have been unnecessarily perplexed by the last pair [sc. astronomy, *ta phainomena*]...; as Aquinas correctly notes, *here* Aristotle is interested only in a special sort of hierarchical relation between *explanans* and *explananda* which is not *simply* a matter of relation of genus to species.'

[50] Mignucci (1975, 178-84) suggests that the principles of the subordinate science will be proved by the super-ordinate science; Barnes (1994, 136) rightly points out that if all such principles were provable then the subordinate science would not be a separate science at all, but simply a proper part of the superordinate science; but that does rule out the possibility of some of the subordinate science's principles being so demonstrable (the ones which do not explicate the definitions of the proper objects of the domain, for example; but even the latter may turn out to be at least partially demonstrable: see n. 33 above). Aristotle nowhere says anything of the kind directly; but see 42-7; and T17.

[51] There may be a sense in which arithmetic is prior to geometry for Aristotle (*Metaph.* M 3, 1078a9-13 certainly seems to suggest this: 'insofar as something is concerned with things prior in account and simpler, to that extent it is more precise, for this is the simple; so what is without magnitude is more precise than what involves magnitude, while the latter is more so if it is without motion, and if it involves motion, the more so if it involves the primary motion, for that is the simplest and is uniform'); but as regards such properties as proportionality or equality, they seem clearly co-ordinate.

[52] The examples here are a little puzzling, although the general point is clear enough.

And this position is reiterated in a later passage:

> T12. Demonstration does not apply to another domain, otherwise than in the way it was stated that geometrical demonstrations apply to mechanics and optics, and arithmetical ones to harmonics. (*Post. An.* 1.9, 76a22-5)

So there is clearly still work to be done in order to make sense of Aristotle's position on the common principles. Matters are not helped here (as elsewhere) by a certain looseness in the terminology. By 'common principles' he sometimes appears to mean not such items as the equals axiom, but more general 'logical' principles such as the Law of the Excluded Middle. For example, in the course of arguing that there cannot be a single science of everything on the model of Platonic dialectic, he says:

> T13. Nor could there be some of the common principles from which everything could be proved (by 'common' I mean, e.g., that everything must be either affirmed or denied); for the kinds (*genê*) of things which are different, and some things hold only of quantities, others of qualities; and it is along with these that things are proved through the common principles. (*Post. An.* 1.32, 88a36-b3)

In other words, all sciences require some proprietary principles of their own; but they can make use of ones which are not. The only thing excluded by T13 is the 'Platonic' idea of there being some superscience which comprehends every other branch of knowledge within its grasp; and on no account does Aristotelian metaphysics, of the type discussed in *Metaph.* Γ and E, do that; it is a science which in a sense deals with everything; but it does not deal with everything to do with everything. Thus at *Metaph.* Γ 3, 1005a19-b8, Aristotle claims that investigation of 'the so-called axioms' of the domains of knowledge 'belongs to the philosopher' – and the axioms in this case too turn out to be principles like that of non-contradiction.

But this raises another issue, which is worth briefly treating here: what is the precise status and function of such principles for Aristotle? Ross (1949, 531) detects a difference between proving X from Y and proving X through Y (see n. 25 above), where to prove from Y is to use Y as a premiss while to prove through Y is

---

Aristotle does consider the curved line more perfect than the straight (*Cael.* 1.2, 269a19-30); whether that means that it is also more beautiful is another question. The same passage deals with the issue of contrariety (1.4, 270b32-271a33) as it applies to straight and circular *motions* (although not to the lines themselves); and as Barnes says (1994, 132), 'contrariety is a relation holding between things *qua* beings' (cf. n. 31 above). At *Metaph.* B 2, 996a29-b1 and M 3, 1078a31-b6 Aristotle deals with the notion of beauty in mathematics, but neither passage is much help. But one may speculate that, insofar as aesthetic considerations apply to mathematical objects, they do so in virtue of more than merely their mathematical properties (perhaps because they exhibit certain proportional facts which have a far broader extension).

to employ Y as a rule of inference. This distinction is also suggested by the last sentence of the following passage:

> T14. Proper too are the things which the science assumes to exist, about which it studies those things which belong to it *per se*, as arithmetic studies units and geometry points and lines: for they assume both that these things are and what they are. But as regards their *per se* attributes, what each signifies is assumed, e.g. arithmetic assumes what odd and even or square and cube are, and geometry what irrationality and deflexion and verging[53] signify; but that they are is shown through the common [principles] and from the things which have been demonstrated; and the same thing holds in astronomy. (*Post. An.* 1.10, 76b3-11)

'From the things which have been demonstrated' is a little odd – one would expect Aristotle to say that conclusions are demonstrated from the indemonstrables: but perhaps he is thinking of chains of inference of the sort one finds in arithmetic and geometry, where each stage (apart from the first) takes for its premisses propositions demonstrated at the previous stage.[54] But even so, this distinction of sense between the two prepositional phrases is extremely fragile, and there are numerous cases (some cited by Barnes: 1994, 139)[55] where the distinction appears to break down,[56] as it does in the following passage:

> T15. Every demonstrative science is concerned with three things: the things which it posits as existing (and these are the kinds (*genê*) whose *per se* attributes it studies); the so-called common axioms, the primary things from which they demonstrate; and thirdly the attributes of which it assumes the signification of each. (*Post. An.* 1.10, 76b11-16)[57]

---

[53] Deflexion is deviation from a straight path; a finite straight line verges to all those points which it would pass through if it were extended beyond its actual limit; see Barnes (1994), 139.

[54] See Mignucci (1975), 198-9.

[55] 'Aristotle uses "from" of the common axioms (e.g. 75a42; 76b14; 77a27) and "through" of the premisses (e.g. 78a30; *Top. A* 1 [i.e. 1.1], 100a26)'; add to the first group the passages from *Metaph.* B 2 quoted in n. 46; and *Post. An.* 1.32, 88b27-9 (T17).

[56] Moreover, as Barnes also notes, there is no clear ancient separation between axioms and rules of inference as such; although Aristotle is clearly dimly at any rate aware of it: as he points out in *Post. An.* 1.11, 77a10-21, the Principle of Non-Contradiction rarely appears as a premiss in proofs, although in a sense it is fundamental to all proofs; cf. *Metaph.* Γ 3-5; see further n. 59.

[57] See T5; and cf. *Post. An.* 1.10, 76a31-6:
> In each domain those things of which it is not possible to prove that they are I call 'principles'; therefore what the primary things and those derived from them signify is assumed; but as regards existence, in the case of principles it is assumed, while in the case of the others this is proved; so for instance what a unit is or what the straight and also what a triangle is [is assumed]; but we assume the existence of the unit and of magnitude, while the others are proved.

T15 reinforces some of the claims of T14 about what gets to be assumed and what proven; but it also claims of the 'so-called common axioms'[58] that things are demonstrated *from*, and not through them, contrary to Ross's basic distinction. Moreover, the passage (1.7, 75a42: T5) which Ross is commenting on when he introduces the distinction (1949, 531) is one he has to explain away (since 'from' is used there of the common axioms) by pointing out that 'such axioms [sc. as the equals axiom] are frequently used as premises in Euclid (and no doubt were used in the pre-Euclidian geometry A. knew)' (see n. 25). This may be true, but the question precisely is, can Aristotle allow them to be used as such?

In discussing whether there can be a single super-science on the model of Platonic dialectic (a question which is also central to *Metaph.* Γ and E), Aristotle writes:

> T16. All the sciences share with one another in respect of the common [axioms] (by 'common' I mean what they use as though demonstrating from them, not the subjects about which they prove, nor what they prove); and dialectic shares in all of them, as would any one which attempted to prove the common [axioms], such as everything is either affirmed or denied, or that equals taken from equals [leave equals], and things of that sort. But dialectic does not deal with things defined in this way, nor is it confined to some single domain. (*Post. An.* 1.11, 77a26-32; cf. T18)

He adamantly rejects the idea of such a super-science: none of these fundamental principles (Principle of Non-Contradiction [PNC], Law of Excluded Middle [LEM]) can be demonstrated – indeed, as he says at *Metaph.* Γ 4, 1006a5-11), it is a mark of ignorance to suppose that they can. But equally, properly understood, the *Metaphysics* never suggests that the principles of the special sciences as such can be established by metaphysics. Rather what first philosophy does is to establish the very general conceptual scaffolding within which such sciences can be elaborated; and it does this in part by establishing in a non-demonstrative manner ('refutationally' as he puts it) the fundamental principles of that architecture.[59] Consequently

> T17. If this is clear,[60] then it is also clear that it is not possible to demonstrate the proper principles of each domain: for such principles would be principles of everything, and the science of them would be sovereign over everything. For one who knows on the

---

[58]   On the 'so-called', cf. *Metaph.* Γ 3, 1005a19-b8: above, 40.

[59]   'But surely such principles can on occasion turn up as premises of a demonstration, as PNC does in *reductio* proofs?' Surely so, at least in modern sentential calculus presentations; but Aristotle was not of course working with such a logic (although he does allow that PNC may figure as a premise in an argument if the conclusion is of that form: *Post. An.* 1.10, 77a10-21; the passage is very obscure: see Barnes, 1994, 145-7) and in any case they do not supply any content to the arguments, as Aristotelian first principles surely should.

[60]   Sc. 'it is not possible to demonstrate anything in an unqualified way otherwise than from its principles': 1.9, 76a13-15; T10.

basis of higher reasons knows in a superior manner. Consequently if he knows in a superior, indeed in the most superior, manner, then that science will be superior or most superior. (*Post. An.* 1.9, 76a16-22; and cf. *Post. An.* 1.10, 76a31-6: n. 49)

But there is no such sovereign science; and this entails that the principles, some or all of them, of the special sciences be *sui generis*. But of course that rejection of the possibility of a Platonic superscience of dialectic is perfectly compatible with supposing that some of the principles, of some of the sciences, are borrowed from higher-order, more general sciences.

III

Let us pause to take stock. The principles of any science will be proper to that science. They will consist in part of I1-predications which are by definition (see above, 26-7) proper to it; and if they also make use of existence assumptions, as T14 and T15 say, those assumptions too will be tied to the domain in question (there is no room in anthropology for propositions like 'there are frogs'). Hence the sciences ought to be (and Aristotle argues that they are) hermetically-sealed; and there will be no kind-crossing. And yet for all that Aristotle allows that there can be such a thing 'in a way'; consider again *Post. An.* 1.7, 75b8-11 (T6):

> the domain must either be the same without qualification, or at least in a way, if the demonstration is going to cross; and it is clear that it is impossible in any other way, since the extreme and the middle terms must be from the same domain. (cf. T8)

'The extreme and the middle terms [i.e. *all* the terms that figure in the syllogisms] must be from the same domain' because otherwise we cannot have a scientific explanation at all. Now, if the domain is 'the same without qualification', then there are no kinds to cross; but there may be if it is the same 'in a way'. What might that mean?

An obvious suggestion, in the case of the subordinate sciences, would be that the subordinate science was a proper part of the superior. But that will not do (see n. 50 above): optics contains all sorts of propositions regarding rays, light, etc.[61] which are no part of geometry. Perhaps then optics contains as part of itself a proper part of geometry? That is more promising – but again it appears to violate the original strictures that Aristotle placed on the sciences – for the premisses of geometry as such will not be true *per se* of the objects of optics. Geometry is an abstract science in a very real sense for Aristotle: it deals with the spatial properties

---

[61] I refer to standard Greek mathematical optics, of the sort exemplified by Euclid's *Optics* – Aristotle may have had a somewhat different conception, at least of the material of the subject (consider his view that 'light is the actualization of the diaphanous [medium]': *De An.* 2.7, 419a11-12); but his general view its formal properties was no doubt similar.

of magnitudes abstracted from their physical instantiations.[62] In a later chapter (which again deals with, and rejects, the possibility that there could be in any genuine sense a single set of principles from which all the truths of all the sciences follow), he writes:

> T18. It is evident even in this case[63] that it is not possible [sc. for there to be a unified totality of principles], since we have shown that principles of things which differ in kind themselves differ in kind.[64] For the principles are of two kinds, those from which and those concerning which: those from which are common, while those concerning which are proper, e.g. number and magnitude.[65] (*Post. An.* 1.32, 88b25-9; cf. T8)

A little earlier, Aristotle once again spelled out the conditions on the independence of a science:

> T19. A single science is that which is of a single domain (*genos*), the things which are composed of the primary things and are parts or *per se* attributes of them.[66] Sciences differ from one another if their principles are neither derived from the same things,[67] nor the principles of one from those of the other. An indication of this is when one arrives at the indemonstrables: for these must be in the same domain as what is demonstrated. (*Post. An.* 1.28, 87a38-b3)

Geometry is about (among other things) lines and their properties. Optics is about certain kinds of physically-realized straight lines and *their* properties, some of which will be straightforward consequences of the geometry.[68] Equally, in mechanics,

---

[62] See Mueller (1970); Lear (1982); but now see also Netz (forthcoming); and see Lennox (1986), 31-44.

[63] 'This case' is the supposition that there is a unified totality of first principles, although not every conclusion relies on all of them (1.32, 88b15-21): they would be 'related', although different principles would function in different departments.

[64] The reference is presumably to 1.7 and 1.28, 87a38-b3 (T19).

[65] Note that the usage of this sentence also conflicts with the Ross thesis: n. 25, and 31 above.

[66] This sentence is adduced by McKirahan (1992, 57-8) in support of the view that domains include both the subject-items and their attributes; and this is indeed what the text plainly says. But as Barnes (1994, 190-91) notes, '[T]his is singular', and appears to contradict 1.7, 75a42 (T5), and what is implied by *Metaph.* B 2, 997a5-9, 21-2; I am inclined to regard it as an aberration – but it is worth noting that in any demonstration, the middle terms will function as both predicates and subjects (in different premisses).

[67] Presumably 'derived from the same things' here means not 'deduced from the same axioms' (which would be oxymoronic), but 'constructed from the same terms'; see Barnes (1994), 191.

[68] Cf. *Phys.* 2.2, 193b23-194a12, a passage discussed in Lennox (1986), esp. 194a7-12: 'the more physical of the mathematical sciences, such as optics, harmonics and astronomy, make this clear too: for they are in a way the converse of geometry. For while geometry considers physical lines, but not *qua* physical, while optics considers the

applying the principle of the parallelogram of forces (cf. ps.-Arist., *Mechanics* 1, 848b1-35), we can determine the velocity of a composite motion as the vector-sum of its components by geometrical reasoning. But what is the status of the geometrical axioms in relation to such sciences? Crucially, must they actually form a part of them?

To this the answer is, I think, 'no'. Consider again the opening sentence of T8: 'of the things which are used in the demonstrative sciences, some are proper to each science while others are common; but common in virtue of analogy, since they are useful only insofar as they belong to the domain which falls under the science'. In other words, if I make use of the equals axiom in an arithmetic proof, I make use of it in its arithmetic form

(EA)   Equal numbers subtracted from equal numbers leave equal numbers;

rather than in that of its Euclidian generalization

(EG)   Equals subtracted from equals leave equals.

It is EA, rather than EG, which actually functions in the argument. But, it will be objected, EA is not primitive and immediate, since it can be shown to be a consequence of EG.

This is precisely what I want to deny on Aristotle's behalf. Or rather, even if EA can be derived from EG, that does not show that, in the context of arithmetical derivations, EA is not primitive and, in a sense, immediate. Let us suppose that, *sub specie* an arithmetic demonstration, the appropriate principle to use is EA; and also that it is, *sub* that demonstration, immediate (i.e. it holds in some suitable sense immediately of numbers). But how can it be immediate if it is derived from EG? It is worth recalling the technical definition of immediacy noted above (26): a proposition AaB is immediate just in case there is no X such AaX and XaB, and A holds *per se* of X and X of B and X explains A's holding of B. One might initially suppose (as indeed I did) that EG cannot function like that in relation to EA for logical reasons; and in some cases indeed that seems to be right: typically, the basic geometrical facts which inform mechanics and optics cannot be integrated into the sciences in question in the form of terms in demonstrative syllogisms. Suppose that 'AaB' represents some (interpreted) fact of geometry as it applies to optics (e.g. the angle of incidence = the angle of reflection): this, as it is a principle of optics, will be immediate just in that the premiss cannot be 'thickened' by the imposition of intermediate terms.[69] But, as it turns out, this is not the case in regard to the relation between EA and EG; and EA can in fact be derived syllogistically from EG as follows:

---

mathematical line, but *qua* physical rather than mathematical'; see also n. 82.

[69]   On 'thickening', see *Post. An.* 1.15; 1.19; Barnes (1994), 169-70.

[B]   (1)   being such that, when equal and when subtracted from equals, equals
              remain, belongs to all magnitudes;
       (2)   magnitude belongs to all numbers
hence
       (3)   being such that, when equal and when subtracted from equals, equals
              remain, belongs to all numbers;

and that, while no doubt clumsy, exhibits the paradigmatic demonstrative
syllogistic form of Barbara. Thus, on the face of it, the admittedly cumbrous (1)
could be introduced to arithmetic, which, along with (2), would yield EA as a
derivative principle. Moreover, it seems plausible to suppose that both (1) and (2)
involve *per se* attributions, albeit in different domains. Thus it is not the case that
EG can be excluded from arithmetic on the grounds that it can play no directly
syllogistic role in the establishment of arithmetic axioms (although in plenty of
other cases that does indeed seem to be the case).[70] Still, one might reasonably
argue that inferences such as [B] misrepresent in a certain sense the relations that
hold between the special and the general truths in such cases, which is (or ought to
be) one of analysis;[71] or to put it another way, in virtue of the fact that numbers are
magnitudes, we should be able to substitute 'number' for 'magnitude' throughout
such principles and obtain a subordinate principle (and this will apply equally in
those cases where the relation between the general principle and its subordinate
derivative cannot be represented syllogistically).

Moreover, this is the case even if the special truths can be shown to follow
deductively from the general in the domain of some suitable super-science of
quantity: for the domain of that science will include numbers and magnitudes, but
considered only as types of quantity. This in turn suggests another way in which
it makes sense to suppose that, within the domain of arithmetic as such, EA is a
proper, immediate, *per se* principle: for it holds of numbers *as such*, i.e. part of
what is to be a number (namely a quantity) entails it definitionally. This is why
the separate versions of the principle are related, as Aristotle says (T8),
analogically: their domains are different, but certain separate facts about the
separate domains are structurally isomorphic with one another[72] (see further

---

[70]   As Galen saw, while Alexander did not (see Barnes, 1985, and Hankinson, 1994, esp.
       61-4): syllogistic cannot handle inferences involving multiple generality, unless (as in
       the case of B) those generalities can all be shoved into the predicate of the major
       premiss. The axiom in question (Euclid's cn 1), which cannot be expressed
       syllogistically, is 'things equal to the same thing are equal to one another': Galen,
       Introduction to Logic 1.5.
[71]   On analysis, see Robinson (1953); Hintikka and Remes (1974).
[72]   This sense of 'analogy' is prominent in Aristotle's biological works, and indeed has
       persisted into modern biological classification. Thus, animals' hair, birds' feathers and
       fishes' scales are related by analogy, and likewise bones and fish-bones (*Historia
       Animalium* 1.1, 486b17-21; cf. *Parts of Animals* 1.4, 644b8-12; *Mete.* 4.9, 387b1-6,

T20).[73] And although B3 is derivable from B1 and B2, and each of them hold *per se*, they hold *per se* for different sciences. That is why, considered as a principle of arithmetic, EA (or B3) is not just derivatively *per se* – it is so immediately: there is no way in which EA can be 'thickened' by way of an intermediate truth *of arithmetic*. Another way of putting it is that, whenever anyone derives EA as a special case of EG, he does so not as an arithmetician, but as a quantity-theorist – and similar strictures hold when one employs geometrical reasoning in optics or mechanics, or arithmetical reasoning in harmonics. Moreover, this analysis has the further advantage of minimizing the distance between the subordinate cases and those involving co-ordinate science (such as arithmetic and geometry in the case of proportional alternation): for the latter can now be seen to be a complex type of the former – there is a superordinate science, quantity-theory, which provides the explanation as to why the interpreted principles hold in two subordinate sciences.

IV

I want finally to apply the results of this investigation to what is perhaps the most recalcitrant case of them all, (f) of 38-9 above. First, a long passage, which confirms and supports much of the recent analysis:

T20. The reason why differs from the fact in another way[74] when each of them is studied by way of a different science. Of this kind are all those which stand in a relation to one another such that one is subordinate to the other, as optics is to geometry, mechanics to

---

quoting Empedocles); menstrual fluid is analogous to semen (*Generation of Animals* 1.19, 727a3); there is in bloodless animals a fluid analogous to blood (ib. 726b2-5; *Parts of Animals* 1.5, 645b3-11). The central idea involved is that things related analogously are related in terms of form and function, but are not simply variants on the same thing. If this implication is carried over into our passage, it confirms the strong sense in which EA is distinct from its counterpart in geometry – and from EG.

[73] Indeed, the relations may I think be even closer than that without necessarily compromising the separateness of the sciences; 'mortality' as predicated for humans is surely more than merely analogous to its homonym predicated of, say, horses: for it is a direct consequence of the animality we share with horses. The situation is not the same as it apparently might be in the case of longevity (n. 6); of course, whether or not the properties in question are genuinely identical or merely, as one might say, phenotypically the same will be (as indeed it should be) an empirical one, turning on issues of causality; see further *Post. An.* 2.16-18. But unless all the basic principles of a given science are commensurately universal (which seems impossible), as a matter of logic the science will involve *per se* properties whose extension is wider than that of some of its subjects (on commensurate universals, see n. 5).

[74] I.e. other than that mentioned earlier (above, 25), in which a commensurate universal may be read in either direction to produce one syllogism 'of the fact' and one 'of the reasoned fact'.

stereometry, harmonics to arithmetic, and observational to mathematical astronomy ... .
In these cases it is for the observational [sciences] to know the facts and for the
mathematical ones to know the reason why; for the latter possess demonstrations of the
reasons why, while they are often unaware of the fact, just as those who study the
universal are frequently unaware of some of the particulars because of lack of
observation. These are the ones which, while they are distinct as regards their essence,
none the less make use of certain forms; for mathematical sciences are concerned with
forms, and not related to a particular subject-matter, since even if geometrical problems
are related to some particular subject-matter, they are not so at any rate *qua* that subject
matter. There is something which stands to optics as the latter does to geometry, as for
instance in the study of the rainbow. For it is for the natural scientist to know the fact,
and for the student of optics (whether optics without qualification, or mathematical
optics) to know the reason why. And many sciences which are not subordinate exhibit
this relation, for instance medicine to geometry: for it is for the doctor to know that
circular wounds heal more slowly, but for the geometer to know the reason why. (*Post.
An.* 1.13, 78b35-79a16)

It is the last example which is the most difficult one. Indeed, Barnes (1994, 160)
states baldly: 'on any account of kind-crossing, this violates the thesis of *A* 7 [i.e.
1.7: T5, T6, T11]'.[75] But first some general remarks are in order.

In T20 Aristotle states (not for the first time: cf. *Post. An.* 1.9, 76a10-15, T10
above) that (at least in some cases) the relation between super- and subordinate
sciences is such that the latter state the facts while the former give the reasons. This is
obviously problematic, since science is, as we have seen (23-8 above), by definition
for Aristotle an explanatory enterprise: to be in possession of a science just is to be
able to produce the proper explanations in the domain. Yet if what Aristotle says here
is taken at face value, he appears to be claiming that there are some sciences, namely
the subordinate ones, which simply state facts without giving reasons.

But this cannot be the case; and it is noticeable here that Aristotle appears to
countenance a three-stage hierarchy of at least some of the sciences: just as optics
stands to geometry, so 'the study of the rainbow'[76] stands to optics in general; and
similar hierarchies seem to be constructible for harmonics and possibly also for
astronomy.[77] At the lowest level of the hierarchy, we would have something like
systematized empirical observation (that is how the moon's phases go, or where
Orion rises;[78] this is a pipe that produces a sound of pitch an octave higher than that

---

[75]   Mignucci (1975), 323-4, agrees.

[76]   The phenomena of which Aristotle himself treats with some mathematical sophistication
       at *Meteorology* 3.2, 371b26-72a10; 3.4-5, 373a32-77a28; see n. 79.

[77]   So Ross (1949), 554-5; Barnes (1994), 159-60, supposes that Aristotle refers to a
       bipartite astronomy in two different ways; but there seems no reason why, even if this is
       true for the texts as we have them (as it may well be), Aristotle could not have supposed
       such a threefold structure to hold; cf. nn. 48-9.

[78]   I.e. the sort of information contained in the early astronomical almanacs, or
       parapegmata; see Dicks (1970), 84-9.

one), something which as Ross says 'is only by courtesy called a science' (1949, 555), an organized, but not explanatorily organized, collection of empirical data. But even in the case of respectable Aristotelian applied sciences (i.e. the middle ones in triads such as iridology/optics/geometry,[79] or – perhaps better – empirical optics/geometrical optics/geometry), it is still going to be the case in some cases that the super-science provides the account in virtue of which the theorems of that science (or at any rate some of them) hold.

Take the phase-structure of the moon. The first stage is simply to observe and record its regularity (this would belong to observational astronomy).[80] Next comes the hypothesis that the moon is spherical, which, along with other facts (such as that it shines by reflected light, and that its orbit takes it between the earth and the sun), will account for the appearances. That hypothesis (since it concerns *the moon*) is proper to astronomy, but to mathematical rather than observational astronomy – and it explains the fact in the familiar manner. But it does so by applying a perfectly general theorem of geometry (or perhaps rather of geometrical optics? the waters become muddy here), and it is that geometrical theorem which in turn explains (or at least underlies) the particular fact regarding the moon, since while it does refer *specifically* to *the moon*, it is none the less a *general* fact about *sphericity*.

We may now view mathematical astronomy, appropriately, as something intermediate between observational astronomy and pure geometry (cf. T3). Unlike the observational astronomer, who (at least in some cases, and certainly as such) merely knows the facts, the mathematical astronomer understands them. Unlike the former, he knows the reasons, in virtue of knowing (a fragment of) geometry, why they hold. On the other hand, the pure mathematician can fail to know that the moon exhibits such a phase-structure because (at the limit) he may fail to know that there is such a thing as the moon, or (more plausibly perhaps) may never have reflected on its shape ('they are often unaware of the fact, just as those who study the universal are frequently unaware of some of the particulars because of lack of observation': T20). Thus he knows a fact *de dicto* about all spheres, and knows it in the strongest demonstrative sense; but for all that he may fail to have all kinds of *de re* knowledge of actual spheres.[81] The mathematical astronomer, then, practices one

---

[79] It is worth glancing at Aristotle's geometrical treatment of the rainbow and other related phenomena in *Meteor*. 3 to unpack the relations involved here: 'we must borrow the proof that vision is reflected from air and other smooth-surfaced things just as it is from water from what has been proved in optics' (*Meteor*. 3.2, 372a29-32); but the reason why the halo is always 'a circle or a segment of a circle' is shown by geometrical analysis (3.3, 372b34-373a19), as is the fact that the rainbow can never exhibit an arc of greater than a semi-circle (3.5, 375b16-377a11); this passage is discussed in a similar context by Lennox (1986), 44-9; and I should note that my general account of subordination in the sciences is indebted to his in that article.

[80] This is presumably the phase of '*ta phainomena*': however, see nn. 16, 49.

[81] This case parallels the 'Paradox of Universal Knowledge' (thus Gifford, 1999) discussed by Aristotle in *Post. An*. 1.1, 71a17-30 (cf. *Pr. An*. 2.21 67a8-30, the passage

of those disciplines which, while being 'distinct as regards their essence, none the less make use of certain forms'; and the forms are supplied by the abstract science.[82]

What, finally, about the last case of T20? Aristotle explicitly says that it does not involve subordination: there is no such thing as geometrical medicine on the analogy of geometrical optics, although we would surely allow that medicine may borrow from physiology, biology, biochemistry, molecular biology, chemistry and perhaps even physics.[83] And presumably the reason for this is that the case in question is exceptional: medicine does not in general look to geometry for its explanations; there is no plausible science of geometrical medicine (i.e., there is no properly unified part of the science which is geometrical, in that it applies geometrical reasoning, by contrast with optics and mechanics). None the less, there is an alleged case in which the geometer supplies the doctor with the reason why: circular wounds heal more slowly than those of any different configuration.

This claim was controversial in antiquity, both factually and explanatorily. The fact was controverted on empirical grounds by Asclepiades; but Herophilean doctors upheld it, and maintained that it was a function of the fact that circular wounds have the smallest perimeter/surface area ratio of any plane figure.[84] This latter is probably the explanation envisaged by Aristotle (although Philoponus, while reporting this interpretation, prefers an alternative: in a circular wound the parts that are healing are further separated from one another and nature has difficulty knitting them together; *In An. Post.* 182,21-3).[85] Suppose at any rate that it is. The mere geometrical fact that the circle has the smallest perimeter/area ratio

---

Gifford focuses on): someone may know that all triangles have an angle-sum 2R, but not know it of *this* triangle as such, since he has never encountered it.

[82] Conversely, the (astro-)physicist will know the relevant mathematical facts, but not (*qua* physicist at any rate) necessarily know the mathematical reasons for them: 'is astronomy distinct from, or a part of physics? For it would be absurd if the physicist knew the essence of the sun and the moon, but none of their *per se* attributes, and in any case physicists obviously do talk of the shapes of the sun and the moon, and whether the earth and the cosmos are spherical or not' (*Phys.* 2.1, 193b25-30). For the shape of the cosmos, see *Cael.* 1.1-4, 2.4; for the sphericity of the earth see *Cael.* 2.14, 297a8-98a20: this is deduced on the basis of both physical and geometrical considerations (earth falls by nature, and so tends to accrete as closely to the centre of the cosmos as possible, equally in all directions; but the solid all of whose surface points are equidistant from the centre is a sphere), as well as on the basis of celestial observations (of the form of the shadow of the earth on the surface of the moon during a lunar eclipse, and of the different altitudes of stars at different latitudes) that also presuppose abstract geometrical competence.

[83] And so in his own way would Galen, for example, have done.

[84] See Cassius, *Problems* 1 = von Staden (1989), 411-12 (T 236).

[85] It is not clear whether Philoponus's alternative is a genuine one; but the thought may be that wounds (as opposed to skin lesions) are not two-dimensional plane surfaces, and so we need some other account; but that in itself destroys the direct link with plane geometry (we would have to distinguish between cylindrical and conical wounds, for instance).

on its own won't do any medical work: it requires some further postulates to show why it is relevant to the healing case. Rapidity of healing is proportional to the perimeter/area ratio, and this (presumably) because wounds heal by the accretion of material from the edges, which will in turn be as function of the length of the edge (i.e. the perimeter) and the amount of space (the area) to be filled in (for ease, consider the 'wound' simply to be the removal of a patch of skin). And all the latter considerations are proper to medical science.

The question then becomes: Does this violate the stipulations against kind-crossing? I do not see that it does. The argument supplying the reason for the fact will have geometrical content; but in exactly the same way as in the cases of the genuine subordinate sciences such as optics, that content will be formal only; the material will be specified by the domain, and the formal principle regarding perimeter/area ratios particularized to medicine – it is circular *wounds* which heal in this way (and, of course, they need not have done: it is an *empirical* fact – if indeed it is one – that they do so). Indeed, at this point it helps to consider how reason-giving enters in at two distinct stages here, one of them proper to medicine and one not. Why do circular wounds heal the slowest of all? Because they are circles and circles have the smallest perimeter/area ratio. Why do circles have the smallest perimeter/area ratio? Because this a geometrically provable fact about circles. This is the sense in which the 'higher' science (higher incidentally, and in this case – or at most a few others – only, otherwise it would properly be superordinate) provides the reason why: it does not provide the reason why within the actual context of the practical science itself – and hence the latter can be, subject to Aristotle's own theoretical strictures, genuinely a science in its own right. Thus, I conclude, even the medical case does not break Aristotle's own rules.

But at this point it might be asked what those rules now really amount to. We cannot cross kinds; but kind-crossing now seems to have been characterized in such a way that it is something which is actually rather difficult to do (and all sorts of things that look as though they involve it in fact don't). But I do not think this is quite right. What matters is how the content derived from the other sciences is stipulated. Bryson's mistake (at least on Aristotle's account – it makes no difference of course if Aristotle is *right* about this) was to think that he had proved something by way of a geometrical principle alone, whereas what he had done was to employ one derived quite generally from the (nameless) science of quantity. Since he was unaware of this, he was unaware of the precise status of the principle in question (and exactly the same applies to people using EA unaware that it is a special case of EG). To have produced a non-sophistical proof, he would have had to flag his principle as such, and show how it related to the general quantitative principle. But he would not have had to include the quantitative reasoning as such within his science, any more than the doctor, *qua* doctor, needs to exhibit the geometry of circles in his own science, although he does of course need to know of it, at any rate factually: recall the two-stage explanatory process sketched above: the doctor makes use of the perimeter/area theorem as a *fact*, which is in turn used to *explain* a fact about wounds; the explanation of the geometrical fact is relegated, quite properly, to geometry as such. Thus it is after all possible (indeed in a sense necessary) to produce explanations wholly internal even to the subordinate sciences; EA really is a *per se* axiom of number-theory. But it is not, in another sense, entirely free-standing; and in order fully to understand not only the derivations of his own science, but also how they themselves fit into, and are dependent upon truths of, a larger picture, he must know those further facts about its dependence.

One last point suggests itself. I remarked earlier that apodeictic syllogistic is a poor tool for formalizing typical arguments in the abstract sciences; yet it is quite good at exhibiting certain sorts of explanatory relations that hold between predicates and the properties they represent (think again of the sphericity and phase-exhibition case). That is, it can well handle cases of causal dependence. What it is much less well-equipped to do (and this emerges from a consideration, e.g., of the relations that hold between EG on the one hand and EA and its siblings on the other) is to model the explanation of reductive analysis when that reduction takes the form of a many-one rather than a one-one relation. Such analysis is of course the meat and drink of modern science: we think of the reduction of Galileo's law of falling bodies, and of Kepler's laws of planetary motion, to Newtonian mechanics – each of the former are (with some suitable adjustments) special cases (or at least approximately so) of the latter.[86] It is precisely that model of explanation which Aristotle's vision of separate, compartmentalized sciences, albeit ones which stand in some relations to each other, is least fitted to capture. And that fact in turn, I believe, to a large extent accounts for the difficulties and obscurities in his account of the crossing of kinds.[87]

References

Barnes, J. (1985), 'Uma terceira espécie de silogismo: Galeno e a logica de relações', *Análise* 2.1, 35-61.
Barnes, J. (1994), *Aristotle: Posterior Analytics* (2nd edn), Clarendon Press, Oxford.
Barnes, J. (1995) (ed.), *Cambridge Companion to Aristotle*, Cambridge University Press, Cambridge.

---

[86] On the issue of the precise logical relationship between the Galilean and Keplerian laws and Newtonian mechanics, see Nagel (1970); I agree with him that the fact that the reductions are not absolute (that, e.g., Galileo's law makes acceleration invariant, while Newton's has it vary as the inverse square of the distance between the gravitationally attractive bodies) does not invalidate the idea of such reductions; the same of course goes for the relationship between Newtonian and Einsteinian mechanics.

[87] I should like to thank the participants at the Colloquium for their helpful and searching questions, and in particular my commentator, Lindsay Judson, for comments at once critical and courteous, which helped me to sharpen – I hope – the points I am trying to make.

Demoss, D., and Devereux, D. (1988), 'Essence, existence, and nominal definition in Aristotle's *Posterior Analytics* II 8-10', *Phronesis* 32, 133-54.

Deslauriers, M. (1990), 'Aristotle's four types of definition', *Apeiron* 23, 1-26.

Dicks, D.R. (1970), *Early Greek Astronomy to Aristotle*, Cornell University Press, Ithaca.

Gifford, M. (1999) 'Aristotle on Platonic Recollection and the Paradox of Knowing Universals: *Prior Analytics* B.21 67a8-30', *Phronesis* 44, 1-29.

Gotthelf, A., and Lennox, J.G., (1987) (eds), *Philosophical Issues in Aristotle's Biology*, Cambridge University Press, Cambridge.

Hankinson, R.J. (1987), 'Causes and empiricism', *Phronesis* 32, 329-48.

Hankinson, R.J. (1994), 'Galen and the logic of relations', in L.P. Schrenk (ed.), *Aristotle in Late Antiquity* (Studies in Philosophy and the History of Philosophy 27), Catholic University of America Press, Washington.

Hankinson, R.J. (1995a), 'Philosophy of science', in Barnes (1995), 109-39.

Hankinson, R.J. (1995b), 'Aristotelian science', in Barnes (1995), 140-67.

Hankinson, R.J. (1997) '"*Sêmeion* e "*tekmêrion*". L'evoluzione del vocabulario di segni e indicazioni nella Grecia classica', in S. Settis (ed.), *I Greci*, 2.2: *Definizione*, Einaudi, Turin, 1169-87.

Hankinson, R.J. (forthcoming), 'Avant nous le déluge: Aristotle's notion of intellectual grasp'.

Heath, T.L. (1925), *The Thirteen Books of Euclid's Elements* (2nd edn), Cambridge University Press, Cambridge (3 vols).

Heath, T.L. (1949), *Mathematics in Aristotle*, Clarendon Press, Oxford.

Hintikka, K.J.J., and Remes, U. (1974) (eds), *The Method of Analysis*, Reidel, Dordrecht.

Inwood, B. (1979), 'A note on commensurate universals in Aristotle's Posterior Analytics', *Phronesis* 24, 320-29.

Judson, L. (1991a), 'Chance and "always or for the most part" in Aristotle', in Judson (1991b).

Judson, L. (1991b) (ed.), *Essays on Aristotle's Physics*, Clarendon Press, Oxford.

Kirwan, C. (1971), *Aristotle: Metaphysics, Books Gamma, Delta, and Epsilon*, Clarendon Press, Oxford.

Kretzmann, N. (1982) (ed.), *Infinity and Continuity in Ancient and Medieval Thought*, Cornell University Press, Ithaca.

Kullmann, W. (1974), *Wissenschaft und Methode: Interpretationen zur aristotelischen Theorie der Naturwissenschaft*, de Gruyter, Berlin.

Kung, J. (1982), 'Aristotle's *de Motu Animalium* and the separability of the sciences', *Journal of the History of Philosophy* 20, 65-76.

Lear, J. (1982), 'Aristotle's philosophy of mathematics', *Philosophical Review* 91, 161-92.

Lennox, J. (1986), 'Aristotle, Galileo, and "mixed sciences"', in W.A. Wallace (ed.), *Reinterpreting Galileo*, Catholic University of America Press, Washington.

Lennox, J. (1987), 'Divide and explain: the *Posterior Analytics* in practice', in Gotthelf and Lennox (1987), 90-119.

McKirahan, R. (1978), 'Aristotle's subordinate sciences', *British Journal for the Philosophy of Science* 11, 197-220.

McKirahan, R. (1992), *Principles and Proofs*, Princeton University Press, Princeton.

Mignucci, M. (1975), *L'Argomentazione Dimostrativa in Aristotele*, Antenore, Padua.

Mueller, I. (1970), 'Aristotle on geometrical objects', *Archiv für Geschichte der Philosophie* 52, 156-71; repr. in J. Barnes, M. Schofield and R. Sorabji (eds), *Articles on Aristotle III: Metaphysics*, Duckworth, London, 1979, 96-107.

Mueller, I. (1982), 'Aristotle and the quadrature of the circle', in Kretzmann (1982).

Nagel, E. (1970), 'Issues in the logic of reductive explanations', in H.E. Kiefer and M.K. Munits (eds), *Mind, Science and History*, State University of New York Press, Albany, 117-37.

Netz, R. (forthcoming), 'Aristotle's *Metaphysics* M3: realism and the philosophy of QUA'.

Nussbaum, M.C. (1978), *Aristotle's de Motu Animalium*, Princeton University Press, Princeton.

Robinson, R. (1969a), 'Analysis in Greek Geometry', in Robinson (1969b) 1-15.

Robinson, R. (1969b), *Essays in Greek Philosophy*, Oxford University Press, Oxford.

Ross, W.D. (1949), *Aristotle's Prior and Posterior Analytics*, Clarendon Press, Oxford.

Scholz, H. (1975), 'The ancient axiomatic theory', in J.Barnes, M. Schofield and R. Sorabji (eds), *Articles on Aristotle I: Science*, Duckworth, London, 50-64: English translation of 'Die Axiomatik der Alten', *Blätter für deutsche Philosophie* 4 (1930), 259-78.

Staden, H. von (1989), *Herophilus: the Art of Medicine in Early Alexandria*, Clarendon Press, Oxford.

Tiles, J.E. (1983), 'Why the triangle has two right angles *kath' hauto*', *Phronesis* 27, 1-16.

Tredennick, H. (1960), *Aristotle: Posterior Analytics*, Loeb Classical Library, Heinemann, London/Harvard University Press, Cambridge, Mass.

Wallies, M. (1909) (ed.), *Ioannes Philoponus in Anal. Post. et Anonymus in Anal.Post. 2* (Commentaria in Aristotelem Graeca vol. XIII.1), Reimer, Berlin.

Chapter Four

The Place of Zoology in Aristotle's Natural Philosophy

James G. Lennox

1. Introduction

In 1987 David Balme wrote an essay that my title is intended to bring to mind, 'The Place of Biology in Aristotle's Philosophy'. In it he hoped to open up

> ... the possibility that we might gain light upon these [philosophical] concepts – such as substance, form, species, essence, logos – by examining their reference in biology, together with the arguments around them.[1]

What Balme was not doing, which his title might have led one to expect, was situating Aristotle's various animal studies within Aristotle's 'map' of *epistêmai*. This, in brief, is what I am currently attempting to do.

To be more precise: I am asking how Aristotle saw his various books about animals to be related and how he situated them within natural philosophy. Does he conceive of them as a unified investigation, and if so how should we conceptualize that unity? How are these studies, however and to whatever degree they are unified, related to his other investigations of nature? And what is to be included in an investigation of animals? In particular, would the *De Anima*, the studies gathered in our *Parva Naturalia* (*PN*), the *De Incessu* and *De Motu Animalium*, or *Meteorology* 4 be within, or outside, its boundaries?[2]

There are reasons for us to expect Aristotle to address this problem directly and systematically. There are, after all, familiar texts that argue that first philosophy, natural philosophy and mathematics are united as theoretical sciences and distinct

---

[1]   Balme (1987b), 11-12. Later (17) he refers to 'reciprocal influence between the biological and the metaphysical treatises'.

[2]   Thanks to the perceptive remarks of my commentator at the Keeling Colloquium, Lindsay Judson, I realized that the way I had presented the problem at the conference was question-begging, foreclosing on the possibility of some plausible answers. In revision I have tried to leave room for those solutions initially, and consider them as options in the body of the paper.

in specific ways from practical and productive sciences. A number of those same texts spell out the differences between these three theoretical sciences. Similarly, a number of texts in the corpus make a case for their being a number of mathematical sciences, and specify ways in which they are both united as mathematical disciplines and distinguished from each other.[3] So one would not be surprised to find texts in the corpus that similarly discuss the ways in which different investigations of nature are at once parts of a single investigation and yet distinct from each other in various ways.

Aristotle does not, however, address these questions directly and systematically. Nevertheless there are ways of exploring these questions indirectly, by focusing attention on certain kinds of texts. I will here enumerate five of these, though in this paper I will focus most of my attention on the first three. They are:

1. Cross-references within the works reporting investigations of animals.
2. Passages that refer to an ordered sequence of natural investigations.
3. Three passages, two in the *Parva Naturalia* and one in *De Partibus*, which discuss the relationship between an investigation of health and disease and the investigation of nature.
4. Discussions of the relationship between geometry and arithmetic, on the one hand, and between these and optics, mechanics, astronomy, harmonics on the other.
5. Passages that discuss the need for a distinct investigation of the soul over and above ensouled things, and a distinct investigation of uniform living parts from a purely material perspective.

2. Cross-references

Our first task is to consider the question of the unity of Aristotle's investigation of animals and of the relationship of the various investigations to one another, a task for which I have found a careful reading of the 'zoological' cross-references to be useful. Often they are exploited in a superficial way in the hope of being able to provide a chronology for these works. Read within their contexts as contributions to Aristotle's research, however, they can help provide a better understanding of the internal conceptual and methodological relationships envisioned by Aristotle among his investigation of animals.[4]

---

[3]   Regarding the former subject the canonical text is *Metaphysics* E 1; on the latter, slightly different pictures emerge from *Posterior Analytics* 1.9-13, *Physics* 2.2 and *Metaphysics* M 3.

[4]   And it helps, in that respect, to avoid thinking of them as references to 'treatises', and more as references to various distinct investigations and types of information.

In the *De Partibus*, the most commonly referred to investigation is that into the generation of animals (there are ten references). The references are invariably looking forward *from Parts of Animals* (PA) to *Generation of Animals* (GA), including, of course, the reference in the very last lines of *PA*. This need have nothing to do with the order in which the actual investigations were carried out, nor with the actual order in which these *logoi* were prepared. However, this is the order clearly dictated by his methodological pronouncements in *PA* 1.1:

> It seems we should begin, even with generation, precisely as we said before: first one should get hold of the phenomena concerning each kind, then state their causes. For even with house building, it is rather that these things happen because the form of the house is such as it is, than that the house is such as it is because it comes to be in this way. For generation is for the sake of substantial being, rather than substantial being for the sake of generation. That is precisely why Empedocles misspoke when he said that many things are present in animals because of how things happened during generation – for example, that the backbone is such as it is because it happened to get broken through being twisted (640a10-22).

Methodologically, the study of generation must be posterior to the study of that which is to be generated – *generation is for the sake of being*; being is the cause, coming into being the effect (the methodology is defended on ontological grounds at *PA* 2.1 646a25-646b19).[5] That the references in *De Partibus Animalium* all look forward to the *De Generatione Animalium* reflects Aristotle's peculiarly teleological understanding of the methodological/conceptual structure of animal inquiry. I will illustrate briefly with one example from *De Partibus*, which gives us two other internal cross-references as a bonus. It is from chapter 10 of book IV.

> At the end of what is called the trunk are the parts concerned with the discharge of both dry and moist residues. Nature makes use of the same part in the discharge of the moist residue and in connection with copulation, alike in both females and males, in (with few exceptions) all the blooded animals, and in all the live-bearing ones. This is because the semen is something moist and a residue – let this be assumed for now (τοῦτο δὲ νῦν ὑποκείσθω); later it will be proven (ὕστερον δὲ δειχθήσεται). And of the same character too are the menstrual discharge in females and that by which the males emit semen.[6]

---

5   Though there are relatively few references in any of the other treatises to the *first* book of *De Partibus*, there is an especially valuable reference to this passage at *GA* 5.1 778a29-b6 (see Düring, 1943, 30-31). It is valuable in part because it refers to this passage as having been said κατ' ἀρχὰς ἐν τοῖς πρώτοις λόγοις. The plural may suggest that some or all of the 'chapters' gathered together in 'our' *PA* 1 were intended to be so; the reference as a whole certainly suggests that *PA* 1 was viewed as an preliminary not merely to the rest of *PA*, but to *GA* as well. This, in turn, indicates a vision of these works as parts of a single project.

6   Both here and at a16 below I am translating γονή as 'semen'. I think it is clear, despite the problematic syntax of a13, that it actually refers to male semen in both texts. I thus prefer Düring's reading to the conjectures of Peck, Platt and Ogle. See Düring (1943),

(These things too will be defined later [διορισθήσεται ... ὕστερον]; for now let it only be assumed [νῦν δ' ὑποκείσθω μόνον] that menstrual fluid in females is a residue.) The menstrual fluid and the semen are both moist in nature, so it is in accord with our account that the discharge of things that are the same and alike be assigned to these parts.

Both how the parts concerned with the seed and embryo are arranged internally and in what manner they differ become apparent with the help of the inquiry about animals and the dissections, and will be stated later in the works on generation. But that the configuration of these parts is necessarily for their activity is not hard to see (689a4-20).

Two things are to be assumed here and proved elsewhere: (a) that in all blooded, live-bearing animals semen is both moist and a residue and (b) that the menses of the female are likewise residual. This is in fact the subject of a long and complicated discussion in *GA* 1.18-19. When one looks to it, one realizes that it would be impossible for Aristotle to establish these claims here in *PA* 4.10 without losing the thread of argument. On the other hand, it is important to the argument here that these premises be posited, since Aristotle is attempting to establish that the moist, residual character of seed is the reason why nature uses the same organ for two functions. Without these assumptions, then, the grounds for his basic causal premise would be undermined.

In the second part of this passage, Aristotle points to a division of labor between the animal *historiae*, the dissections, and the studies of animal generation that is also revealing. The former two – so often, as here, referred to in conjunction – will make apparent (i) the arrangement of the internal organs connected with generation and (ii) their differences from one group of organisms to another. What is thus made apparent in the *Histories* and *Dissections* is to be *stated* in *De Generatione*, which will then define the male and female contributions to generation and demonstrate their properties. The investigation represented by the *De Partibus*, finally, shows that the configuration of these parts is determined in relation to their activities (τὰ σχήματα τῶν μορίων τούτων πρὸς τὴν ἐργασίαν ἀναγκαίως). Each of the four works makes a distinct contribution to an understanding of the reproductive organs of blooded organisms.

Such a passage strongly suggests that each of the 'works' referred to represents a distinctive contribution to a single enterprise, and provides considerable insight into how Aristotle conceives the 'internal' structure of the biological project. The inquiries (or 'histories') and dissections are not, or at least not primarily, referred to as '*logoi*' or accounts. It is not too anachronistic, I think, to say that Aristotle refers to them as if they were databases, if one assumes that typical databases have complex organizations dictated by discipline-specific purposes. We are not referred to them for discussion or explanation, but for the appearances regarding specific sorts of differences regarding a certain part from one kind of animal to the next.[7]

---

193. Note that at a18 the more generic τὸ σπέρμα is used where the contrast is *not* with the female's contribution to generation, the menses, but rather with the embryo.

[7]   For details on the ways in which the data are organized, see my (2001), and Gotthelf (1988).

There is a fundamental division, justified by reference to the teleological priority of being to generation, between the study of the structures and functions of the actual parts of mature organisms and the study of their generation. This is respected concretely in the regular putting off of discussion about how the uniform parts arise out of blood, and how the reproductive parts are arranged and function, to a distinct work, one which is to be studied after *PA*, even if that means we have simply to assume in the *PA* discussion points to be established there.[8]

So much for the different tasks of these different works – what, if anything, makes them parts of a single investigation? One obvious answer, the answer one would anyway expect after reading *Posterior Analytics*, is they are all investigations of a single *genos*, the *genos* of animals.[9] This is an important necessary condition for a single science; I think the important question it raises is why this investigation is then divided into so many distinct sub-investigations, unlike (say) Meteorology or Cosmology. And since it is so subdivided, how should we think of these subdivisions being related? Is it simply by their all being related to a single class of objects, or is there more to their unity? There is more – in fact, much more – and we can get at it by asking what each investigation does for the others, and how that in turn dictates its own structure. I have already discussed the ways in which the *PA* and *GA* contribute to one another and how that in turn shapes each of them. Another example, which I have discussed in past research,[10] is the ways in which the *Historia Animalium* is shaped by the nature of Aristotle's explanatory goals. It was one of David Balme's most important insights that the repeated failure of historians of science to understand that great work was due to the fact that they tended to look at it neither in connection with the explanatory aims of *PA* and *GA*, nor in connection with Aristotle's own views about definition and explanation.[11] Once one does so, it becomes clear that to understand it you need to see it as part of an explanatory science of a very special sort.

3. ἡ περὶ τῶν ζῴων μεθόδος: the systematic study of animals

Suppose, then, that a detailed examination of all such passages were to give us a picture of a methodologically tightly organized investigation of animals as a distinct scientific domain. How are we to conceive of it in relation to the other inquiries into nature and the reports of the results of those inquiries that have come down to us? A fairly obvious and straightforward way into this question is to look

---

[8] Both *PA* and *GA* also make a small number of backward references to works on respiration, locomotion, and sense-perception, which with varying degrees of difficulty can be matched to passages in our *PN*.

[9] As Judson noted in his commentary.

[10] Especially in Lennox (1987) and Lennox (2001).

[11] Stated most clearly, I think, in Balme (1987a).

closely at those texts in which an investigation of animals is explicitly discussed, whether on its own or in comparison with other investigations. If one limits oneself to passages that speak generally about the investigation of animals, or animals and plants, as a single investigation, this task is not terribly daunting.

An obvious place to begin is with the well-known reference in *Meteorology* 1.1. Aristotle has just canvassed different aspects of the investigation of nature in ways that encourage us to think of the investigations that lie behind our *Physics*, *De Caelo*, and *Generation and Corruption* as a methodologically unified project, since he says that 'meteorology' is 'a part of the same systematic study' (μέρος τῆς μεθόδου ταύτης, 338a26). The passage concludes by looking 'ahead' to certain other investigations.

> Having dealt with these subjects, we must study whether we are somehow able, in the appropriate manner (κατὰ τὸν ὑφηγημένον τρόπον),[12] to give an account of animals and plants, both in general and separately. For having given an account of these things, we may perhaps have reached the goal we set before ourselves at the outset (339a5-9).

Myles Burnyeat and Andrea Falcon have each discussed this passage in recent work.[13] Neither of them, however, comments on the fact that it is left an open question whether we will be able 'in the appropriate manner' to give an account of animals and plants.[14] That this is left as an *open* question here leaves room for, and provides a motivation for, *PA* 1.1. Recall that in the introductory preamble to that book, Aristotle declares that its purpose is to provide certain standards for the inquiry into nature (ὅροι τῆς περὶ φύσιν ἱστορίας),

> ... such that by referring to them one can appraise the manner of its proofs ... (639a12-15)

---

[12]   Compare *EN* 1108a3; *Pol.* 1252a17, 1256a2, 1260a4. The idea is to do something in the manner in which you have been instructed or guided by some set of precepts or norms. So after the use of this phrase at *Pol.* 1252a17, Aristotle tells us that the method he has in mind is to divide composites into their incomposite constituents.

[13]   Burnyeat's discussion is in his (2004); Falcon's is in a draft of a paper which he graciously shared with me, and will be incorporated in his (forthcoming). I am grateful for the opportunity to see these discussions in advance of publication and for permission to refer to them. Falcon and I are in full agreement that, as he puts it, 'Aristotle does not think of the study of animals and plants as an independent and self-contained science', if by that is meant that that study is part of natural philosophy, and heavily dependent on other parts. This does not preclude, of course, principles and methods distinctive of the sub-domains, any more than the unity of mathematics precludes special principles and methods for arithmetic and geometry.

[14]   The text reads θεωρήσωμεν εἴ τι δυνάμεθα κατὰ τὸν ὑφηγημένον τρόπον ἀποδοῦναι περὶ ζῴων καὶ φυτῶν, καθόλου τε καὶ χωρίς. I think Falcon downplays the tentativeness in this remark by translating ' ... we will consider what account we can give, in accordance with the method indicated ... '.

and at the end of chapter four, he concludes by proclaiming:

> We have said how the systematic study of nature (τὴν περὶ φύσεως μέθοδον) should be judged, and in what way the study of these things might proceed methodically and with greatest ease (ὁδῷ καὶ ῥᾷστα). Further, about division we have said in what way it is possible by pursuing it to grasp things in a useful manner, and why dichotomy is in a way impossible and in a way vacuous. (644b16-20)

As Andrea Falcon rightly notes in his discussion of these passages, the lack of any explicit mention of animals in these programmatic remarks, given the thoroughly zoological content of the discussion, demands explanation. Concretely, it is clear that Aristotle's focus is entirely on animals; but it is the investigation of *nature* for which he claims to be providing standards of judgment. I want to pursue this point, because I think it suggests a way of thinking about locating Aristotle's animal investigations within his general science of nature.

Chapter 5 of *De Partibus* opens with a contrast between the investigation of natural substances that are ungenerated and imperishable and those that partake of generation and perishing, acknowledging the value and divinity of the former objects, but the greater scientific accessibility of the 'perishable plants and animals' around us. Having already discussed the astronomical appearances, he goes on, we must now discuss animal nature (περὶ τῆς ζωικῆς φύσεως).

If we were to read this as a recommendation of the order of investigation of nature, on a par with that which opens the *Meteorology*, there is a fairly glaring omission here: according to the *Meteorology*, it is *meteorology* that is supposed to follow the study of the heaven, and the investigation of living things is to follow meteorology. But it seems clear that the purpose of the opening lines of *PA* 1.5 is to introduce a stirring piece of advocacy for the study of animals (cf. τὴν ζήτησιν περὶ ἑκάστου τῶν ζῴων, 645a23), despite our initial disgust at the ugliness of some of the creatures and at the necessity of cutting through flesh and blood vessels full of blood to study bones, livers, and kidneys. Initially, the audience might fairly respond that, given the inherently distasteful nature of such a study, the greater cognitive access to its objects is insufficient motive. Thus Aristotle marshals all his rhetorical skills to convince us that, with an appropriately philosophical (that is, teleological) perspective, one sees beauty even in the most lowly of animals. As Darwin was to say, in a piece of advocacy aimed at a similarly skeptical audience some 2300 years later, 'there is grandeur in this view of life'.[15] Beginning with the stark contrast between a study of the eternal heavenly bodies and the 'animals and plants around us' sets up this passage perfectly; to mention meteorology would ruin the effect.

Chapter 5, then, makes it clear that in some sense Aristotle has been focused on animal nature and a zoological inquiry all along. But then why do the more programmatic passages in the first four chapters speak as if he is elaborating standards for natural investigation in general?

---

[15] Darwin (1859), 490.

The answer, I want to suggest, is this. Most of the prescriptions of *De Partibus* 1 concern how to apply Aristotle's general philosophy of nature and of science to the investigation of *living* nature. To do so requires modes of investigation, and accounts of necessity, cause, division and demonstration, which are distinctive even within the investigation of nature. *But this does not imply that they are not to be viewed as the standards for natural investigation generally*. For Aristotle may well be defending a viewpoint similar to that of one of the most philosophically astute evolutionary theorists of the last generation, George Gaylord Simpson. Simpson concludes an essay, devoted in part to a critical evaluation of a form of reductionism he found prevalent among physicists, with the following thought.

> I suggest that both the characterization of science as a whole and the unification of the various sciences can be most meaningfully sought in quite the opposite direction [from that of the physicist/reducionist], not through principles that apply to all phenomena but through phenomena to which all principles apply. Even in this necessarily summary discussion, I have, I believe, sufficiently indicated what those latter phenomena are: they are the phenomena of life. Biology, then, is the science that stands at the center of all science.[16]

To apply Simpson's insight to our problems: Aristotle can, without comment, refer to a discussion of the distinctive standards necessary for the study of living things as the standards for natural inquiry *because the standards that apply to animals will include standards that would be missed completely if one were to focus solely on principles that apply to natural change in general*. Moreover, since one must appeal to the actions of hot and cold on the composites of moist and dry in biology, such *generally* applicable principles (and their limitations) will be discussed as well. For Aristotle (as for Simpson) only a fully articulated *zoological* method will provide us with a complete set of standards for natural science; only someone with a bias toward reductionism would assume otherwise.

With this suggestion for understanding the purpose of *PA* 1 in hand, let us now return to the concluding lines of the *Meteor.* 1.1 narration of studies of nature. It concludes with the claim that once the investigation of animals and plants is concluded, we may, perhaps, have reached the τέλος τῆς ἐξ ἀρχῆς ἡμῖν προαιρέσεως πάσης – the goal we set before ourselves from the beginning. This remark rightly stresses the continuity of the study of living things with the other aspects of natural philosophy. Burnyeat asks (2004, 23-4) whether 'Aristotle might not believe that his chosen order of study is an appropriate response to an orderly universe, in which the elements and mixtures at the lower levels exist for the sake of plants and animals.' But if that is the way the natural world is ordered, then it is in the study of animals that we should find the complete arsenal of explanatory tools, not in

---

[16] Simpson (1964), 107. The title of Simpson's collection of essays, *This View of Life: The World of an Evolutionist* is, of course, a conscious echo of the sentence from Darwin cited earlier.

meteorology and not in cosmology. But again, that does not mean that it is *outside* natural philosophy – it means it is *exemplary* natural philosophy, its fully articulated heart and soul.

If this turn of phrase in the *Meteorology* indicates that the study of life may be in some sense the goal of natural philosophy and not simply its dénouement, a passage near the close of *On Length and Shortness of Life* indicates that the study of living things can also be view as a *methodos* with its own goal.

> But now, with respect to the various animals, we have stated the cause of both length of life and shortness of life; it remains for us to study youth and old age, and life and death. For having defined these things the investigation about animals (ἡ περὶ τῶν ζῴων μεθόδος) would have achieved its goal (τέλος). (*Long.* 6, 467b5-9).

But if this passage identifies the *telos* of the systematic investigation of animals, how are we to understand its relationship to the remaining animal studies? Are we to assume that these studies of the causes of life's nature, duration, waxing and waning conclude a series that began with the *De Partibus* and *De Generatione*? Are we to picture the *Historia Animalium* or the *Dissections* as part of the *methodos*?

A passage near the beginning of *De Sensu* (436a1-4) would seem to pose insuperable problems for that assumption. For it begins with a backward reference to a completed study of 'soul by itself' (περὶ ψυχῆς καθ' αὐτήν) and about each of its powers part by part (κατὰ μόριον), and announces that what is to follow is an investigation of animals and of everything having life (τὴν ἐπίσκεψιν περὶ τῶν ζῴων καὶ τῶν ζωὴν ἐχόντων ἁπάντων). This opening would seem to encourage us to see the *De Anima* preceding study of life, death and ageing, and to expect the so-called 'zoological works', and perhaps a colleague's work on plants, to *follow*. And of course that is not at all what follows; nor is it what is suggested by the close of *On Length and Shortness of Life*.

Fortunately, the opening lines of *De Sensu* go on to further specify the investigation to follow as focused specifically on the distinctive and common activities (πράξεις) of living things. We have to take as established what was said about the soul and go on to study those activities of animals that are 'the common/shared features of body and soul'. The features enumerated are by no means a perfect match for everything in our *Parva Naturalia* – no mention is made of dreams, for example; while spirit, desire and appetite, which are not treated, *are* mentioned. But investigations of sense perception, memory, and the pairs waking/sleeping, youth/old age, inhaling/exhaling, and life/death, which do follow, are explicitly noted. So it seems that the opening lines of *De Sensu* look forward only so far as the end of these studies of the common activities of body and soul.

In general, all this fits well with the overall program for an investigation of animals provided in *PA* 1.1 and 5 and *HA* 1.1-6. There is a clear division of differentiae into parts and activities (and a less clear distinction between activities, ways of life, and character traits), and *PA* 1.5 closes with a discussion of divisions laying out general modes of activities and their distinctive realizations in different forms of animals, arguing that these are to take priority, in teleological explanation, over the divisional laying out of parts.

Thus the passage in *Long.* 6 with which I began this section, a discussion that looks forward to the *telos* of the animal *methodos*, can be read in two ways, either of which is unproblematic. Either its claims are implicitly restricted to the completion of the study of the 'common and distinctive activities' of animals referred to at the beginning of *De Sensu*; or it *is* the *telos* of the entire animal investigation, but only in the sense that the entire investigation of animals is complete only when we have understood these activities, which should be studied only after the investigation of the parts which mostly exist for the sake of these activities. For present purposes, we do not have to decide between these options.

Yet another reference to the investigation of animals and plants in relation to other natural investigations concludes *Meteorology* 4. It is clear from the opening lines of Alexander's *Commentary* on *Meteorology* 4 that questions of its authenticity and place within the corpus were already being debated in the late Hellenistic period. I am convinced that it is Aristotle's work, and I am not entirely convinced that it is out of place as the last book of the *Meteorology*.[17] One reason for supposing *Meteor.* 4 is where it belongs is that its final chapter serves as a self-conscious segue into animal inquiry – which is just what the opening chapter of *Meteor.* 1 would lead us to expect. Moreover, without a serious discussion of the production and material nature of uniform bodies which included uniform biological parts, such a segue would be impossible.[18]

Be that as it may, I believe *Meteor.* 4.12 provides further insight into the place of biological inquiry within the general inquiry into nature. The chapter opens looking forward:

> Since we have determined these things [i.e. the material nature of uniform bodies], let us state one by one what flesh, or bone, or the other uniform things are; for we grasp their kinds – the kind from which the nature of each of the uniforms is constituted – through their generation. For uniform bodies arise from the elements, and the whole works of nature are composed of uniform bodies as matter (389b23-8).

---

[17]   Contrary to the opinion of most commentators, who follow Alexander; cf. his words at (1899), 179.3-6: 'The book entitled the fourth of Aristotle's *Meteorology*, though it *is* a work of Aristotle's, does not belong to the meteorological treatise; for the things discussed in it are not appropriate to that work. On the contrary, as far as the matters discussed are concerned, it should follow *On Generation and Corruption*.' As far as I can tell, David Furley was the first to make the above point: '...the introduction to *Meteorologica* announced that biology should follow meteorology. If *Meteor.* 4 is Aristotle's prolegomenon to his biological works, then it is not out of place at the end of the *Meteorologica*.' (Furley, 1989, 148). The argument has more recently been reinforced by Eric Lewis's introduction to his (1996), 9-15.

[18]   See Gill (1997), 148.

There is an interesting parallel in this chapter to the problem discussed earlier regarding *PA* 1. Explicit reference to the investigation of organisms is again conspicuously absent throughout most of the chapter – though it is obvious from Aristotle's examples that 'the whole works of nature' referred to here are animals and plants. The emphasis is on distinguishing ontological levels understood in terms of relative layers of matter and form, and the relative clarity of functional 'for the sake of' relations at the higher vs. the lower levels. However, after echoing its opening lines, the chapter concludes as follows:

> If, then, we have a grip on the kind of each of the uniform things, we must take up the question what each one is specifically, for example, what blood, flesh, seed, and each of the others, is; for in this way we will know on account of what each one is, and what each is; if, that is, we have a grip on either the matter or the account, but most of all both, of their generation and destruction, as well as whence the change originates. And having made these things clear, we must study in like manner the non-uniforms, and finally (τέλος) the things constituted from these such as mankind, plant, and the other such things (390b15-22).

This is a pretty clear look forward to the biological project as described in the opening lines of *GA*. There (715a1-17) he describes the project in causal terms: what has been accomplished in *PA* is the understanding of the *logos* (since the *logos* and that for the sake of which as goal are the same (a8-9)) and the matter (since for animals their parts are their matter (a9-12)); what will be accomplished in *GA* is an account of the parts involved with generation and generation's motive cause (a12-17). Moreover, the conclusion of *Meteor.* 4 stresses that its explanatory resources are insufficient for the task ahead (390b10-14).

What these passages clearly evidence is that the work accomplished in *Meteor.* 4 is done *in part* so that we will go into the investigations of animals and plants with a sound understanding of the material constitution of uniform biological parts, and the sorts of causal processes that give rise to them. It lacks the resources and the focus to be part of the biological project, but it is something upon which it can depend, and presuppose.

All of the passages discussed in this section, in different ways, suggest that Aristotle sees the study of animals as both continuous with certain other natural investigations and yet distinct both in subject matter, methods and principles. *Parva Naturalia* is characterized both as dependent upon *De Anima* and, at least in part, a sort of capstone of the investigation of animals. *Meteorology* 4, on the other hand, while providing much needed material understanding of the uniform parts of animals, lacks the resources to be considered a part of that study – Furley's term 'prolegomenon' seems precisely correct. *Meteorology* 4 carves up the world in terms of elemental compounds and their emergent dispositions and interactions, without regard for the functions and goals that actually tell us what a living part precisely is. And yet it provides important resources for the explanations of *PA*, *GA* and *PN*. How to understand this sharing of resources across disciplinary boundaries is our next task.

4. The *Physikos* and the Physician

In the last section I discussed a passage at the beginning of the *De Sensu*, and thus at the beginning of our *Parva Naturalia*, which refers to the completion of the study of the activities common to body and soul as the goal of the study of animals. That same passage continues by looking forward to another investigation, however.

> It is also up to the *physikos* (the 'natural scientist') to look into the first principles of health and disease; for neither health nor disease can come to be in the absence of life. Hence most investigators of nature complete their study looking into the first principles of medicine, and doctors who approach their art philosophically start from those aspects of nature that concern medicine (*Sens.* 1. 436a18-436b2).

Similarly, in *PA* 2.7 a discussion of 'fluxes occurring in the head" is curtailed by referring to another investigation:

> For when the nourishment vaporizes up through the blood vessels, the residue that undergoes cooling because of the potential of this region produces fluxes of phlegm and serum. ... However, the appropriate place to speak about these things – to the extent that it is up to the natural philosopher to speak about them – is in discussions of the origins of disease (653a1-3, 8-10).

A somewhat more detailed claim about the connection between natural science and medicine concludes *De Respiratione*. It will be noticed that the above passage does not put off the discussion to a theoretical medicine, but rather to an investigation of the principles of disease by the *natural philosopher*. What the natural philosopher provides to medicine are the *results* of a *theoretical* investigation of the causes of health and disease.

> About life and death, and investigations akin to these, we have spoken more or less completely. But about health and disease it is not only for the physician *but also for the natural philosopher as well to discuss their causes up to a point*. And that by which they and their studies differ must not escape our notice, since the facts attest that, up to a point, the subject is a shared one (ἐπεὶ ὅτι γε σύνορος ἡ πραγματεία μέχρι τινός ἐστι, μαρτυρεῖ τὸ γινόμενον). That is, those physicians who are skilled or inquisitive (κομψοὶ καὶ περίεργοι) discuss nature to a certain extent and expect to grasp their principles there, and the finest (οἱ χαριέστατοι) of those who study nature generally conclude with the principles of medicine (*Resp.* 21, 480b22-31, emphasis added).[19]

This may be a part of Aristotle's project left unfulfilled at his death. Be that as it may, these passages are useful for seeing how Aristotle himself thinks about the

---

[19]   For the overriding importance of these passages to the revival of an Aristotelian approach to comparative anatomy in Padua and Bologna in the Renaissance, I refer the reader to the wonderful study by Schmitt (1985).

borderlines between distinct, yet related, investigations. Medicine requires certain first principles, and in particular those that identify the causes of health and disease, that it apparently does not itself provide, but 'takes' from another investigation. In particular, its study of health and disease requires causal principles regarding, presumably, the operations of the organs of human beings. Now the natural philosopher who is not focused on providing foundations for medicine will focus more or less exclusively on the proper, healthy functioning of the organism. Thus, in *PA* 2.7 the discussion of the causes of fluxes and phlegm in the region around the brain is cut short and we are referred to a special branch of natural investigation that provides foundations for medicine. What it will do is study not only the causes of the proper functioning of the human organs, but also the causes of their malfunctioning or premature decay, and in general the causes of disease. These causes will be referred to and cited in medicine, but establishing these causes as the causes of disease is the task of a medically oriented *physikos*.

These passages tell us something about the border between biology and medicine. Note again, however, that the stress is not on the investigation of animals and (keeping in mind the importance of herbs and roots to Greek medicine) plants – as we saw earlier with *PA* 1 and *Meteor.* 4.12, the contrast is between the *methodos* of the *physikos* and that of the physician. This lack of stress is not, in my view, because Aristotle fails to recognize the distinctive nature of the investigation of living things. Many of the passages reviewed in this essay make it clear that he does. As I have stressed repeatedly, given the centrality of functionally organized matter/form unities in his natural philosophy, there is no need for such emphasis.[20] The paradigmatic *physikos* deploys all four causes, all three necessities, and thinks of form in functional terms and matter in teleological terms. But there may be a more local explanation for it being the *physikos* who here supplies the causes. Given the emphasis in Greek medicine on the role of such environmental factors as climate and bodies of water, medicine will presumably *not* look *solely* to the study of animals and plants for its principles, but also to meteorology.

There is also, in these three passages, more than a hint that Aristotle is thinking of the relationship between medicine and the theoretical investigation of nature by analogy with the relationship between optics and geometry, or harmonics and arithmetic. Physicians, at least the skilled, inquisitive and philosophical ones, look to the *physikos* for their first principles and causes, rather than supplying them themselves. But we now need to think of the *physikos* investigating organic

---

[20] Recall *Met.* E 1 1025b35-1026a6. Its goal is to demarcate natural philosophy from mathematics and first philosophy or theology by again stressing that its objects are 'like the snub'. Its list of examples is 'nose, eye, face, flesh, bone, animal generally, leaf, root, bark, plant generally', after which he concludes: 'for of none of these is there a *logos* without change, but they always include matter. So it is clear how one ought to seek and define "the what it is" in natural investigations, and why it is even up to the natural philosopher to study some aspects of soul, whichever aspects cannot be without matter.' The focus on life is obvious. I will return in my conclusion to this comment about soul.

structures and functions *qua* healthy or diseased. He will be 'the more medical of the natural scientists', if you will.[21] On the other hand there will be physicians who are selecting just those principles from the study of nature that are appropriate for their subject, while ignoring the rest. The physician studies the fact, the *physikos* supplies the reason why. It is here, rather than in trying to understand the connection of the investigation of animals to the wider investigation of nature, that Aristotle's thinking about the subordinate mathematical sciences bears fruit.

In fact, if we compare those passages in which Aristotle distinguishes *historia* from the investigation of causes with these passages where the 'medical physiologist' and the 'philosophical physician' are distinguished, some interesting results emerge. Recall that in a number of key passages, upon which some of my early papers were focused, *HA* is described as investigating the facts regarding the differentiae and properties of animals, in some way preliminary to causal investigations. Yet this distinction is developed without any hint of there being two sciences with one supplying first principles for the other. The *genos*, after all, is the same – and indeed, as I have been at pains to show, the *HA* discusses the very features of animals that will be identified as causes in the other treatises; and it is clearly organized for the purposes of achieving causal demonstrations. The causal principles are *not* borrowed from another domain – causal inquiry will aim toward determining which among the differentiae and attributes are causally fundamental or, put otherwise, are in the τί ἐστι.

Medicine and natural philosophy, on the other hand, are related in a manner akin to the subordinate sciences and mathematics. Medicine is restricted to human beings, as optics is restricted to the mathematical aspects of visual phenomena. Medicine does not (on Aristotle's model) investigate the causes of its phenomena – natural philosophy does that. To put it in the language of the *Posterior Analytics*, the fact and the reason why are in this case studied by different sciences. The causes of disease are not to be found in the *genos* of medicine, but in the *genos* studied by the natural philosopher. As is implied by *Posterior Analytics* 1.13, sometimes the distinction between causal and 'factual' investigation is internal to a single science, and sometimes it is not.

5. Tentative conclusions

Chapters 7-13 of *Posterior Analytics* I view the 'subordinate' sciences as exceptions to the rule that each science is concerned with a single *genos* with principles proper

---

[21] Most interestingly, it appears that the Renaissance anatomists and physicians who relied on these passages for their understanding of the foundations of medicine in natural philosophy interpreted this relationship according to the model of the mixed or subordinate sciences discussed in *An. Post.* 1.13, *Phys.* 2.2 and *Metaph.* M 3. See Schmitt (1985).

to it. I have assumed, throughout this discussion, that there is an *epistêmê* of nature, and have taken it as open for discussion whether Aristotle imagined that, within that natural science, the theoretical investigations of animals possessed sufficient unity – conceptual, explanatory and methodological coherence – to count as contributions to one science; such that their connections to other aspects of natural philosophy are of an entirely different order.

Now one might ask whether this is a question that has a meaningful answer; and one might also wonder whether it is a question about which Aristotle cared.[22] To this point I have simply assumed that the answer to both questions is 'yes'. But I will here address them directly. Of course not all questions about disciplinary boundaries are fruitful. But if the success of an investigation depends on starting from the correct set of first principles and deploying the correct set of concepts and methods, then locating that investigation correctly is critical. As for whether Aristotle cared about such matters, it seems we have clear evidence that he did. His principal reason for writing *PA* 1, as far as I can see, is that he felt that the study of animals required its own proper 'standards' (*horoi*) – the understanding of causality and necessity that might have worked if animals were just chance combinations of elements or atoms was not sufficient for this study; nor was the understanding of division that might have worked in pure mathematics. Moreover, texts such as *Metaph.* E 1 and *Phys.* 2.2 show that mapping such disciplinary boundaries was a task to which Aristotle devoted a great deal of attention.

I have argued that one line of evidence for the 'one science of living things' thesis, under utilized for this purpose, consists of the cross-references within the animal investigations themselves. This evidence is not just evidence that there is a coherent science, but actually gives us details of the 'internal' structure of that science. A second line of evidence consists of passages where the investigation of animals (or, sometimes, animals and plants) is explicitly mentioned in relationship to other natural investigations. These passages suggest both that there is an identifiable *methodos* of animals that is nevertheless a central, perhaps exemplary, part of natural philosophy in general.

Aristotle's thought about the structure of natural investigation appears to have been influenced by his reflections on the mathematical sciences. Such reflections provide, on the one hand, a telling contrast – once one takes seriously that living things are material bodies essentially organized for their activities, while mathematics is viewed as a science organized around quantitative attributes properly studied in separation from change and matter. But, on the positive side, one hears echoes of his discussions of the 'subordinate' mathematical sciences in his attempts to delineate the boundary between natural philosophy and medicine.

Conspicuous by its absence from the outline of the investigation of nature in *Meteorology* 1.1 is any reference to a separate investigation of the soul. Burnyeat, like Webster and Lee (see their footnotes to 339a8) before him, assumes that the

---

[22]   As Lindsay Judson in fact did in his comments on this essay.

reference to the study of animals and plants *includes* such a reference.[23] That may be a plausible assumption, but it covers up an important question: namely, why is there a *separate* treatise on the soul, and how should we conceive of it in relation to the animal investigations themselves? One thing is certain: *PA* 1.1 (641a33-b10) is emphatic that the investigation of reason and thought is not part of natural science.[24] And lest we think this an aberration, let me remind you that it finds a clear echo in *Met.* E 1 (see n. 20). We thus have a clear statement that at least part of the *scientia de anima* does not fall within the bounds of the natural investigation of animals. Given, moreover, that 'soul' is a *genos* of Aristotle's ontology that spans the generable and the eternal, it seems bound to have a scientific status that is problematic and puzzling. Indeed, after stressing the supreme importance of understanding the soul at the beginning of *De Anima*, he warns us:

> But it is in every respect among the most difficult tasks to grasp any secure belief about it (402a10-11).

Amen to that.

References

Alexander of Aphrodisias (1899), *In Aristotelis Meteorologicorum libros commentaria*, ed. Michael Hayduck, Reimer, Berlin (*Commentaria in Aristotelis Graeca* 3.1).

Balme, D.M. (1987a), 'Aristotle's Use of Division and Differentiae', in A. Gotthelf and J. G. Lennox (eds), *Philosophical Issues in Aristotle's Biology*, Cambridge University Press, Cambridge, 69-89.

Balme, D.M. (1987b), 'The Place of Biology in Aristotle's Philosophy', in Gotthelf and Lennox, op. cit., 9-20.

Broadie, S. (1998), 'Νοῦς and Nature in *De Anima* III', in J.J. Cleary and W.C. Wians (eds), *Proceedings of the Boston Area Colloquium in Ancient Philosophy* 12 [for 1996], University Press of America, Lanham, 163-76.

Burnyeat, M.F. (2004), 'Aristotle on the Foundations of Sublunary Physics', in F.A.J. de Haas and J. Mansfeld (eds), *Aristotle, On Generation and Corruption Book 1, Proceedings of the 15th Symposium Aristotelicum*, Clarendon Press, Oxford, 7-24.

Darwin, Charles (1859), *On the Origin of Species by means of Natural Selection*, Murray, London.

Düring, I. (1943), *Aristotle's De Partibus animalium: Critical and Literary Commentaries*, Elander, Göteborg: reprinted Garland, New York, 1980.

Falcon, A. (forthcoming), *Aristotle and the Science of Nature. Unity without Uniformity*, Cambridge University Press, Cambridge.

---

[23]   'This is a large scale map of Aristotle's natural philosophy, beginning with the *Physics*, going on to *De Caelo* and *De Generatione et Corruptione*, pausing here for the *Meteorologica*, looking forward to *De Anima* and the biological works' (2004, 13).

[24]   For contrasting views of what to make of this, see Lennox (1999), and Broadie (1998).

Furley, D.J. (1989), 'The Mechanics of *Meteorologica* IV: A Prolegomenon to Biology' in id., *Cosmic Problems: Essays on Greek and Roman philosophy of nature*, Cambridge University Press, Cambridge, 132-48.

Gill, M.L. (1997), 'Material Necessity and *Meteorology* IV 12', in W. Kullmann and Sabine Föllinger (eds), *Aristotelische Biologie: Intentionen, Methoden, Ergebnisse*, Steiner, Stuttgart, 145-61.

Gotthelf, A. (1988), '*Historiae* I: Animalium et Plantarum' in W.W. Fortenbaugh and R.W. Sharples (eds), *Theophrastean Studies*, Transaction, New Brunswick, 100-135.

Lennox, J.G. (1987) 'Divide and Explain: the *Posterior Analytics* in practice', in A. Gotthelf and J.G. Lennox (eds), *Philosophical Issues in Aristotle's Biology*, Cambridge University Press, Cambridge, 90-119.

Lennox, J.G. (1999), 'The Place of Mankind in Aristotle's Zoology', *Philosophical Topics*, 27, 1-16.

Lennox, J.G. (2001), 'Between Data and Demonstration: the *Analytics* and the *Historia Animalium*', in id., *Aristotle's Philosophy of Biology*, Cambridge University Press, Cambridge, 39-71.

Lewis, E. (1996), *Alexander of Aphrodisias: On Aristotle* Meteorology *IV*, Duckworth, London.

Schmitt, C.B. (1985), 'Aristotle Among the Physcians' in A. Wear, R. K. French and I. M. Lonie (eds), *The medical renaissance of the sixteenth century*, Cambridge University Press, Cambridge, 1-16.

Simpson, G.G. (1964), *This View of Life: The World of an Evolutionist*, Harcourt, Brace and World, New York.

Chapter Five

Between the Hippocratics and the Alexandrians: Medicine, Philosophy and Science in the Fourth Century BCE

Philip J. van der Eijk

1. Introduction

Greek medicine in the fourth century BCE is an important and rich field, both from the point of view of the history of medicine and science and also, as we will see in this paper, from a more strictly philosophical perspective, with many interesting questions about scientific methodology, intellectual development and interaction. In the late fifth and fourth century, there was a very considerable body of medical theory and practice over and above the medical activities of the Hippocratic physicians, which presents interesting connections with what went on in the philosophical schools of the time. And during the fourth century medicine acquired, to a greater extent than the Hippocratic writings, features that prompted later writers such as Galen to label its main protagonists as 'rationalists', i.e. practitioners of a medicine based on a theory of nature, displaying a considerable degree of systematicity and following explicitly articulated epistemological and methodological procedures.

Yet historians of philosophy have not paid much attention to the medical writers of the fourth century,[1] nor have the medical interests of the philosophers in this period attracted great scholarly interest.[2] It is usually treated as a transitional episode between what is seen as the foundation period of Greek 'scientific' or 'rational'

---

[1] With the notable exceptions of Hankinson, who has written extensively on philosophical aspects of Diocles (see especially his 1995, 1998, 2002, and forthcoming), and Frede, who has dealt more generally with the philosophical nature of Greek medicine in his (1986) and with Diocles in particular (1980) and (forthcoming). For older studies see especially the publications by Jaeger listed in the Bibliography.

[2] An excellent exception is Tracy (1969); see also the older studies by Poschenrieder (1882) and (1887); Kalthoff (1934); Schuhl (1960); Marenghi (1961) and (1965); Flashar (1962); Mitropoulos (1964). For some more recent discussions see next note.

medicine as laid by the Hippocratic writers in the late fifth and early fourth century, and the spectacular anatomical and physiological discoveries made by the Alexandrian medical scientists Herophilus and Erasistratus around the turn of the fourth to the third century. With a few, mostly recent exceptions,[3] medical historians at best cast a casual glance at Plato and Aristotle, and occasionally also at Theophrastus and Strato – presumably because they were not medical writers in the strict sense.[4] The fate of other, more strictly medical, writers from the late fifth and fourth century outside the Hippocratic Corpus, such as Philistion, Acron, Euryphon, Diocles, Evenor, Praxagoras, Chrysippus, Philotimus, Xenophon, Mnesitheus and Dieuches, or of some of the twenty-odd medical authors mentioned in the Anonymus Londiniensis, has hardly been better, their contributions to the field usually being summarized in the form of an uninspiring catalogue of their main opinions.

One main reason for this is, of course, to be found in the fragmentary nature of the evidence, which makes this field particularly difficult and often frustrating. Much of the material we have survives only in bits and pieces, indirectly preserved in sources of sometimes questionable reliability. Yet the situation is by no means hopeless. As a matter of fact, we have quite a lot of evidence, some of it of good quality, especially when we broaden the definition of what 'medicine' actually involves (see below), and it affords us to obtain a reasonable impression of what must have been an extensive body of medical literature existing alongside the Hippocratic writings. The study of this material requires great care and especially patience, but is ultimately very rewarding. Before discussing some of its more salient aspects, let us take stock of what it comprises.

2. The men and their works

The following survey, which lays no claim to exhaustiveness, lists the main authors and, where applicable, works of the late fifth and fourth century BCE concerned with the area of medicine, human physiology and related fields, sometimes extant (indicated by *) but in most cases known to us only indirectly.

---

[3] Such as Longrigg (1993), which has chapters on medicine in the Academy and in the Lyceum (in which Diocles is treated as closely associated with Aristotle and his school), or Harris (1973), which gives ample space to Aristotle. More recently, Lloyd (2003) has devoted separate chapters to Plato and Aristotle, while Nutton (2004) discusses the fourth century in his chapter 'From Plato to Praxagoras'. For more specialized studies see Debru (1982), Preus (1983), Cootjans (1991), Kollesch (1997), and Althoff (1997) and (1999).

[4] Thus in a modern textbook such as Conrad et al. (1995) not more than two pages are devoted to Aristotle, and nothing is said about Theophrastus, Strato and other Peripatetics, nor indeed about later authors such as Alexander of Aphrodisias or John Philoponus.

Plato[5]
- * *Timaeus* (especially 72d ff.)

Speusippus

- ὅμοια (*Similars*)[6]

Aristotle and Pseudo-Aristotle[7]

- * *History of Animals* VII, 602b12-605b21, on animal diseases
- περὶ ὑγιείας καὶ νόσου (*On Health and Disease*)
- ἀνατομαί (*Dissections*)
- ἰατρικά (*Medical [issues]*, in two books)
- *(?) ὑπὲρ τοῦ μὴ γεννᾶν (*On Failure to Generate Offspring*, possibly identical with the extant *History of Animals* book X)
- περὶ βοηθημάτων (*On Remedies* – quoted in a Latin source as *De adiutoriis*)
- * περὶ πνεύματος (*On Breath*)
- προβλήματα (*Problems*, i.e. the lost *Problemata* to which Aristotle often refers, as distinct from the preserved but presumably post-Aristotelian collection known as *Problemata physica*, for which see below)
- *Menoneia* (i.e. the lost 'Aristotelian' doxography on the causes of disease reported in the *Anonymus Londiniensis*; see below)

Theophrastus[8]

- * περὶ ἰλίγγων καὶ σκοτώσεων (*On Vertigo and Dizziness*)
- περὶ λειποψυχίας (*On Fainting*)
- περὶ πνιγμοῦ (*On Choking*)
- περὶ παραλύσεως (*On Paralysis*)
- περὶ ἐπιλήψεως (*On Epilepsy*)
- περὶ λοιμῶν (*On Plagues*)
- περὶ μελαγχολίας (*On Melancholy*)

---

[5] For a discussion of scattered passages on medicine in other works of Plato, such as the *Phaedo, Charmides, Phaedrus, Republic*, etc. see Vegetti (1995).

[6] See Tarán (1981), especially pp. 66 ff. and frs. F6-27.

[7] For references and a discussion see van der Eijk (1999a), 493-4; see also van der Eijk (1995a), 452-3.

[8] Based on the list printed in Fortenbaugh et al. (1992), vol. 2, pp. 106-109; see also the discussion by Sharples (1995), 3-8. Editions with translation and commentary of the extant works *On Sweats, On Dizziness* and *On Fatigue* can be found in Fortenbaugh, Sharples and Sollenberger (2003); and a collection of studies (by Debru, Vogt, King and Roselli) of these Theophrastean works can be found in Fortenbaugh and Wöhrle (2002).

- περὶ παραφροσύνης (*On Derangement*)
- περὶ ἐνθουσιασμοῦ (*On Inspiration*)
- * περὶ κόπων (*On Fatigues*)
- περὶ ὕπνου καὶ ἐνυπνίων (*On Sleep and Dreams*)
- * περὶ ἱδρώτων (*On Sweats*)
- περὶ τριχῶν (*On Hairs*)
- περὶ ἐκκρίσεως (*On Excretion*)
- περὶ πνευμάτων (*On Breaths*)
- περὶ γήρως (*On Old Age*)
- * *Inquiry into Plants*, book IX

Strato[9]

- περὶ τοῦ πνεύματος (*On Breath*)
- περὶ φύσεως ἀνθρωπίνης (*On Human Nature*)
- περὶ ζωογονίας (*On Generation of Living Beings*)
- περὶ ὕπνου (*On Sleep*)
- περὶ ἐνυπνίων (*On Dreams*)
- περὶ νόσων (*On Diseases*)
- περὶ κρίσεων (*On Crises*)
- περὶ δυνάμεων (*On Faculties*)
- περὶ λιμοῦ (ἰλίγγου Reiske) καὶ σκοτώσεων (*On Hunger* (or: *Vertigo*) and *Dizziness*)
- περὶ κούφου καὶ βάρεος (*On Sense of Lightness or Heaviness*)
- περὶ ἐνθουσιασμοῦ (*On Inspiration*)
- περὶ τροφῆς καὶ αὐξήσεως (*On Nutrition and Growth*)

Problemata physica (i.e. the extant early Peripatetic collection attributed to Aristotle)[10]

- * 1. ὅσα ἰατρικά (*Problems concerned with medical matters*)
- * 2. ὅσα περὶ ἱδρῶτα (*Problems concerned with sweat*)

---

[9] Based on the titles printed in Wehrli (1969).

[10] On this work see Flashar (1962) and Louis (1991-1994). I have listed here only those sections which are clearly designated as belonging to the domain of medicine (including physiology), even though other books also contain much of medical interest (e.g. book 30, chapter 1, on melancholy, or book 18, chapter 1, on sleeplessness and concentration failure), and some books are concerned with subjects like botany (book 20), foodstuffs (books 21-2), climate (book 14 'on mixtures', book 26 on winds) and environment (books 23-5 on water and air) which clearly have a medical relevance. The dating of the *Problemata* is still disputed (with Louis making a renewed but in my view not very persuasive case for Aristotle), and some material may well be of a third century origin; see Nutton (2004), 144-7.

- * 3. ὅσα περὶ οἰνοποσίαν καὶ μέθην (*Problems concerned with wine-drinking and drunkenness*)
- * 4. ὅσα περὶ ἀφροδίσια (*Problems concerned with sexual activity*)
- * 5. ὅσα ἀπὸ κόπου (*Problems concerned with the effects of fatigue*)
- * 6. ὅσα ἐκ τοῦ πως κεῖσθαι καὶ ἐσχηματίσθαι συμβαινει (*Problems concerned with the effects of lying down and taking up positions*)
- * 7. ὅσα ἐκ συμπαθείας (*Problems concerned with the effects of sympathetic reaction*)
- * 8. ὅσα ἐκ ῥίγους καὶ φρικῆς (*Problems concerned with chill and shivering*)
- * 9. ὅσα περὶ ὑπώπια καὶ οὔλας καὶ μώλωπας (*Problems concerned with bruises, scars and weals*)
- * 10. ἐπιτομὴ φυσικῶν (*Summary of physical problems*)
- * 11. ὅσα περὶ φώνης (*Problems concerned with the voice*)
- * 31. ὅσα περὶ ὀφθαλμούς (*Problems concerned with the eyes*)
- * 32. ὅσα περὶ ὦτα (*Problems concerned with the ears*)
- * 33. ὅσα περὶ μυκτῆρα (*Problems concerned with the nose*)
- * 34. ὅσα περὶ τὸ στόμα καὶ τὰ ἐν αὐτῇ (*Problems concerned with the mouth and what is in it*)
- * 35. ὅσα περὶ τὰ ὑπὸ τὴν ἀφήν (*Problems concerned with the effects of touch*)
- * 36. ὅσα περὶ πρόσωπον (*Problems concerned with the face*)
- * 37. ὅσα περὶ ὅλον τὸ σῶμα (*Problems concerned with the whole of the body*)
- * 38. ὅσα περὶ χρόαν (*Problems concerned with complexion*).

Diocles of Carystus[11]

- ἀνατομικόν or ἀνατομαί (*On Anatomy*, or *On Dissection(s)*)
- Ἀρχίδαμος (*Archidamus*, dealing *inter alia* with the use of olive oil in personal hygiene)
- ἐπιστολὴ προφυλακτικὴ πρὸς Ἀντίγονον (*Letter on the Prevention of Disease*, addressed to Antigonus)
- ὀψαρτυτικά (*Cookery*)
- πάθος αἰτία θεραπεία (*Affection, Cause, Treatment*)
- περὶ ἀφροδισίων (*On Sexual Activity*)
- περὶ γυναικείων, or γυναικεῖα (*Matters Related to Women*, at least three books)
- περὶ ἐκκενώσεων (*On Evacuations*, quoted in Latin as *De egestionibus*)
- περὶ ἐπιδέσμων (*On Bandages*)
- περὶ θανασίμων φαρμάκων (*On Lethal Drugs*)
- περὶ θεραπειῶν, or θεραπεῖαι, or θεραπευτικά (*On Treatments*, at least four books, quoted in Latin as *De curationibus*)
- περὶ καταρρῶν (*On Catarrhs*)

---

[11] For further details about these titles (some of which are uncertain) see van der Eijk (2000), xxxiii-xxxiv.

- περὶ λαχάνων (*On Vegetables*)
- περὶ πέψεως (*On Digestion*)
- περὶ πυρετῶν (*On Fevers*, quoted in Latin as *De febribus*)
- περὶ τῶν ἔξωθεν θεραπειῶν, or περὶ τῶν ἔξωθεν παθῶν (*On External Remedies*, or *On External Affections*, title quoted in Arabic source)
- περὶ τῶν κατὰ ἰατρεῖον, or κατ᾽ ἰατρεῖον (*On Things in the Surgery*)
- προγνωστικόν (*On Prognosis*, referred to in Latin as *liber prognosticus*)
- ῥιζοτομικόν (*On Rootcutting*)
- ὑγιεινὰ πρὸς Πλείσταρχον (*Matters of Health addressed to Pleistarchus*)

Praxagoras of Cos[12]

- ἀνατομή (*Dissection*, or *Anatomy*)
- φυσικά (*Matters related to Nature*)
- αἰτίαι, πάθη, θεραπεῖαι (*Affections, Causes, Treatments*, quoted in Latin as *De causis atque passionibus et curationibus*)
- περὶ νούσων (*On Diseases*, at least three books, quoted in Latin as *De morbis*)
- διαφοραὶ τῶν ὀξέων (*Different Kinds of Acute Diseases*)
- νοῦσοι ἀλλότριοι (*Foreign Diseases*, at least two books, quoted in Latin as *Passiones peregrinae*)
- περὶ ἐπιγινομένων (*On Things Supervening [on Diseases]*)
- περὶ συνεδρευόντων (*On Things Accompanying [Diseases]*, at least two books)
- θεραπεῖαι (*Treatments*, at least four books, quoted in Latin as *Curationes*)

Mnesitheus of Athens[13]

- παθολογικός (*Account on Affections*)
- περὶ τῶν ἐδεσμάτων, or περὶ ἐδεστῶν (*On Foods*)
- ἐπιστολὴ πρὸς Λύκισκον περὶ παιδίου τροφῆς (*Letter to Lyciscus on the Rearing of the Child*)
- περὶ κωθωνισμοῦ (*On Tippling*)
- περὶ τῶν περιττωμάτων (*On Residues*)[14]
- περὶ στεφανῶν (*On Garlands*, quoted in Latin as *De coronis*)

---

[12] See Steckerl (1958), 5 and Capriglione (1983), 16-17 (but I have found no evidence for Steckerl's and Capriglione's claim that Praxagoras wrote a work entitled ἐπιδημίαι). Some of the titles here show striking similarities with those listed for Diocles, suggesting a kind of trend, although it is not in all cases entirely certain that the source-author is quoting the title of the work accurately.

[13] See Bertier (1972), 151.

[14] Note the similarity of this title with the prominent use of the concept of περίττωμα in Aristotle, Diocles, Anonymus Londiniensis and the *Problemata*. The term περίττωμα is not found in the Hippocratic writings, and looks like a new development in 4th century medicine; see Thivel (1965).

Other medical writers of the late fifth/fourth century (in alphabetical order):

Abas (or Aias)
Aegimius of Elis
Alcamenes of Abydos
Alcmaeon of Croton
Chrysippus of Cnidus
Dexippus of Cos
Dieuches
Diphilus of Siphnus
Eudemus
Euryphon of Cnidus
Evenor
Fasitas of Tenedos
Herodicus of Cnidus
Herodicus of Selymbria

Hippo of Croton
Menecrates
Ninyas the Egyptian
Petron of Aegina
Philistion of Locri
Philolaus of Croton
Philotimus (or: Phylotimus)
Pleistonicus
Polybus
Thessalus
Thrasymachus of Sardis
Timotheus of Metapontus
Xenophon

3. A variety of agendas and overlaps: Philosophy, science, medicine

This survey, however superficial and uninformative, is illuminating in that it gives us an idea of what was on the agenda(s) in this period – and also that the agendas of people we normally think of as 'philosophers' present very substantial overlap with those of people usually regarded as medical writers in the stricter sense. We find Aristotle, Theophrastus, Strato (and other Peripatetics) writing about phenomena such as epilepsy and melancholy, and we find authors like Diocles and Praxagoras writing on areas such as physics and botany. I am not suggesting that this was all one undifferentiated field or that there are no specific variations in interest, scope, methodology, emphasis or amount of detail between the different writers and works of this period. However, I would argue that any such differences (as well as similarities) have to be identified and assessed from one individual case to another, and generalizations *a priori* in terms of 'medicine' and 'philosophy', 'practical' vs. 'theoretical', or 'clinical' vs. 'scientific' etc., are often quite inadequate, if not misleading. As has been pointed out elsewhere in this volume by André Laks, and recently also elsewhere, for the earlier period, by Geoffrey Lloyd,[15] 'philosophy' and 'medicine' are headers which may easily conceal the very substantial overlap that existed between the various areas of activity – and which continued to exist, though to a varying extent and in spite of fluctuating levels of specialization, throughout antiquity. People who have gone down in the textbooks as 'philosophers', such as Empedocles, Democritus, Parmenides, Pythagoras, Plato,

---

[15] Lloyd (2002); for what follows see also van der Eijk (forthcoming) and the Introduction to van der Eijk (2005a).

Aristotle and Theophrastus, but also later writers such as Sextus Empiricus and John Philoponus, took an active interest in subjects commonly associated with medicine, such as the anatomy and the physiology of the human body, embryology and reproduction, youth and old age, respiration, the physiology of sense-perception and nutrition, the causes of disease and of the effects of food, drink and drugs on the body, etc. Furthermore, as Lloyd points out, we must consider for what reasons this was so, what claims Greek thinkers themselves were making with regard to their engagement with these areas of study and in what terms they defined their own activities and underlying purposes and ambitions – and in all this, we should be careful not to make premature generalizations, but to remain alert to the possibility of there being a great variety of such reasons and claims. 'Philosophy' is, of course, a notoriously problematic label concealing a whole range of different projects, but even for 'medicine' varying and often rival definitions were given in the classical period (and beyond), both by practitioners and outside observers – as far as the evidence allows us to make such a distinction. These differences had major implications for the shaping of agendas, the establishment of methods and procedures and the formulation and presentation of ideas in different textual genres, on varying occasions and to varying audiences.

An awareness of these issues can already be found in the ancient sources themselves. Thus according to the Roman author Celsus (1st century CE), it was under the umbrella of 'philosophy' (*studium sapientiae*) that people began to take an interest in the study of health and disease, and it was only when the physician Hippocrates 'separated' the art of healing from this theoretical study of nature that medicine was turned into a domain of its own for the first time.[16] This perception of the early development of medicine and its overlap with 'philosophy' was not peculiar to Celsus, but was more widely shared in antiquity. Thus Plato was regarded as a great authority in medicine, not only in the eyes of Galen (for whom Plato was the only author to be on a par with Hippocrates), but also in the opinion of the Anonymus Londiniensis, the medico-doxographical work surviving on a papyrus dating to the first century CE but going back at least as far as the early Peripatetic school, i.e. Aristotle's pupil Meno, if not – as Daniela Manetti and Olof Gigon have argued – to Aristotle himself.[17] The Anonymus puts Plato's views on the human body and on the origins of diseases as expounded in the *Timaeus* first before discussing the doctrines of other, major Greek medical writers.[18] Likewise, Aristotle and Theophrastus continued to be regarded as authorities in medicine by medical writers of later antiquity such as Galen, Soranus, Oribasius and Caelius Aurelianus.

It would be quite wrong to regard these ancient perceptions as nothing more than later, anachronistic distortions or to believe that these medical interests of

---

[16] Celsus, *On Medicine*, Preface, section 8.
[17] See Manetti (1999), 98-9 and Gigon (1983), 511.
[18] Anon. Lond. XIV 11 ff.; see the analysis by Manetti (1999), 118-25.

'philosophers' were nothing more than eccentric curiosity. We have to study, as unbiasedly as possible, the reasons why Greek thinkers, even if they were not practising 'healers', were no less interested in these areas than in the movements of the celestial bodies or the origins of earthquakes. And it would be equally wrong to believe *a priori* that their interests in the medical area were limited to theoretical study or the pursuit of knowledge for its own sake without extending to 'clinical' or 'therapeutic' practice. Some are known to have put their ideas into practice, such as Empedocles, who seems to have been engaged in substantial therapeutic activity, or Democritus, who seems to have carried out anatomical research on a considerable scale and even to have attempted experimental trials of the effects of foods and drugs on the body (although the evidence is somewhat dubious here). Of course, I am not suggesting that we call people such as Empedocles, Democritus, Pythagoras, Alcmaeon, Plato, Aristotle and Theophrastus 'doctors', but this is largely because that term conjures up associations with a type of professional organization and indeed specialization that only developed later, but which are inappropriate to the actual practice of the study of, and care for, the human body in the periods concerned.

4. Medicine and the life sciences in the Academy and the Lyceum

While this view seems now increasingly to be taken on board by students of archaic and early classical thought, matters are different when we come to the fourth century, which is still generally regarded as a period of increasing specialization and 'division of labour' (*Arbeitsteilung*). This view seems particularly inspired by the various attempts at constructing 'hierarchies' of sciences as undertaken in the early Academy and in the Lyceum. Yet even here we need to be careful not to make *a priori* (over-)statements, e.g., about the supposed differences between Plato's and Aristotle's interests in medicine on the one hand and those of medical writers of the relevant period on the other. As for Plato, important new perspectives on what he has to say on medical topics – and in what contexts, and why he is interested in them at all – have recently been developed by Vegetti and Lloyd.[19] And as far as Aristotle and the early Peripatetics are concerned, there now is a similar scholarly development towards reassessment of their activities in the area of medicine and related fields, arising *inter alia* from a most welcome joint effort by historians of philosophy and historians of science, especially medicine and biology.

I say 'most welcome', because for many decades there was a rather unfortunate disciplinary dividing line between philosophers and historians of medicine, with the former usually regarding the medical aspects of Aristotelian thought as philosophically uninteresting, while the latter often shied away from Aristotelianism because it was believed to be philosophy not medicine. Yet over

---

[19]   Vegetti (1995); Lloyd (2003), 142-75.

the last two decades, Aristotle's 'zoological' works have enjoyed a remarkable revival of attention, inspired – at least partly – by a very stimulating dialogue between Aristotelian scholars and historians of biology;[20] and there are now encouraging signs that the later sections of Aristotle's *Parva naturalia* dealing with longevity, youth and old age and respiration (which are probably the most neglected of the whole Corpus Aristotelicum) are also at long last beginning to get the attention they deserve.[21] Likewise, the whole area of early Peripatetic thought on the life sciences has received a major boost from the combined efforts of Project Theophrastus and from students of ancient medicine directing their attention to Theophrastus' physiological opuscula, (Debru, 2002 and 2005), 'Aristotelian' medical doxography (Manetti, numerous publications, especially 1999, on the Anonymus Londiniensis), the *De spiritu* (Roselli, 1992), the *Problemata* (Jouanna, 1996) and Strato (Repici, 1988).[22]

The issues here are more complicated and more controversial than with Plato. One of the key points on which scholars are divided is the question about the systematicity of Aristotle's and other Peripatetics' practice in these fields, i.e. to what extent it can be fruitfully connected with other parts of their work, most notably their theoretical and epistemological views on the nature and procedures of scientific inquiry (such as analysis, explanation and definition). The alternative would be to regard them rather as a number of *ad hoc*, relatively unsystematic and compartmentalized activities. Yet for all the controversy, there is a consensus that Aristotelian science has had a profound impact on the development of medicine in antiquity, and indeed the middle ages and the early modern period. It made and facilitated major discoveries in the field of comparative anatomy, physiology, embryology, pathology, therapeutics and pharmacology. It provided a comprehensive and consistent theoretical framework for research and understanding of the human body, its structure, workings and failings and its reactions to foods, drinks, drugs and the environment. It provided fruitful methods and concepts by means of which medical knowledge could be acquired, interpreted, systematized and communicated to scientific communities and wider audiences. And through its development of historiographical and doxographical discourse, it placed medicine in a historical setting and thus made a major contribution to the understanding of how medicine and science originated and developed.

The reasons why this is so, though, still deserve closer attention. It is one thing to remind ourselves that Aristotle was the son of a distinguished Macedonian court physician and had a keen interest in medicine and biology, which he passed on for further development to the members of his school. Yet this is not the whole story,

---

[20] Especially the work of A. Gotthelf (1985) and (1987), and J. Lennox (1999), (2001a) and (2001b) must be mentioned here; see also Kullmann and Föllinger (1997), and Cunningham (1999).

[21] See King (2001); Morel (2000), (2002a) and (2002b).

[22] For Project Theophrastus, see especially the studies mentioned in n. 7 above.

nor does it fully explain the rather peculiar ways in which Aristotle, in his many analogies between different areas of human inquiry and productive skill, characterizes the medical *tekhnê*.[23] One potential explanatory factor here (but this requires further research) is Aristotle's familiarity with earlier and contemporary medical thought (Hippocratic Corpus, Diocles of Carystus) – which is now more widely accepted to have been very considerable[24] – and his acknowledgement of the extent to which doctors contribute to the study of nature. This generous attitude is reflected in the reception, and critical evaluation, of medical ideas in Aristotle's own research[25] and in the interest he and his followers took in the historical development of medicine.

Yet a further reason may be found in Aristotle's views on the status of medicine as a science and its relationship to biology and physics, which I believe have sometimes been misinterpreted, even to the extent that no independent medical research was thought to have taken place within the Aristotelian school. It is true that Aristotle was one of the first to spell out the differences between medicine and physics; but the point of the passages in which he does so (in the *Parva naturalia*: 436a17 ff.; 463a3 ff.; 480b22 ff.) is to stress the substantial overlap that existed between the two areas.[26] It is further important to realize that Aristotle is making this point in the context of a theoretical, physicist account of psycho-physical functions, where he is wearing the hat of the *phusikos*, the 'student of nature'. Yet that does not prevent him from wearing different hats on different occasions and from dealing with more specialized medical topics in a different, more 'practical' context. That such practical contexts existed, is suggested by the fact that in the indirect tradition Aristotle is credited with several writings on medical topics and with a number of medical doctrines.[27] As in the case of the more specialized works on harmonics, acoustics, mechanics, optics, etc. attributed to Aristotle in the catalogues and the indirect transmission, here, too, in the case of the medical works, there is no *a priori* reason to believe that Aristotle did not write them. The burden of proof lies on those who deny the authenticity of these works; and since they are lost, the primary basis for questioning their authenticity seems to have been a tacit distinction between 'philosophy' and 'science' and the assumption that these writings were too 'specialized' and 'unphilosophical' for the mind of Aristotle, who would have left it to his pupils (such as Theophrastus, Meno, and Eudemus) to deal with the technical details. There is, however, little evidence for this assumption, which has every appearance of a prejudice and does not do justice to the fact that Aristotle's 'philosophical' writings themselves contain a large

---

[23]   For a recent study see Cordes (1994), 170-84. For references to older studies see van der Eijk (1995a), 447 n. 3.

[24]   Cf. Oser-Grote (1997) and (2004).

[25]   For a case study see Coles (1995) and McGowen Tress (1999).

[26]   For a full analysis of these passages see van der Eijk (1995a) and (1999a), from which the present observations are derived.

[27]   See the survey above and the references in n. 7.

amount of 'technical' detail (a good example of this is *Generation of Animals* book V, discussed elsewhere in this volume by James Lennox).

So there is good reason to take Aristotle's and other early Peripatetics' activities in the area of medicine more seriously. For the fourth century, such a project would concentrate on the reception, transformation and further development of medical knowledge in the works of Aristotle and the early Peripatetic school. This would comprise Aristotle's views on the status of medicine, his characterization of medicine and medical practice, and his use and further development of medical knowledge in the areas of anatomy, physiology and embryology, as well as his attitude to Hippocratic and other medical writers. It would also cover the (largely neglected) medical works of the early Peripatos, such as the medical books of the *Problemata* and the *De spiritu* and the works of Theophrastus and Strato on human physiology, pathology and embryology listed above.

Yet such a project would also have major spin-offs for later periods. It would, for instance, have implications for further study of the development of medical thought in the Peripatetic school in the period 300 BCE-100 CE and its impact on major Hellenistic medical thinkers such as Praxagoras, Herophilus, Erasistratus, the Pneumatists and the Empiricists. It would further provide a new perspective on the question of Galen's Aristotelianism, comprising the role of Aristotelian terminology, methodology, philosophy of science, teleological explanation and medico-biological views in Galen's work. Vice versa, it would provide a framework for research into the impact of developments in medicine after Aristotle on later Aristotelian thought and on the interpretation of Aristotle's works in late antiquity. We may think here of the role of medicine in the Imperial Peripatos and of the reception of medical ideas – such as the Alexandrian discoveries of the nervous system and of the cognitive function of the brain, or the medical theories of Galen – within the later Aristotelian tradition and in the interpretation of Aristotle's works (especially *De Anima*) by ancient commentators such as Alexander of Aphrodisias, Themistius, Simplicius, John Philoponus and Stephanus of Alexandria.[28]

That project, however, is still in an early stage,[29] and it would be rash to anticipate its results. Let us therefore move on and, having considered the medical interests of people usually regarded as 'philosophers', let us approach the subject from the opposite angle by considering the 'philosophical' interests of some fourth century medical writers – although it will by now have become clear that I regard this distinction between 'medical' and 'philosophical' as highly artificial and problematic.

---

[28] See Todd (1977) and (1984).
[29] For this project see http://historical-studies.ncl.ac.uk/research/projects/project_42/index.htm. For some related studies see chs. 5-9 in van der Eijk (2005a).

5. Medical writers of the late fifth and fourth centuries

Again, for the study of the Hippocratic writers – or at least those that are dated to the fifth and early fourth century – it is now increasingly acknowledged that the agendas of some of these writers were very similar to, or at least coterminous with, the activities and pursuits of Presocratic 'philosophers' such as Empedocles, Diogenes and Anaxagoras.[30] The fact that these medical writers and their works have, in the later tradition, been associated with Hippocrates and placed under the rubric of medicine[31] can easily obscure the genuine possibility that they themselves had rather different conceptions of the disciplines, settings or contexts in which they were working. Thus the authors of such Hippocratic works as *On the Nature of Man*, *On Fleshes*, *On the Nature of the Child*, *On Places in Man* and *On Regimen* – and outside the Hippocratic Corpus one may cite the Pythagorean writer Alcmaeon of Croton – emphatically put their investigations of the human body in a physicist and cosmological framework. Some of these men may have had very little 'clinical' or therapeutic interests; for others, the discussion of the human body and its reactions to disease and treatment was situated in a wider context in which medicine was just one of the several areas of study.[32]

A further relevant point here, which I already alluded to, is that what counted as medicine in the fifth and fourth centuries BC was still a relatively fluid field, for which rival definitions were continuously being offered – evidence for this being provided in the Hippocratic writings just mentioned. 'Medicine', just as 'philosophy', was not a monolithic entity. There was very considerable diversity among those involved, in whatever way or capacity, in health and healing in the Greek world, not only between the 'rational', 'philosophically inspired' medicine as we find it in the Hippocratic writings and what is sometimes called the 'folk medicine' practised by drugsellers, rootcutters, faith healers etc., but even among more intellectual, elite physicians themselves. And one of the crucial points on which they were divided was precisely the 'philosophical' nature of medicine, i.e. the question to what extent medicine should be built on the foundation of a theory of nature, the world and indeed the universe. It is well-known but interesting in this

---

[30]　See van der Eijk (1999b) and (forthcoming).

[31]　I am referring here not only to the problems surrounding the so-called 'Hippocratic question', which most scholars have now taken on board, but also to the more specific question of the 'unity' within the Hippocratic writings, i.e. the question whether there is any intrinsic connection between these works that binds them together more closely than with non-Hippocratic medical and other non-medical writers (such as some of the Presocratic philosophers). For a discussion of this problem see the Introduction to van der Eijk (2005a).

[32]　Thus it has repeatedly been claimed (though this view has been disputed) that the Hippocratic works *On the Art* and *On Breaths* were not written by doctors or medical people at all, but by 'sophists' writing on *tekhnai* (fields of systematic study with practical application) for whom medicine was just one of several intellectual pursuits.

connection that the first attestation of the word *philosophia* in Greek literature occurs in a medical context – chapter 20 of the Hippocratic work *On Ancient Medicine* – where it is suggested that this is not an area with which medicine should engage itself too much. The polemical tone of the treatise suggests that such 'philosophical' approaches to medicine were becoming rather popular, and this is confirmed by the extant evidence such as that provided by the Hippocratic treatises mentioned above. There were a number of medical authors for whom 'philosophy' in this sense was an essential part of their project, even if they did not refer to their work by this term.

Again, the recognition of this side of the overlap between 'medicine' and 'philosophy' can already be found in the ancient sources themselves, e.g. in Aristotle (in the *Parva Naturalia* passages mentioned above), and also in the doxographical tradition of 'Aëtius', where in the context of 'physics' a number of 'medical' writers such as Diocles, Herophilus, Asclepiades etc. are cited alongside 'philosophers' such as Aristotle and the Stoics for their views on such topics as change, the soul, the ruling part, respiration, dreams, monstrosities, fertility and sterility, twins and triplets, the status of the embryo, mules, seventh-month children, embryonic development, and the causes of old age, disease and fever.[33] Accordingly, recent scholarship in ancient philosophy has increasingly appreciated that the medical writers, in addition to reflecting a perhaps derivative awareness of philosophical issues, also made contributions to philosophical thinking in a stricter sense, e.g. in the areas of epistemology, sign theory, causal explanation, physics, logic, etc.[34]

When we try to apply these insights to the fourth century, we are faced with several difficulties. First, there is the problem, already referred to, of the fragmentary nature of the evidence (although recent scholarship, mentioned above in notes 8, 10, 11, 12 and 13, has done much to examine and present the evidence as usefully as possible). Yet, for all the problems inherent in the study of fragmentary material, I would argue that there is at least one respect in which these medical writers compare favourably to the authors of the Hippocratic Corpus.[35] The considerable number, size and substance of fragments preserved from their works gives us opportunities to form a picture of what *individual* medical writers were up to, which we do not have in the case of the Hippocratic Corpus. For in the present state of Hippocratic studies, one is faced with the problem that it has become effectively impossible to appreciate the role of individual doctors in the formation of Greek medicine. The Hippocratic Corpus is now viewed as a heterogeneous collection of treatises by a great number of different, and in most cases anonymous, authors, none of whom can with any certainty be identified with the historical Hippocrates. Even though in a few cases we can, with a reasonable degree of

---

[33] See Runia (1999).
[34] See especially the publications by Hankinson and Frede mentioned in note 1 above.
[35] I have made this point also in van der Eijk (2000a), viii.

certainty, assign different works in the Corpus to one and the same author, this comes nowhere near the number of treatises which people such as Diocles and Praxagoras are reported to have authored. And even though of some of these works we have not more than a few lines, the titles give us an idea of the wide range of their scientific interests and literary activity which we simply cannot gain in the case of the writers of the Hippocratic Corpus.

This brings us to a second point, the question of specialization. There certainly is reason to believe that, especially towards the end of the fourth century, different branches of scientific activity began to be more clearly distinguished from each other. Within medicine, too, there is evidence to suggest that the subject was in the process of being specialized and divided into distinct sub-areas, e.g. medicine being sub-divided into a therapeutic and a hygienic part (treatment of the sick and preservation of health), or therapeutics being sub-divided into surgery, pharmacology and dietetics, etc.[36] However, specialization of subjects is not the same thing as the emergence of specialist practitioners, and there is no reason to believe that individual people were unable to be active in more than one specialism. Indeed, more or less simultaneously with this development towards specialization, we can observe an increasing tendency among some authors towards what we might call a comprehensive or indeed 'encyclopaedic' coverage of a whole range of different areas. Aristotle himself is, of course, a case in point, and Theophrastus and other Peripatetics follow suit, while in 'medicine', we find people like Diocles, Mnesitheus and the late fourth century writer Dieuches crossing disciplinary boundaries and stretching the limits of their fields of expertise by writing about topics such as child-rearing, food preparation and cookery, gourmandry and wine-drinking, etiquette, the wreathing of flowers, as well as providing regimens for specific activities such as gymnastics, travelling and seafaring. Clearly, the medical writers of this period were expanding their territory and their claims to competence, trying to have a finger in a larger number of pies and to address a wider clientele – an expansion which was probably one of the main provocations of Plato's harsh condemnation of dietetics in the *Republic* (403e ff.). They wrote popularizing documents in the form of letters and poems about healthy living, thus disseminating their ideas more widely and having greater influence on society.

6. Diocles of Carystus

Diocles of Carystus is probably the best example in this period of a 'medical' writer whose steps we can trace in a wide variety of fields.[37] About 240 'fragments' (i.e. both direct quotations and indirect reports) testifying to his work and ideas have survived. His interests ranged widely, and as the table above shows, he is

---

[36]   For a discussion see van der Eijk (1999d).
[37]   For what follows see also van der Eijk (2000a) and (2001).

reported to have written extensively and on a great variety of areas such as anatomy, physiology, digestion, fevers, prognostics, pathology, therapeutics, bandages, gynaecology, embryology, surgery, dietetics, hygiene and regimen in health, foods, wines, herbs, vegetables, olive oil, drugs, poisons, sexuality, and possibly also – as some fragments suggest – mineralogy and meteorology.

The history of Dioclean scholarship has been that of a pendulum swinging from wild speculation to aporetic, indeed paralysing scepticism. After all the sweeping attempts – ancient as well as modern – to pigeon-hole him as a 'Sicilian' doctor, an 'Aristotelian', a Dogmatist, an Empiricist, or even a Sceptic, there followed the period of the 'Probleme um Diokles von Karystos'[38] and the 'Skandalon der Jaegerischen Vernunft'.[39] It was clear how Diocles ought not to be viewed or studied, but it was difficult to turn this awareness into something more constructive. With the fragments newly collected, presented and commented upon, it is hoped that the pendulum can now start to swing back again in the other direction, although it would be desirable if speculation could be kept under some control and be checked against the evidence. Such an approach should help to strip Diocles of all the labels he has been invested with in antiquity as well as in modern times, and stay clear of the unhelpful (and largely insoluble) debate about Diocles' date and relationship to Aristotle.[40] In particular, it should encourage the study of Diocles not primarily as a member of this or that 'school' or 'tradition', but as a thinker and writer with an identity and personality of his own.

That does not mean, of course, that we should isolate Diocles from his intellectual context, and as I have argued elsewhere, there are good reasons to believe that he was well in touch with the medical and philosophical thinkers of his time, that he knew a number of the Hippocratic writings and that he was familiar with, and to, Aristotle and Theophrastus.[41] Furthermore, he appears to have positioned himself prominently in the intellectual debates of the fourth century, and to have played a major role in the communication of medical views and precepts to wider audiences in Greek society by means of highly civilized literary writings and, unusually for medical prose, in the Attic dialect.

We have no explicit evidence for the way in which Diocles defined himself or his own activity, nor do we have *verbatim* statements on the nature and aims of the medical art. Yet we do have some explicit, critical and at times almost

---

[38] Kudlien (1963).

[39] A variation on Jaeger's own use of the expression 'Skandalon der historischen Vernunft', by which he was referring to scholars' misunderstanding of Diocles' role in the history of thought; see Jaeger (1938a) and (1938b), critically discussed by von Staden (1992).

[40] On this see van der Eijk (2001), xxxi-xxxviii.

[41] See van der Eijk (2001), xxxi-xxxviii, where I argue that the evidence does not allow us to rule out any reasonable pair of dates within the fourth century. Theophrastus mentions a Diocles in his work *On Stones* (Diocles, fr. 239 vdE), although it is not absolutely certain that this refers to Diocles of Carystus.

'programmatic' pronouncements on matters of methodology. He comes across as someone who tries to preserve a subtle balance between theoretical and empirical tendencies. He clearly had a keen interest in 'the phenomena' and in the practical aspects of medical care, and rated the results of long term medical experience very highly. Yet at the same time, Diocles was known for his theoretical and philosophical outlook and for his tendency to base his medical views on a general theory of nature (cf. frs. 61, 63, 64). That, in combination with the impressive range of subjects he dealt with, the almost encyclopaedic coverage of the subject of medicine and allied sciences such as botany, biology, and possibly mineralogy and meteorology, the considerable size of his literary production and the stylistic elegance his work displayed, may well have been the reason why he was referred to in Athens as a 'younger Hippocrates' or as 'second in fame and age to Hippocrates' – his tendency to relate his medical views to more general theoretical views on nature being similar to the 'Hippocrates' referred to by Socrates in the well-known passage in Plato's *Phaedrus* (270cd). From the remains of his work Diocles emerges as a very self-conscious scientist with a keen awareness of questions of methodology, a fundamental belief that treatment of a particular part of the body cannot be effective without taking account of the body as a whole (fr. 61) or of the essence of disease (fr. 63), and a strong desire for systematization of medical knowledge. Diocles' use of notions such as *pneuma*, humours and elementary qualities, his use of inference from signs (fr. 56), his references to obscure causes (fr. 177), his interest in cognition, sense-perception and locomotion, and even within the field of dietetics his endeavours to develop and systematize dietetics into a detailed regimen for health and hygiene aimed at prevention of disease – all this confirms the 'theoretical', 'rationalizing' nature of Diocles' medical outlook.

Yet, as we have seen, there was also a tradition in antiquity that represented Hippocrates as being hostile to philosophy, indeed as the one who liberated medicine as an empirical, practical art aimed at treatment of diseases from the bondage of theoretical philosophical speculation. And there is that side to Diocles as well (cf. fr. 2): for Diocles insisted that the use of theoretical concepts and explanatory principles constantly has to be checked against the empirical evidence, and that their appropriateness to individual circumstances has to be considered time and time again in each individual case. Diocles' reputation as the first to write a handbook on anatomy, providing detailed descriptions of all the parts of the human body, including the female reproductive organs, his status as one of the leading authorities in the area of gynaecology, as well as the fame of some of his surgical instruments and bandages all suggest that we are dealing not only with a writer, communicator and thinker, but also with an experienced practitioner.

Yet whatever the title of 'younger Hippocrates' means, it certainly does not mean, and perhaps was not meant to suggest, that Diocles faithfully followed the footsteps of the Father of medicine in all respects. For as several fragments of his works bear out that, whatever the authority of Hippocrates may have been in Diocles' time, it did not prevent Diocles from taking issue with some ideas and practices that are similar to what is to be found in texts which we call Hippocratic.

Diocles can therefore be regarded as an independent key figure in the interaction between medicine and natural philosophy (at least in its epistemological results) in one of the founding periods of Greek science, who long exercised a powerful influence on later Greek medicine. He was an important bridge figure between Hippocratic medicine and Aristotelian biology, and as such he provided a major impetus to Hellenistic medicine, especially to Erasistratus. I would say that his influence on later medicine was particularly prominent in the (further) development of (comparative) anatomical research; in physiology and embryology, especially concerning the notion of *pneuma*; in regimen in health, and more generally in his views on food (preparation), cookery, sports and in general the quality of life (later authors such as Athenaeus, Galen and Oribasius regarded him as the leading authority in these fields); in the development of gynaecology, where, again, a later author such as Soranus often mentioned him as one of the major authorities; and finally, I would say, in the systematization of medicine as a science and in his views on the methodological and epistemological aspects of medicine.

7. Praxagoras of Cos and Mnesitheus of Athens

Similar observations can be made with regard to Praxagoras of Cos, who lived presumably somewhat later than Diocles and who is usually mentioned in the handbooks of the history of medicine mainly for his 'discovery' of the difference between veins and arteries, his pulse-lore, his assumption of the so-called 'vitreous' humour, and his views on vascular anatomy and the cognitive role of the heart. Again, he seems to be one of those medical authors who, simply because a collection of the fragments was published some time ago, has been largely neglected.[42] Yet a renewed collection and examination of the extant material (about 120 fragments are included in Steckerl) would be very worth while. Among some of the more striking features are a strong interest in classification (mainly in the area of humoural physiology), an awareness of different kinds of symptoms, several references to dissection and also the use of *analogismos*, a kind of inferential reasoning on the basis of visible phenomena. Praxagoras further presents an intriguing example of a doctor who provides a connection between Hippocratic medicine – after all, he came from Cos –, Alexandrian medicine – he was the teacher of Herophilus – and Hellenistic philosophy – the latter because of his close association with Chrysippus and the early Stoa.[43] A new, overall assessment of Praxagoras' role in the history of ideas is certainly called for.

My third example of a medical personality is the fourth century Athenian physician Mnesitheus, the fragments of whom were collected by Hohenstein in

---

[42] See the studies by Steckerl (1958) and Capriglione (1983). Not much recent work has been done on Praxagoras; the only title I am aware of is Nickel (2005).

[43] See the recent analysis by Tieleman (2003).

1935 and later by Janine Bertier in her *Mnésithée et Dieuchès* of 1972. Even more than in the case of Diocles and Praxagoras, our knowledge of Mnesitheus' doctrines is severely limited and distorted by the fact that the source-authors in whom the evidence is preserved had very selective interests and corresponding modes of reporting. Thus in the case of Mnesitheus, most fragments are concerned with diet and especially food and drink – what to eat and when, how to prepare it, and how to get rid of it if it troubles you. Yet here, too, a closer look at the surviving evidence shows some interesting features, such as a strong preoccupation with classification and taxonomy, using the method of division, and an interest in comparative anatomical research.

Much more could be said on the achievements of these individual writers.[44] In the rest of this paper, however, I would like to concentrate on themes rather than people, and illustrate by means of examples what I perceive to be some major developments characterizing the medical (and biological/physiological) texts that have been preserved from this period, which in my view represent innovative tendencies compared to the Hippocratic writings and which clearly also reflect an awareness of, and possibly have contributed to, developments in 'philosophy'. I will first deal with a number of aspects of what I would call the systematization and sophistication of medicine, especially in epistemological, methodological and theoretical respects. I will then turn to the development of empirical research and the relationship between reason and experience. Finally, I will make some more general observations about the character of medicine in the fourth century.

8. Classification and division

A first feature is the striking interest displayed by some authors in classification by means of division (*dihaeresis*). Thus in a little-known passage (frs. 10-11 Bertier), Mnesitheus sets out an elaborate classification of the constituents of the medical art. We have two versions of this fragment, one preserved in Galen's *Therapeutics to Glauco* and one in the commentary on this work by the late sixth century CE medical/philosophical writer Stephanus. I print the Galenic version first, followed by Stephanus' comments:

> Now, Hippocrates was also the first of all those we know to write this (i.e. that medical competence should be based on a knowledge of the healthy state of the body). As many of his successors as understood his writings commented on them at length, and one of them was Mnesitheus of Athens, a man not only quite knowledgeable in all the other arts but also second to none as far as methodical practice of healing is concerned. This Mnesitheus, beginning from the primary and highest genera, sees fit to divide them by species and genera and differentiae (ἀπὸ τῶν πρώτων καὶ ἀνωτάτω γενῶν ἀρξάμενος ἀξιοῖ τέμνειν αὐτὰ κατ᾽ εἴδη τε καὶ γένη καὶ διαφοράς). Then in turn we divide in a

---

[44]   For some remarks see Nutton (2004), ch. 8.

similar way what has been divided, then divide these again in the same way, until we arrive at a species such that after we have divided it we are left with something single in number and indivisible. (vol.11 3.7-17 Kühn)[45]

Stephanus comments as follows:

This (i.e. the method of division) was also practised by Mnesitheus, who had a thorough understanding of philosophy and all other disciplines as well, and who also won the highest honours in medicine. After Hippocrates, this man was the first to bring healing into line with a method (μεθόδῳ τὴν ἰατρικὴν συστήσασθαι), and he did so by using precisely this kind of division. Now, if we may, let us bring his division into the centre of our discussion. Well, Mnesitheus used to say that the physician either preserves the health of the sound or else treats the diseases of the infirm. He preserves health by the use of likes, whereas he eliminates diseases by the use of opposites, and in both cases he eradicates the causes of diseases. Now, these causes are excesses in either quantity or quality. Quantity is observed either in *pneuma* or in liquids, and quality in turn is either pungent or salty or acid or bitter or hot or cold. Moreover, each of these is in turn brought about <by different> causes. For the humours have come to be such as they are either through the nature that from the beginning adheres (?) in accordance with the original composition, or else through some acquired temperament that has subsequently gone wrong. <...> Thus the season alters the type of the humours. Now, who does not know that the season of summer is well suited to bile, and that of winter to phlegm and, for that matter, that of spring to blood and that of autumn to the atrabilious humour? Further, the place has as much influence as the season, and so do the age and the type of regimen, depending on whether it is of one kind or another. For that matter, types of afflictions also influence the humours. These arise either in the soul or in the body. <...> of the soul, or else by immoderate sexual activity. The fact is that excessive sexual indulgence, since it dissipates the *pneuma* that is the substratum of the soul, could be called a psychic distress. For that matter, brooding no less than grief can produce in the humours the qualities we have mentioned. Now Mnesitheus carried out this division in this manner and finally arrived at things that it is impossible to divide.' (pp. 32.30-36.5 Dickson)

Stephanus goes on to comment on Galen's view that the incorrect use of division leads to gross therapeutic errors, and then, somewhat later, he says again: 'We have given an account of the division practiced by Mnesitheus, and we have shown the incompetence of those who practise division badly in these matters.' (p. 40,8-9 Dickson).

There are a number of textual and interpretive problems with this fragment which would require much more discussion than I can offer here.[46] A more fundamental question is whether the fragment represents Mnesitheus' practice of division faithfully – which is not the same thing as saying that we have a *verbatim* quotation here. Stephanus' later version is much longer and more elaborate than

---

[45]   Translation Dickson (1998), 31-3, modified.
[46]   See Bertier (1972), 13-23 and 160-65 and Dickson (1998), 30-39.

Galen's, and this raises the question what Stephanus' sources for this information were. Stephanus' work is generally believed to be substantially based on Galen,[47] and this raises the suspicion that the additional information that goes beyond what Galen says here is a later projection or systematization by Stephanus in the light of the medical views of later times.[48] This may well be possible. Yet I do not see a specific reason to question the authenticity of this report. The terminology used in the report is in accordance with what we hear from other sources (frs. 12, 13 and 14) about Mnesitheus' distinction between *chumos* and *chulos*, with the former referring to the perceptible quality (flavour or taste) of a substance (which need not be a fluid itself), whereas *chulos* would refer ontologically to any fluid or moisture qua being liquid (this distinction is also made by Theophrastus, fr. 419). In the present passage we find the word *chumos* used several times, but always in relation to the perceptible qualities (and qualitative changes) of the humours mentioned earlier on (pungent or salty or acid or bitter or hot or cold), whereas the more neutral term *hugron* is used just to refer to fluids in their liquid state. A further reason for taking the report somewhat more seriously is the fact that Mnesitheus would not be a very obvious name for Stephanus or indeed Galen to use as a cover-up for fabrication. Compared to most other fragments of Mnesitheus, the present passage is one of the very few more specific characterizations of Mnesitheus' views. Most other references to Mnesitheus in Galen are in the context of the familiar lists of 'Dogmatist' or 'Rationalist' authorities to whom Galen appeals for authoritative backing of views he wishes to promote, where Mnesitheus is not more than a name. By contrast, when it comes to his divisionist skills, Galen praises Mnesitheus also elsewhere (fr. 9), and this suggests that Mnesitheus did have a certain reputation for his usage of this technique – and understandably so, as we shall see in a minute. Moreover, it is quite possible that Stephanus relies on other Galenic passages which we no longer have. Another possibility is that Rufus of Ephesus was an intermediary source, as Wellmann suspected.[49] We can only speculate here, as it is hard to say how much of Mnesitheus' work was available in late antiquity. Galen's contemporary Athenaeus of Naucratis, who often quotes Mnesitheus in his *Deipnosophists* for his views on foods, seems to have had access to his work *On Foods*, from which he produces some sizeable quotations, and Oribasius in the mid 4th century CE has preserved several excerpts from Mnesitheus' dietetic writings. I would therefore not wish to exclude the possibility that Stephanus had access to Mnesitheus' work either directly or through an intermediary source other than Galen.

If this is accepted, we have here one of the earliest attempts at systematization of the art of medicine (μεθόδῳ τὴν ἰατρικὴν συστήσασθαι) by means of division. It is divided into two branches, preservation of health and treatment of illness, each of

---

[47] See Duffy (1983), 12-13.
[48] For a similar difficulty in Stephanus see the discussion in van der Eijk (2001), 120-22.
[49] Wellmann (1901), 55; see also van der Eijk (2001), 105, 122 and 275.

which is said to be based on the principles of similarity and opposition, which are addressing the (potential) causes of disease. These causes are subdivided into quantitative and qualitative factors, and each of these two is then subdivided into further factors, with most attention being given to qualitative factors, i.e. qualitative changes to the humours brought about by factors such as climate, season, physical activity but also by mental factors exercising influence on the humours through the intermediary of *pneuma*.[50] Thus we get a kind of stemma,[51] which is still a far cry from the detailed ramifications found in later authors such as Galen, but which still marks something new compared to what we find in the Hippocratic writers. The emerging pathophysiological picture itself is fairly traditional, with humours and primary and secondary qualities playing a major role and environmental and life-style factors being considered of great relevance. What is new and interesting, though, is the explicit distinction between physical and mental causes of (bodily) health or sickness, and the mediating role of *pneuma*, which is said to be the 'substrate of the soul' (τῆς ψυχῆς ὑποκείμενον). One might take a sceptical line here and argue that this smells like a later, Galenic interpretation. However, the psycho-physical role of *pneuma* is exactly one of those innovations in medico-physiological thought of the fourth century, figuring prominently in Aristotle's (later?) works and also in Diocles, especially fr. 150.[52]

There is more evidence for a strong interest on Mnesitheus' part in classification and division, notably in the area of dietetics, especially vegetables and fish, which is discussed extensively by Bertier.[53] But the use of the technique was more widespread. Thus Mnesitheus' division between affections of the soul and affections of the body as causes of illness reminds us of another late fourth century source, the (source of the) Anonymus Londiniensis, who makes the same distinction in his discussion of 'affections' (*pathê*) in the first surviving section of his work (I 15, 29). Admittedly, that section probably reflects early Stoic terminology, although the Anonymus attributes it to 'the ancients', whom he explicitly distinguishes from the 'more recent ones', the Stoics (οἱ δὲ νεώτεροι, τοῦτ' ἔστιν οἱ Στωικοί, II 22). We are on safer ground, though, when we come to the second section of the papyrus, which represents the Anonymus' account of what he presents as 'Aristotle''s survey of earlier doctrines about the causes of disease and which is sometimes referred to as the 'Menoneia'. Whether that survey actually goes back to Aristotle himself or to his pupil Meno is not so relevant now: it is clear that we have a strongly Aristotelian, Peripatetic piece of doxography, very similar (though not entirely identical) in method to what we find in Theophrastus'

---

[50] My reading of this section is slightly different from Bertier's, who takes the external factors as affecting the pathological process as a whole, not just the qualitative changes of the humours (1972, 17).

[51] This is brought out well in Bertier's presentation of the fragment (1972), 16-17 and 162-3.

[52] See van der Eijk (2001), 286.

[53] Bertier (1972), 34-48.

De sensibus,[54] and using medical terminology strongly reminiscent of the *Problemata*. The details of the diairetic structure set out here have been studied with great care and in great detail by Daniela Manetti (1999). Basically, there are two types of explanations for diseases, one being the 'residues of nutriment' (*perittômata*), the other 'the elements' (*stoikheia*). 'Aristotle' subsequently presents a whole range of thinkers, including Hippocrates and Plato (but not Diocles) and puts each of them under one of these two rubrics, but with various subdivisions, e.g. according to the number of 'elements' they assumed, or according to different kinds of disease. Remarkably, the Anonymus, who for most of the time restricts himself to a bare report of 'Aristotle''s views, suddenly intervenes when it comes to the doxography on Hippocrates (V 35 ff.), where he disagrees with 'Aristotle''s version of Hippocratic doctrine and replaces it with his own. This is an interesting example of a critical reaction to the straightjacketing effect of the Aristotelian classification, and an expression of the awareness that such a schematized representation does not do justice to the position in question. The Anonymus might also have taken issue with 'Aristotle''s account of Plato, which resembles only very partially Plato's own typology of corporeal diseases into three categories (*Timaeus* 81e7 ff.), viz. (1) an unnatural surfeit, or shortage, or displacement of the elements, (2) diseases due to a reversal and corruption of the normal process of nutrition through blood, and (3) diseases that arise from breath, phlegm or bile. We have yet another, related example of the use of division and classification here. And Plato, too, introduces various subdivisions of these classes and subsumes a number of diseases known from medical literature under these headings. He adds a further distinction between diseases of the body and diseases of the soul (86b1 ff.), and subdivides mental illness between 'madness' (*mania*) and 'stupidity' (*amathia*).[55]

A fourth example of division is provided by Praxagoras' division of humours or moistures into different kinds, which is testified by Galen (fr. 21) and illustrated in greater detail by Rufus of Ephesus (fr. 22):

> Praxagoras had a peculiar way of giving names to the humours, (calling them) sweet, equally mixed, and vitreous. These belong to the species (*idea*) of phlegm. Others he named acid, sodic, salty and bitter; these become manifest when one tastes them; yet others he named leek-green because of their colour, or yolk-like because of their thickness; others he called corrosive, because it contributes to being corroded, or stationary, because they remain in the vessels and do not pass through into the flesh, on account of the fact that stationary humours are thin and venous. On the whole, Praxagoras calls every moisture a humour. Mnesitheus however calls the former (moisture) a juice, but the faculty of causing taste, whether it is in something dry or something wet, he calls flavour.

---

54   See now the analysis of this work by Baltussen (2000).
55   For discussions of Plato's typology of disease see Longrigg (1993), ch. 5 and Lloyd (2003), ch. 6.

This fragment accords well with Galen's report (fr. 21) that Praxagoras distinguished ten different humours – or eleven, if one included blood – and Galen claims to have devoted a separate treatise to Praxagoras' humoural theory, which, although lost, gives us some reason to believe that he was relatively well informed about the topic. The fragment lists eleven different names, even though the criteria by which the identification of these eleven humours is arrived at are rather different in nature, ranging from colour and taste to effect on their environment and movement. (It is interesting that some of the categories here correspond to those mentioned by Mnesitheus.) Furthermore, phlegm is labelled as an *idea*, a species or kind, under which three of the eleven humours are apparently subsumed; and which of the eleven is blood is not immediately obvious. But it may just be that Praxagoras was explaining the naming of the various humours rather than giving ontological criteria. Unfortunately, the evidence is too scanty to allow us to go much further.

A final, though dubious example of classification by division can be found in the *Letter to Antigonus* attributed to Diocles (fr. 183a), where we find a division of the body into four sections (head, chest, belly, bladder) corresponding to four types of diseases with corresponding sets of symptoms and prophylactic measures. However, the authenticity of the *Letter* is disputed.[56]

Of course, divisions of these types can already be found in some of the Hippocratic writings, with their various binary and quaternary schemata, most notably in the work *On the Nature of Man*. Still, it is fair to say that the scale on which the technique is applied by medical writers of the fourth century, especially considering the fragmentary evidence, marks a new development.[57] The reasons for the use of this technique may vary from one case to another, and it is difficult to prove 'influence' here, but it is tempting to relate this to the epistemological developments and the methodological procedures developed in the Academy and the Lyceum.

9. Classificatory terminology

A related form of 'systematization' of medicine is the attempt at establishing a correct usage of classificatory terminology. We have already seen Mnesitheus' distinction between *chumos* and *chulos*, which can be paralleled with a fragment in Theophrastus (fr. 419). The Anonymus Londiniensis devotes the first section of his work to terminological distinctions between *nosos, diathesis, hexis, pathos*, etc.,

---

[56] See van der Eijk (2001), 352-8.
[57] Cf. Bertier (1972), 23: 'La différence qui le (i.e. Mnesithée) sépare des auteurs du Corpus, réside plutôt dans ses procédés d'exposition. Sous ce rapport, il obéit à un souci d'exhaustivité, d'analyse, de déduction des concepts dont les médecins du Corpus ne lui ont pas fourni le modèle.'

and various meanings of the same term (e.g. soul, affection, movement, etc.). Then there are Diocles' attempts to arrive at a systematic catalogue and nomenclature for plants, vegetables and other edible substances – efforts which gave rise to the belief that Diocles was the first writer of a herbal or 'Kräuterbuch' (cf. frs. 193a, 205, 206a, 207, 208). In this connection, we should also mention Speusippus, Plato's successor as head of the Academy, for his detailed interests in plant classification as set out in his 'Similars' (*Homoia*), of which a considerable number of fragments survive in Athenaeus' *Deipnosophists*. Identification, description, definition, comparison with similar items and corresponding classification – these are clear tendencies in the medicine and life sciences of the fourth century, and it is, again, an obvious inference to relate this to developments in the Academy and the Lyceum.

10. Pathology: signs, symptoms, causes

A further area in which we find clear evidence for attempts at systematization is the identification, description, explanation and treatment of pathological phenomena. Here, the Hippocratic nosological treatises had made only rudimentary attempts at distinguishing between disease, symptoms, signs, causes, etc. Diocles and Praxagoras clearly try to be more consistent in terminology and description. Both are reported to have authored works with the words *Pathos, Aitia, Therapeia* in the title (although the order in which the words are mentioned differs somewhat), and also the title of Mnesitheus' work *Pathologikos* points in the same direction. Most of our evidence here relates to Diocles' work, suggesting that he adopted a careful distinction between a descriptive account of the condition (*pathos*), an account of the cause (*aitia*)[58] and a recommendation of a particular treatment (*therapeia*). The most vivid piece of evidence for this is in Diocles' fr. 109, where we find a careful sequence of description and physiological explanation of a disease known as 'melancholic' or 'flatulent'. After Galen's introductory words, we get a long verbatim quotation from Diocles' work:

> Another [affection] occurs in the region of the belly, but it is not like the ones discussed before; some call it melancholic, others flatulent. It is accompanied by the following: after consumption of foods, especially foods that are difficult to digest and that are burning, there are sour eructations, much watery spitting, flatulence, a burning feeling near the hypochondrium, and a gurgling [which happens] not immediately but to people who wait a while; sometimes also strong pains occur in the belly, which in some people extend to the broad of the back. These [symptoms] are alleviated when the foods have been digested, and after eating the same [symptoms] occur again, and often the disturbance occurs both to people when they are fasting and when they have eaten, and when vomiting they vomit raw foods and phlegms that are somewhat bitter, hot and

---

[58] Diocles also uses the word αἰτιολογεῖν, 'state the cause' in fr. 176.32.

sharp, so that also their teeth are set on edge. Most of these [symptoms] occur immediately from youth onwards, but in whatever way they occur, they last for a long time in all [cases].

Galen then goes on to quote from Diocles' account of the cause of the disease:

One must suppose that those who are called flatulent have more heat than is appropriate in the veins that receive the food from the stomach, and that their blood has thickened. That there is an obstruction in the region of these veins is shown by [the fact] that the body does not take in the food, but it remains untreated in the stomach, whereas previously [before the affection arose] these passages received [it] and secreted most of it into the lower [part of the] belly, and [this is also shown] by [the fact] that on the second day the patients vomit, as is the case when the foods are not absorbed into the body. That the heat is greater than is natural one may grasp best both from the burning feelings that they experience and from the administration [of food]; for evidently they benefit from cold foods, and such [foods] usually cool and extinguish the heat.

Galen then goes on to say that 'Following these, Diocles added the rest, too, in the following words:

Some people say that in cases of such affections the mouth of the stomach, which is continuous with the gut, is inflamed, and because of this inflammation it is obstructed and it prevents the foods from going down into the gut at the regular times; when this happens, the foods remain in the stomach longer than they ought to, and they bring about the swellings and burnings and the other [symptoms] mentioned before.

This is what Diocles wrote.'

Note that Diocles begins by a careful description of the symptoms, followed by an account of the underlying physiological processes, which he backs up with an appeal to empirical evidence derived, *inter alia* from the way patients respond to treatment, and with a reference to the views of other people who have examined cases of the disease. The correctness of the physiological explanation is 'shown' (δηλοῖ) or can be 'grasped' (κατανοήσειεν) by means of empirically observable indicators.

The epistemological, inferential significance of the use of these different categories when describing pathological phenomena becomes even clearer in Praxagoras' distinctions between different kinds of pathological phenomena accompanying others. Apparently, he devoted separate treatises to these phenomena, writing about 'supervening' (περὶ ἐπιγινομένων)[59] and about 'accompanying' (περὶ συνεδρευόντων) phenomena. It seems that the first category

---

[59] The title seems once attested, rather unusually, in the aorist (περὶ ἐπιγενομένων, fr. 86), and as such it is listed by Steckerl (1958), 5, but this may be a scribal error (it is not even sure that fr. 86 intends to state the title); in fr. 92, it is quoted in the present tense.

denotes symptoms that occur in addition to an existing condition, whereas the 'accompanying' symptoms are necessarily present and therefore allow inferences as to the nature of the disease.[60] Such inferential reasoning is attributed to Praxagoras by Galen in two fragments (frs. 84, 85) and referred to as *analogismos*, although we have no independent evidence that Praxagoras used this term himself.

More secure evidence for the use of inferential reasoning is provided by Diocles. In fr. 22, we see him drawing an inference about processes of adhesion in the uterus on the basis of an analogy with adhesion between lifeless objects. And in fr. 56, we hear him quoting the famous slogan ὄψις τῶν ἀδήλων τὰ φαινόμενα and drawing an inference about invisible causal connections on the basis of visible manifestations:

> Diocles says: 'The appearances [provide] a view of what is obscure. There are [things] on the basis of whose appearance one can see that fever has occurred in consequence of them, [such as] wounds, inflammations and swollen glands.'[61]

And most strikingly, in fr. 24 we see him drawing an inference about the state of the uterus of women on the basis of repeated dissection of the uterus of mules:

> Why mules are infertile.
> Alcmaeon (...)
> Empedocles [says] that this is because of the smallness and lowness and narrowness of the uterus, which has turned and grown towards the stomach, so that the seed cannot be projected straight into it nor can the uterus receive it, even if it were to arrive there.
> Diocles testifies to this saying:
>   'In the dissections we have often observed that the uterus of mules is of this kind.'
> and [he says] that because of such reasons women, too, can be sterile.

'Often' may be something of a rhetorical overstatement, and there is a question what Diocles may have seen, but there is no reason to dismiss this fragment as insignificant, certainly not when we consider it in combination with other evidence for Diocles' anatomical research (frs. 17-24), some of which is also concerned with

---

[60]   This is what fr. 90 seems to indicate when it speaks three times (once in a direct quote) of 'necessarily' accompanying phenomena (cf. also the use of 'most specific', ἰδιαίτατον). However, the evidence is not quite clear on the precise significance of these terms. In fr. 86, Galen uses the verb 'supervene' (ἐπιγίνεσθαι) in relation to the group of 'accompanying' (συνεδρευόντων) phenomena, and it is unclear from the text whether he attributes to Praxagoras the same distinction as Hippocrates who, according to Galen, used both kinds of symptoms as indicators as to whether the disease would have a good or a bad crisis and whether it will last for a long time or for a short time. Nor is it clear from that fragment that Praxagoras also adopted Galen's category of 'diagnostic' (παθογνωμικά) phenomena, as Steckerl claims (1958, 28).

[61]   For a discussion of some of the difficulties of this fragment see van der Eijk (2001), 123-5. A different reading of the fragment is proposed by Hankinson (forthcoming).

the female reproductive organs (frs. 18, 22, 23), and more generally with Galen's claim that Diocles was the first to write a handbook on anatomy (fr. 17). That handbook may well have been based on comparative anatomical research, practised on a much wider scale than the few isolated references to such practice in the Hippocratic Corpus,[62] and not necessarily by Diocles alone, considering what went on in the Lyceum.

11. The development of empirical research

This brings us to another feature of fourth century medicine, the development of empirical research and fieldwork. Of course, Aristotle's and Theophrastus' achievements in the comparative study of animals and plants have well been documented, but it is less well-known that the medical writers developed similar activities. Unfortunately, the evidence is scanty and only allows glimpses of what may have been research at a very sizeable scale. Apart from Diocles' fragment just quoted, we should mention two fragments of Mnesitheus. In fr. 52, he is reported (by Galen) to be among those who have written about the anatomy of blooded animals, and in particular about the question whether they have a gall-bladder, which Mnesitheus is reported to have denied with regard to the elephant. And in fr. 17,25-6, in a *verbatim* fragment (preserved by Oribasius) about 'the structure of the body' (κατασκευὴ τοῦ σώματος), Mnesitheus says that he is very well aware that in man (as opposed to other animals) there is no distinction between upper and lower stomach. Praxagoras, too, is reported to have referred to 'dissections' (*anatomai*) for his views on the heart and vascular system (fr. 11), on uterine anatomy (fr. 12, again comparing women with other animals), and on thoracic anatomy (fr. 67).

In other areas, we should mention Diocles' fieldwork in the area of vegetables and herbs, displaying considerable geographical variety (and awareness that that may be relevant for the quality of certain fruits or vegetables), and Praxagoras' intriguing work *On Foreign Affections* (*passiones peregrinae*), which suggests a familiarity with diseases from other parts of the world.

12. Reason and experience

Perhaps the most impressive balancing act between reasoning and experience is attested in Diocles' observations on the modes and limitations of causal explanation in his famous 'fragment on method' (fr. 176), taken from his main dietetic work *Matters of Health* and concerned with the 'powers' of substances like foods and drinks to cause effects in the bodies of patients:

---

[62] E.g. *On the Sacred Disease* 11.3-5 (6.382 L.).

'Those, then, who suppose that [substances] that have similar flavours or smells or [degrees of] hotness or some other [quality] of this kind all have the same powers, are mistaken; for it can be shown that from [substances] that are similar in these respects, many dissimilar [effects] result; and indeed, one should also not suppose that every [substance] that is laxative or promotes urine or has some other power is like that for the reason that it is hot or cold or salt, seeing that not all [substances] that are sweet or pungent or salt or those having any other [quality] of this kind have the same powers; rather must one think that the whole nature is the cause of whatever normally results from each of them; for in this way one will least fail to hit the truth.

Those who believe that with every single [substance] one should state a cause why each one of such [substances] is nutritious or laxative or promotes urine or has some other similar power, apparently do not know, first, that for the use [of these substances] something like that is not often necessary, and further, that many of the [things] that are [the case] in some way look like some sort of starting-points by [their] nature, so that they do not admit of the [kind of] account that deals with [their] cause. In addition, they sometimes make mistakes when, while accepting [things] that are not known or are disputed or implausible, they think that they state the cause sufficiently. Therefore, one should not pay attention to those who state causes in this way or to those who believe that one should state a cause for all [things]; rather, one should give credence to the [things] that have been well grasped on the basis of experience over a long time. One should look for a cause [only] of the [things] admitting one, whenever it is by this that what is said turns out to be better known or more reliable.'

These are the words of Diocles, who believes that the powers contained in foodstuffs are known on the basis of experience only and not on the basis of an indication according to mixture or an indication according to humours.

I have dealt with this fragment extensively on several earlier occasions.[63] It is deservedly the most famous of Diocles' fragments, for it testifies, in a rather impressive way, to Diocles' awareness of the limitations of causal explanation, in this case the explanation of the effects of substances like foods, drinks and drugs on the body of the patient. And it may very well be directed against people like Mnesitheus (fr. 22) wishing to straightjacket their material by premature generalizations, at the expense of the variety suggested by empirical observation. If this is correct, we would have another example here, just like the Anonymus Londiniensis mentioned above, of internal debate between the medical writers of the same period regarding the appropriateness of their methodological techniques.

At the same time, fr. 176 does not rule out causal explanation altogether. Indeed, we have already seen that causal explanation features in the title of Diocles' major work on pathology, and the examples we looked at (and more could be cited) show that in his explanations of disease Diocles was quite prepared to go beyond the manifest, though using as many observable clues as possible to give his explanatory account the highest possible degree of 'plausibility'. Furthermore, not even in dietetics is causal explanation out of the question, for in fr. 177 (also taken

---

[63]   See van der Eijk (1996), and (2001), 321-34. See also Frede (forthcoming) and Hankinson (forthcoming).

from Diocles' *Matters of Health*) we can observe Diocles speaking about invisible causes, though again sounding cautionary notes about their relevance, considering the discongruity between causes and effects:

> One may learn this in many other [cases], but particularly also in those of vipers or scorpions and other [animals] of that kind, when one observes how they, though obscure and small of kind, become causes of great dangers and sufferings. Some of these [animals] are not even easy to see on account of a certain smallness and a [physical] strength in which they fall short of the [other] wild animals. Indeed to think how great is [the effect] of the sting of the scorpion and other such [things] that attack the flesh! Some of them produce intense pain, others putrefaction, yet others kill instantaneously. Or [to think of] the injection through the bite of a venomous spider, which causes the whole body to suffer throughout! Indeed one cannot discern the greatness of these [things] on account of the fact that they are so very very small.

The fragment raises numerous textual and interpretive difficulties, and its relationship to fr. 176 is not entirely clear.[64] But it does speak about obscure entities (ἄδηλα) being the causes (αἴτια) of clearly noticeable effects, and about ways of finding out about the identity of these causes (and their *modus operandi*) through inferential reasoning.

13. Conclusion

This account of some features of fourth century medicine has been inevitably selective. There are many more features of the medical writers of this period which deserve more attention. In the area of physiology, for instance, there is the development of the notion of *pneuma* and its relation to blood, the brain and the heart, especially in connection with cognitive processes and mental diseases (a number of fragments attribute this notion to Diocles, Praxagoras and Erasistratus). Then there is the striking preoccupation with the notion of 'excess' (*huperbolê*) and 'residue' (*perittôma*) in Aristotle, the Anonymus Londiniensis, the *Problemata*, Diocles and Mnesitheus. On a more formal level of 'discourse', we can observe an increasing 'textualization' of medical learning and debate, manifesting itself, *inter alia*, in the development of doxography, paraphrase and commentary writing (Aristotle, Theophrastus, but also Diocles);[65] and, as already mentioned above, we can observe how the expansion of the agenda of medicine, its range and coverage including areas like regimen in health, food, cookery,[66] sports, pedagogy, etiquette,

---

[64] For a discussion see van der Eijk (2001), 334-41; for a slightly different view see Hankinson (forthcoming).

[65] For this aspect of Diocles' work see van der Eijk (2001), xxv.

[66] For similarities between Diocles and the food writer Archestratus of Gela see Olson and Sens (2000), xxxi.

brought with it a greater variety of literary genres, such as letters and poems, and an increasing refinement of the language, e.g. by the formation of descriptive compound nouns, adjectives and verbs.[67]

It should by now be easier to understand how medical writers such as Diocles, Praxagoras and others came to be known as 'Rationalists' or 'Dogmatists' in the later tradition. After Kudlien's sobering discussion of these terms,[68] there has been a tendency in scholarship not to attach much value to these labels, and with good justification. For there was no Rationalist 'school' or 'sect' in the sense in which such a thing existed for the Empiricists and the Methodists. But the characteristics I have singled out do all point in the direction of an approach to medicine which is strongly informed by philosophical reflection, especially on matters of epistemology, methodology and formal techniques of analysis and presentation – a reflection which, for all three men we have looked at, seems to have been stimulated by developments in the Academy and the Lyceum.

This inevitably raises questions about 'influence' or 'exchange'. It is impossible to *prove* that people like Diocles or Mnesitheus were 'influenced' by Aristotle, Plato and Speusippus, or vice versa, for the evidence simply does not allow such conclusions. At the same time, it would be perverse to refuse to contemplate even the possibility that Diocles and Mnesitheus – who are both known to have worked in Athens – would have been in touch with these centres of learning (and Diocles is mentioned in Theophrastus' work *On Stones*). I am also not suggesting that the influence went in one direction only, or that these medical writers were not sufficiently independent thinkers to resist influences. Nevertheless, it seems undeniable that medical science in the fourth century, more than that preserved in the Hippocratic Corpus, adopted an epistemological framework and a methodological awareness that was going to be of lasting influence on the later history of medicine. The impact of Aristotelianism was perhaps more directly noticeable, both in the fourth century itself and immediately after. In the case of Herophilus as well as Erasistratus, historical contacts with the Peripatetic school are attested, and some tenets – e.g. the role of *pneuma* in Erasistratus, or the argument about teleological and mechanical explanation in Erasistratus – can hardly be considered in isolation from a strongly Aristotelian background. The influence of Plato and the Academy, apart from the dihairetic technique applied so strikingly by Mnesitheus and others, was perhaps more noticeable in the long term – perhaps we have to wait for that until the first century CE, when the Anonymus Londiniensis (whoever he was) revived interest in Plato's medical doctrines, and to the second century CE, when Galen exalted Plato to the heights of Hippocrates.[69]

---

[67]   See Mnesitheus fr. 17 with Bertier (1972), 23, and Diocles fr. 183a, with van der Eijk (2001), 357.

[68]   Kudlien (1965).

[69]   I am deeply grateful to Bob Sharples for inviting me to take part in the Keeling Colloquium and for his patience in the editing of the proceedings. For comments and

References

Althoff, J. (1992a) *Warm, kalt, flüssig und fest bei Aristoteles. Die Elementar- qualitäten in den zoologischen Schriften*, Steiner, Stuttgart.

Althoff, J. (1992b), 'Das Konzept der generativen Wärme bei Aristoteles', *Hermes* 120, 181-93.

Althoff, J. (1997), 'Aristoteles' Vorstellung von der Ernährung der Lebewesen', in Kullmann and Föllinger (eds), 351-64.

Althoff, J. (1999), 'Aristoteles als Medizindoxograph', in van der Eijk (1999c) (ed.), 33-56.

Balme, D.M. (1985), 'Aristotle Historia Animalium Book Ten', in J. Wiesner (ed.), *Aristoteles. Werk und Wirkung*, vol. 1, De Gruyter, Berlin, 191-206.

Balme, D.M. (1987), 'The place of biology in Aristotle's philosophy', in Gotthelf and Lennox (eds), 9-20.

Balme, D.M. (1991), *Aristotle, History of Animals VII–X*, Harvard University Press, Cambridge Mass. and London.

Balme, D.M. (2002), *Aristotle. Historia Animalium. Vol I: Books I–X, Text*, Cambridge University Press, Cambridge.

Baltussen, H. (2000), *Theophrastus against the Presocratics and Plato. Peripatetic Dialectic in the De sensibus*, Brill, Leiden.

Bertier, J. (1972), *Mnésithée et Dieuchès*, Brill, Leiden.

Bertier, J. (1989), 'A propos de quelques résurgences des Épidémies dans les Problemata du Corpus aristotélicien', in G. Baader, R. Winau (eds), *Die hippokratischen Epidemien. Theorie – Praxis – Tradition. Verhandlungen des Ve Colloque international hippocratique* (Sudhoffs Archiv, Beiheft 27), Steiner, Stuttgart, 261-9.

Bourgey, L. (1980), 'Hippocrate et Aristote: L'origine, chez le philosophe, de la doctrine concernant la nature', in M.D. Grmek (ed.), *Hippocratica. Actes du troisième Colloque international hippocratique*, Éditions du CNRS, Paris, 59-64.

Byl, S. (1980), *Recherches sur les grands traités biologiques: sources écrits et préjugés* (Académie Royale de Belgique, Mémoires de la Classe des Lettres, 2me série, t. 54, fasc. 3), Palais des Académies, Brussels.

Capriglione, J.C. (1983), *Prassagora di Cos*, Il Tripode, Naples.

Clarke, E. (1963), 'Aristotelian concepts of the form and function of the brain', *Bulletin of the History of Medicine* 37, 1-14.

Clarke, E. and Stannard, J. (1963), 'Aristotle on the anatomy of the brain', *Journal of the History of Medicine* 18, 130-48.

Coles, A. (1995), 'Biomedical models of reproduction in the fifth century BC and Aristotle's *Generation of Animals*', *Phronesis* 40, 48-88.

Conrad, L. et al. (1995), *The Western Medical Tradition*, Cambridge University Press, Cambridge.

Cootjans, G. (1991), *La stomatologie dans le Corpus aristotélicien* (Académie Royale de Belgique, Mémoires de la Classe des Lettres, 2me série, t. 69, fasc. 3), Palais des Académies, Brussels.

suggestions I am indebted to my commentator, Manuela Tecusan, and to those who took part in the discussion after its delivery, particularly Geoffrey Lloyd, Jim Hankinson, Jim Lennox, Vivian Nutton and Dominic O'Meara. The research for this paper was financially supported by a Project Grant from the Wellcome Trust.

Cordes, P. (1994), *Iatros. Das Bild des Arztes in der griechischen Literatur von Homer bis Aristoteles*, Steiner, Stuttgart.

Cunningham, A. (1999), 'Aristotle's animal books: ethology, biology, anatomy, or philosophy?', *Philosophical Topics* 27, 17-41.

Debru, A. (1982), 'L'épilepsie dans le *De somno* d'Aristote', in: G. Sabbah (ed.), *Médecins et médecine dans l'Antiquité*, Université de Saint-Etienne, Saint-Etienne, 25-41.

Debru, A. (2002), 'La sueur des corps: le *De sudore* de Théophraste face à la tradition médicale', in Fortenbaugh and Wöhrle (eds), 163-174.

Debru, A. (2005), 'Theophrastus' biological opuscula and the Hippocratic Corpus: a critical dialogue?', in van der Eijk (2005b).

Dickson, K. (1998), *Stephanus the Philosopher and Physician. Commentary on Galen's Therapeutics to Glauco*, Brill, Leiden.

Duffy, J.M. (1983), *Stephanus of Athens. Commentary on Hippocrates' Prognosticon*, Akademie Verlag, Berlin.

Eijk, P.J. van der (1990), 'Aristoteles über die Melancholie', *Mnemosyne* 43, 33-72 [revised and translated into English in van der Eijk (2005a), ch. 5].

Eijk, P.J. van der (1994), *Aristoteles. De insomniis. De divinatione per somnum* (Aristoteles. Werke in deutscher Übersetzung 14/III), Akademie Verlag, Berlin.

Eijk, P.J. van der (1995a), 'Aristotle on "distinguished physicians" and on the medical significance of dreams', in P.J. van der Eijk, H.F.J. Horstmanshoff, P.H. Schrijvers, (eds), *Ancient Medicine in its Socio-Cultural Context*, Vol. 2, Rodopi, Amsterdam, 447-59 [revised and included in van der Eijk (2005a), ch. 6].

Eijk, P.J. van der (1995b), 'Hart en hersenen, bloed en pneuma: Hippocrates, Aristoteles en Diocles over de localisering van cognitieve processen', *Gewina* 18, 214-29 [revised and translated into English in van der Eijk (2005a), ch. 4].

Eijk, P.J. van der (1996), 'Diocles and the Hippocratic writings on the method of dietetics and the limits of causal explanation', in Wittern and Pellegrin (eds), 229-58 [revised and included in: van der Eijk (2005a), ch. 2].

Eijk, P.J. van der (1997), 'The matter of mind. Aristotle on the biology of 'psychic' processes and the bodily aspects of thinking', in Kullmann and Föllinger (1997), 231-258 [revised and included in: van der Eijk (2005a), ch. 7].

Eijk, P.J. van der (1999a), '*On Sterility ('HA X')*, a medical work by Aristotle?', *Classical Quarterly* 49, 490-502 [revised and included in van der Eijk (2005a), ch. 9].

Eijk, P.J. van der (1999b), 'Hippokratische Beiträge zur antiken Biologie', in G. Wöhrle (ed.), *Geschichte der Mathematik und der Naturwissenschaften in der Antike, Band 1: Biologie*, Steiner, Stuttgart, 50-73.

Eijk, P.J. van der (1999c) (ed.), *Ancient Histories of Medicine. Essays in Medical Doxography and Historiography in Classical Antiquity* (Studies in Ancient Medicine 20), Brill, Leiden.

Eijk, P.J. van der (1999d), 'The systematic status of therapy in the Hippocratic Corpus and in the work of Diocles of Carystus' in: A. Lami et al. (eds), *Aspetti della terapia nel Corpus Hippocraticum*, Olschki, Florence, 389-404 [revised and included in: van der Eijk (2005a), ch. 3].

Eijk, P.J. van der (2000a), *Diocles of Carystus. A Collection of the Fragments with Translation and Commentary. Vol. 1: Text and Translation*, Brill, Leiden (Studies in Ancient Medicine 22).

Eijk, P.J. van der (2000b), 'Aristotle's psycho-physiological account of the soul-body relationship', in J.P. Wright and P. Potter (eds), *Psyche and Soma. Physicians and Metaphysicians on the Mind-Body Problem from Antiquity to Enlightenment*, Clarendon

Press, Oxford, 57-77.

Eijk, P.J. van der (2001), *Diocles of Carystus. A Collection of the Fragments with Translation and Commentary. Vol. 2: Commentary*, Brill, Leiden (Studies in Ancient Medicine 23).

Eijk, P.J. van der (2003), 'Aristotle on cognition in sleep', in T. Wiedemann and K. Dowden (eds.), *Sleep* (Nottingham Classical Literature Series / Midlands Classical Series 8), 25-40 [revised and included in: van der Eijk (2005a), ch. 6].

Eijk, P.J. van der (2005a), *Medicine and Philosophy in Classical Antiquity. Doctors and Philosophers on Nature, Soul, Health and Disease*, Cambridge University Press, Cambridge.

Eijk, P.J. van der (2005b), (ed.), *Hippocrates in Context*, Brill, Leiden.

Eijk, P.J. van der (forthcoming), 'The role of medicine in the formation of early Greek philosophical thought', in P. Curd and D. Graham (eds), *Oxford Guide to Pre-Socratic Philosophy*, Oxford University Press, Oxford.

Fiedler, W. (1978), *Analogiemodelle bei Aristoteles*, Grüner, Amsterdam.

Flashar, H. (1962), *Aristoteles. Problemata Physica* (Aristoteles. Werke in deutscher Übersetzung 19), Akademie Verlag, Berlin.

Flashar, H. (1966), *Melancholie und Melancholiker in den medizinischen Theorien der Antike*, De Gruyter, Berlin.

Fortenbaugh, W.W., and Wöhrle, G. (2002) (eds), *On the Opuscula of Theophrastus*, Steiner, Stuttgart.

Fortenbaugh, W.W.; Huby, P.M.; Sharples, R.W.; Gutas, D. (1992), *Theophrastus of Eresos. Sources for his Life, Writings, Thought and Influence*, 2 vols, Brill, Leiden.

Fortenbaugh, W.W.; Sharples, R.W.; Sollenberger, M. (2003) (eds), *Theophrastus of Eresus on Sweat, On Dizziness and On Fatigue*, Brill, Leiden.

Frede, M. (1980), 'The original notion of cause', in M. Schofield et al. (eds), *Doubt and Dogmatism. Studies in Hellenistic Epistemology*, Clarendon Press, Oxford, [repr. in Frede (1987), 125-50].

Frede, M. (1986), 'Philosophy and medicine in Antiquity', in A. Donagan et al. (eds), *Human Nature and Natural Knowledge. Essays Presented to Marjorie Grene on the Occasion of Her Seventy-Fifth Birthday*, Reidel, Dordrecht, 211-32 [repr. in: Frede (1987) 225-42].

Frede, M. (1987), *Essays in Ancient Philosophy*, Clarendon Press, Oxford.

Frede, M. (forthcoming), 'An anti-Aristotelian point of method in three Rationalist doctors'.

Freudenthal, G. (1995), *Aristotle's Theory of Material Substance. Heat and Pneuma, Form and Soul*, Clarendon Press, Oxford.

Gatzemeier, M. (1970), *Die Naturphilosophie des Straton von Lampsakos*, Hain, Meisenheim.

Gigon, O. (1983), *Aristotelis Opera III: Librorum deperditorum fragmenta*, De Gruyter, Berlin.

Gotthelf, A. (1985) (ed.), *Aristotle on Nature and Living Things*, Mathesis and Bristol Classical Press, Pittsburgh and Bristol.

Gotthelf, A., and Lennox, J.G. (1987) (eds), *Philosophical Issues in Aristotle's Biology*, Cambridge University Press, Cambridge.

Gourevitch, D. (1989), 'L'Anonyme de Londres et la médecine d'Italie du Sud', *History and Philosophy of the Life Sciences* 11, 237-51.

Gracia, D. (1978), 'The structure of medical knowledge in Aristotle's philosophy', *Sudhoffs Archiv* 62, 1-36.

Hankinson, R.J. (1995), 'The growth of medical empiricism', in D. Bates (ed.), *Knowledge and the Scholarly Medical Tradition*, Cambridge University Press, Cambridge, 59-83.

Hankinson, R.J. (1998), *Cause and Explanation in Ancient Greek Thought*, Clarendon Press, Oxford.

Hankinson, R.J. (1999), 'Hellenistic biological sciences', in D. Furley (ed.), *From Aristotle to Augustine* (Routledge History of Philosophy, Vol. II), Routledge, London and New York, 320-55.

Hankinson, R.J. (2002), 'Doctoring history: ancient medical historiography and Diocles of Carystus', *Apeiron* 35, 65-81.

Hankinson (forthcoming), 'Diocles of Carystus on causal explanation: Frs. 176–177 vdE'.

Harig, G. (1983), 'Zur Charakterisierung der wissenschaftstheoretischen Aspekte in der aristotelischen Biologie und Medizin', in Irmscher and Müller (eds.), 159-70.

Harris, C. (1973), *The Heart and the Vascular System in Ancient Greek Medicine*, Clarendon Press, Oxford.

Hohenstein, H. (1935), *Der Arzt Mnesitheos aus Athen*, diss., Berlin.

Irmscher, J. and Müller, R. (eds), *Aristoteles als Wissenschaftstheoretiker*, Akademie Verlag, Berlin.

Jaeger, W.W. (1913), 'Das Pneuma im Lykeion', *Hermes* 48, 29-74.

Jaeger, W.W. (1938a), *Diokles von Karystos. Die griechische Medizin und die Schule des Aristoteles*, De Gruyter, Berlin.

Jaeger, W.W. (1938b), 'Vergessene Fragmente des Peripatetikers Diokles von Karystos. Nebst zwei Abhandlungen zur Chronologie der dogmatischen Ärzteschule', *Abhandlungen der preussischen Akademie der Wissenschaften*, Philosophisch–historische Klasse, 1938.3, 1-46.

Jaeger, W.W. (1940), 'Diocles. A new pupil of Aristotle', *Philosophical Review* 49, 393-414.

Jaeger, W.W. (1948), *Aristotle: Fundamentals of the History of his Development*, second edition, Clarendon Press, Oxford.

Jaeger, W.W. (1951), 'Diokles von Karystos. Ein neuer Schüler des Aristoteles', *Zeitschrift für philosophische Forschung* 5, 25-46.

Jaeger, W.W. (1952), 'Diokles von Karystos und Aristoxenos über die Prinzipien', in *Hermeneia. Festschrift für O. Regenbogen*, C. Winter, Heidelberg, 94-103.

Jaeger, W.W. (1957), 'Aristotle's use of medicine as a model in his ethics', *Journal of Hellenic Studies* 77, 54-66.

Jouanna, J. (1966), 'La théorie de l'intelligence et de l'âme dans le traité hippocratique *Du régime*: ses rapports avec Empédocle et le Timée de Platon', *Revue des Études Grecques* 79, 15-19.

Jouanna, J. (1981), 'Médecine et politique dans la *Politique* d'Aristote (II 1268b25-1269a28)', *Ktema* 5, 257-66.

Jouanna, J. (1992), *Hippocrate*, Fayard, Paris.

Jouanna, J. (1996), 'Hippocrate et les Problemata d'Aristote: Essai de comparaison entre *Airs Eaux Lieux*, c. 10; *Aphorismes* III, 11–14, et *Problemata* I 8–12 et 19–20', in Wittern and Pellegrin (eds), 273-94.

Kalthoff, P. (1934), *Das Gesundheitswesen bei Aristoteles*, F. Dümmler, Berlin and Bonn.

Kauder, E., (1960), *Physikalische Modellvorstellung und physiologische Lehre im Corpus Hippocraticum und bei Aristoteles*, Diss. Hamburg.

King, R.A.H. (2001), *Aristotle on Life and Death*, Duckworth, London.

King, R.A.H. (2002), 'Nutrition and fatigue. Some remarks on Theophrastus' *Peri kopôn*', in Fortenbaugh and Wöhrle (eds), 113-21.

Kollesch, J. (1974), 'Zur Säftelehre in der Medizin des 4. Jahrhunderts v.u.Z.', in *Acta*

Congressus Internationalis XXIV Historiae Artis Medicinae, Semmelweis, Budapest, Vol. 2, 1339-42.

Kollesch, J. (1983), 'Zu Aristoteles' Bewertung von Erfahrung und Theorie in der Medizin und ihren Auswirkung auf die Entwicklung der Heilkunde im Hellenismus', in: Irmscher and Müller (eds), 179-82.

Kollesch, J. (1997), 'Die anatomischen Untersuchungen des Aristoteles und ihr Stellenwert als Forschungsmethode in der Aristotelischen Biologie', in Kullmann and Föllinger (eds), 367-73.

Kudlien, F. (1963), 'Probleme um Diokles von Karystos', *Sudhoffs Archiv* 47, 456-64.

Kudlien, F. (1965), 'Dogmatische Ärzte', *RE* Suppl. 10, 179-80.

Kudlien, F. (1985), '"Klassen"-Teilung der Ärzte bei Aristoteles', in J. Wiesner (ed.), *Aristoteles. Werk und Wirkung*, Vol. I, De Gruyter, Berlin, 427-35.

Kullmann, W. (1982), 'Aristoteles' Grundgedanken zu Aufbau und Funktion der Körpergewebe', *Sudhoffs Archiv* 66, 209-38.

Kullmann, W. and Föllinger, S. (1997) (eds), *Aristotelische Biologie. Intentionen, Methoden, Ergebnisse* (Philosophie der Antike 6), Steiner, Stuttgart.

Laks, A. and Louguet, C. (2002) (eds), *Qu'est-ce que c'est la philosophie Présocratique?*, Septentrion, Villeneuve d'Ascq.

Lennox, J. (1999), 'The place of mankind in Aristotle's zoology', *Philosophical Topics* 27, 1-16.

Lennox, J. (2001a), *Aristotle's Philosophy of Biology. Studies in the Origins of Life Science*, Cambridge University Press, Cambridge.

Lennox, J. (2001b), *Aristotle. Parts of Animals*, Clarendon Press, Oxford.

Lesky, E. (1950), *Die Zeugungs- und Vererbungslehren der Antike und ihr Nachwirken*, Steiner, Wiesbaden.

Lloyd, G.E.R. (1968), 'The role of medical and biological analogies in Aristotle's ethics', *Phronesis* 13, 68-83.

Lloyd, G.E.R. (2002), 'Le pluralisme de la vie intellectuelle avant Platon', in Laks and Louguet (eds), 39-54.

Lloyd, G.E.R. (2003), *In the Grip of Disease*, Oxford University Press, Oxford.

Longrigg, J. (1993), *Greek Rational Medicine*, Routledge, London.

López Salva, M. (1996), 'Hippokratische Medizin und aristotelische Handlungs-philosophie: Analogien und Parallelismen', in Wittern and Pellegrin (eds), 203-16.

Louis, P. (1991-1994), *Aristote. Problèmes*, 3 vols, Les Belles Lettres, Paris.

Manetti, D. (1986), 'Note di lettura dell' Anonimo Londinense. Prolegomena ad una nuova edizione', *Zeitschrift für Papyrologie und Epigraphik* 63, 57-74.

Manetti, D. (1994), 'Autografi e incompiuti: il caso dell'Anonimo Londinense P. Lit. Lond. 165', *Zeitschrift für Papyrologie und Epigraphik* 100, 47-58.

Manetti, D. (1999), '"Aristotle" and the role of doxography in the Anonymus Londiniensis (PBrLibr Inv. 137)', in van der Eijk (1999c) (ed.), 95-141.

Marenghi, G. (1961), 'Aristotele e la medicina greca', *Rendiconti del Instituto Lombardo*, Classe di Lettere 95, 141-61.

Marenghi, G. (1965), *Aristotele. Problemi di medicina*, Istituto Editoriale Italiano, Milan.

McGowen Tress, D. (1999), 'Aristotle against the Hippocratics on sexual generation: a reply to Coles', *Phronesis* 44, 228-41.

Mitropoulos, K. (1964), 'Iatrika Aristotelous', *Platon* 16, 17-61.

Morel, P.M. (2000), *Aristote. Petits traités d'histoire naturelle*. Traduction et présentation, Flammarion, Paris.

Morel, P.M. (2002a), 'Démocrite dans les Parva naturalia d'Aristote', in Laks and Louguet (eds), 449-64.

Morel, P.M. (2002b), 'Les Parva naturalia d'Aristote et le mouvement animal', *Revue de Philosophie Ancienne* 20, 61-88.

Nickel, D. (2005), 'Hippokratisches bei Praxagoras von Kos', in van der Eijk (2005b).

Nutton, V. (2004), *Ancient Medicine*, Routledge, London.

Ogle, W. (1897), *Aristotle on Youth and Old Age, Life and Death and Respiration*, Longmans, Green, London.

Olson, S.D., and Sens, A. (2000), *Archestratos of Gela. Greek Culture and Cuisine in the Fourth Century BCE*, Oxford University Press, Oxford.

Oser-Grote, C. (1997), 'Das Auge und der Sehvorgang nach Aristoteles und der hippokratischen Schrift *De carnibus*', in Kullmann and Föllinger, (eds), 333-50.

Oser-Grote, C. (2004), *Aristoteles und das Corpus Hippocraticum*, Steiner, Stuttgart.

Pellegrin, P. (1996), 'Aristote, Hippocrate, Œdipe', in Wittern and Pellegrin (1996), 183-98.

Poschenrieder, F. (1882), *Die platonischen Dialoge in ihrem Verhältnis zu den hippokratischen Schriften*, Thomann, Landshut.

Poschenrieder, F. (1887), *Die naturwissenschaftlichen Schriften des Aristoteles in ihrem Verhältnis zu den Büchern der hippokratischen Sammlung*, W. Gärtner, Bamberg.

Preus, A. (1983), 'Aristotle and Hippocratic Gynaecology', in Irmscher and Müller (eds), 183-96.

Repici, L. (1988), *La natura e l'anima. Saggi su Stratone di Lampsaco*, Tirrenia, Turin.

Rose, V. (1863), *Aristoteles Pseudepigraphus*, Teubner, Leipzig.

Roselli, A. (1992), *[Aristotele]. De spiritu*, ETS, Pisa.

Roselli, A. (2002), 'Theophrastus' *Peri kopôn* and Greek medical theories of fatigue', in Fortenbaugh and Wöhrle (eds), 123-39.

Runia, D.T. (1999), 'The *placita* ascribed to doctors in Aëtius' doxography on physics', in: van der Eijk (1999c) (ed.), 189-250.

Schmitt, C.B. (1985), 'Aristotle among the physicians', in: A. Wear, R.K. French and I.M. Lonie (eds), *The Medical Renaissance of the Sixteenth Century*, Cambridge University Press, Cambridge, 1-15.

Schuhl, P.-M. (1960), 'Platon et la médecine', *Revue des Études Grecques* 73, 73-9.

Senn, G. (1933), *Die Entwicklung der biologischen Forschungsmethode in der Antike und ihre grundsätzliche Förderung durch Theophrast von Eresos*, Sauerländer, Aarau.

Sharples, R.W. (1995), *Theophrastus of Eresus. Sources for his Life, Writings, Thought, and Influence, Commentary Vol. 5: Sources on Biology*, Brill, Leiden.

Sieverts, C.W. (1949), *Die Physiologie bei Aristoteles*, diss., Münster.

Solmsen, F. (1950), 'Tissues and the soul', *Philosophical Review* 59, 435-68.

Solmsen, F. (1957), 'The vital heat, the inborn pneuma and the aether', *Journal of Hellenic Studies* 77, 119-23.

Solmsen, F. (1960), *Aristotle's System of the Physical World*, Cornell University Press, Ithaca and New York.

Solmsen, F. (1961), 'Greek philosophy and the discovery of the nerves', *Museum Helveticum* 18, 150-67 and 169-97.

Spagnolo, A.G. (1992), 'La medicina come modello dell' etica di Aristotele', *Aufidius* 16, 31-40.

Spoerri, W. (1996), 'Médecine et formes de connaissance chez Aristote, *Metaph.* A 1', in Wittern and Pellegrin (eds), 203-16.

Staden, H. von (1992), 'Jaeger's "Skandalon der historischen Vernunft": Diocles, Aristotle, and Theophrastus', in W.M. Calder III (ed.), *Werner Jaeger Reconsidered* (Proceedings of the Second Oldfather Conference, University of Illinois, April 26–28, 1990), Scholars Press, Atlanta, 227-65.

Steckerl, F. (1958), *The Fragments of Praxagoras and his School*, Brill, Leiden.

Tarán, L. (1981), *Speusippus of Athens*, Brill, Leiden.

Thivel, A. (1965), 'La doctrine des *perissomata* et ses parallèles hippocratiques', *Revue de Philologie* 39, 266-82.

Tieleman, T.L. (2003), *Chrysippus on Affections*, Brill, Leiden.

Todd, R.B. (1977), 'Galenic medical ideas in the Greek Aristotelian commentators', *Symbolae Osloenses* 52, 117-34.

Todd, R.B. (1984), 'Philosophy and medicine in John Philoponus' commentary on Aristotle's De anima', *Dumbarton Oaks Papers* 38, 103-10.

Tracy, T.J. (1969), *Physiological Theory and the Doctrine of the Mean in Plato and Aristotle*, Mouton, The Hague and Paris.

Tracy, T.J. (1983), 'Heart and soul in Aristotle', in J. Anton and A. Preus (eds), *Essays in Ancient Greek Philosophy*, Vol. 2, SUNY Press, Albany, 321-39.

Vegetti, M. (1995), *La medicina in Platone*, Cardo, Venice.

Verbeke, G. (1945), *L'évolution de la doctrine du* pneuma, de Brouwer, Paris and Leuven.

Vitrac, B. (1989), *Médecine et philosophie au temps d'Hippocrate*, Presses universitaires de Vincennes, Saint-Denis.

Vogt, S. (2002), 'Theophrast, De vertigine', in Fortenbaugh and Wöhrle (eds), 141-61.

Volprecht, A. (1895), *Die physiologischen Anschauungen des Aristoteles*, diss., Greifswald.

Wehrli, F. (1951), 'Ethik und Medizin', *Museum Helveticum* 8, 36-62.

Wehrli, F. (1967–1969) *Die Schule des Aristoteles. Texte und Kommentare*, 10 vols, 2nd edn, Schwabe, Basel and Stuttgart.

Wellmann, M. (1901), *Die Fragmente der sikelischen Ärzte Akron, Philistion und des Diokles von Karystos* (Fragmentsammlung der griechischen Ärzte, Band 1), Weidmann, Berlin.

Wittern, R. and Pellegrin, P. (1996) (eds), *Hippokratische Medizin und attische Philosophie*, Olms Weidmann, Hildesheim.

Chapter Six

Mathematics as a Model of Method in Galen

G.E.R. Lloyd

Galen's logic and scientific method have attracted a number of important studies in recent years,[1] although the loss of his fifteen-book magnum opus *On Demonstration* inevitably means that conclusions on several aspects of his work in this area must remain tentative. I attempted a provisional survey of the variety of both his concepts and his practices of *apodeixis* in my contribution to the Festschrift for Günther Patzig (Lloyd, 1996). In this study I want to focus more precisely on the texts in the extant works that throw light on Galen's understanding of mathematics as a model of method.

When examined closely, these texts present something of a puzzle. On the one hand he often expresses his admiration for the mathematicians' methods. They provide his star examples of the highest type of demonstration, 'epistemonic *apodeixis*', securing certainty. On the other hand to illustrate those methods Galen gives a bewildering array of examples that do not all by any means conform to the patterns set by the Euclid of the *Elements*. Some of his illustrations do indeed suggest the axiomatic-deductive mode of reasoning we find in the *Elements*. But others belong to areas of what we should call applied mathematics, astronomy, optics, even architecture. The issue I wish to explore here is how clear a grasp of mathematical method does Galen have? Or rather, since we should look at the problem from his point of view, what counts as 'mathematical method' in Galen's eyes? The question derives its importance from the frequency with which mathematics is held up as an ideal: but quite what that ideal comprises is more difficult to pin down than is generally recognized.

Let me begin by reminding you of some of the texts in which Galen insists on the importance of logic. In the pair of treatises he wrote *On the Affections and Errors of the Soul* (*Pecc. Dig.* and *Pecc. Cur.*), the discussion of the latter proceeds by way of an analysis of what it is to be free from error. *Pecc. Dig.* ch. 1 (*CMG* V 4 1 1, 42.2-7, trans. Singer) states:

---

[1]   See especially Barnes (1991), Hankinson (1991a), (1992), Tieleman (2002); and cf. more generally Frede (1987), Donini (1992).

The secure kind of knowledge possessed by the geometer is exemplified by the truths taught in Euclid's *Elements*, beginning with such propositions as 'two times two equals four.' He also possesses the same kind of knowledge in the theory of spheres, which is the next subject taught, and in all the problems solved according to that theory; so also with the theories of cones and gnomons.

That is already an interestingly eclectic selection. It is not as if Euclid spends time on the proposition '2 x 2 = 4', although he states the equality axiom in all its generality in book I and defines multiplication in Def. 15 of book VII, though that book does not open with problems of multiplication but is concerned rather with propositions to do with prime numbers and common measures. As for Sphaerics, we have treatises on that subject by Autolycus of Pitane and by Theodosius of Bithynia, and Euclid's own *Phaenomena* (to which Galen refers elsewhere).[2] Euclid's *Conics* are lost, and so are Aristaeus' *Solid Loci*, but of course we have the first four books of Apollonius' *Conics* in Greek and the later books in an Arabic version. Finally Galen's mention of gnomons here should be taken to refer, not to the arithmetical study of square, oblong and polygonal numbers, but rather to the study of the construction of sun-dials (to which again Galen refers elsewhere).[3]

Galen recognizes, to be sure, that the geometer can make mistakes and contrasts these errors with those that may be committed in the conduct of life – a far more serious matter to do with the knowledge, attainment and avoidance of good and evil. But the general topic of error prompts Galen to take a swipe at one of his favourite targets, the Academic and Pyrrhonian Sceptics, and then to insist on the need for training in logic.

Pecc. Dig. ch. 1 (*CMG* V 4 1 1, 42.15-20; 43.3-7, trans. Singer) continues:

Now, the opinion of the Academics and Pyrrhonists, since they deny the possibility of logical proof in these matters altogether, is that all assent is necessarily hasty, and may also be false. Those philosophers who do believe in proof, however, offer conflicting views on ethical matters, which cannot therefore all be correct ... . The first task for the man interested in becoming free of error is to investigate the question whether matters which are not evident admit of proof by argument. When he finds that they do, the next step is the inquiry into the method of proof – and this is not something to be conducted in a casual manner, but over a long period of time, and in association with men of the highest credentials in terms of veracity, natural intelligence, and education in logical theory.

Of course Galen himself had received just such a training. In *On the Order of My Own Books* ch. 4 (*Libr. Ord.*, *Scr. Min.* II 88.10-12, trans. Singer) he writes of his own great good fortune in the education he received from his father. 'My father

---

[2]   See below 121 on *PHP* VIII ch. 1, *CMG* V 4 1 2, 484.22ff.
[3]   See below 112-13 and 123-4 on *Libr. Prop.* ch. 11 (*Scr. Min.* II 117.1), *Pecc. Dig.* chs 3 and 5 (*CMG* V 4 1 1, 47.12ff., 54.20ff., 59.6-8).

was himself competent in the fields of mathematics, arithmetic and grammar, and reared me in these as well as the other subjects necessary to the training of the young.'[4] A further passage in *On my Own Books* ch. 11 (*Libr. Prop., Scr. Min.* II 115.21-117.20, trans. Singer) elaborates on Galen's early passion for proof. He writes of his desire to learn

> the nature of that method which gives him who masters it the power to recognize whether a self-proclaimed 'proof' really is one, or whether, like some counterfeit coin, it appears similar to the genuine one while being in fact valueless; that method which, at the same time, enables its knower, in any field of inquiry, to find some way of arriving at the discovery of the truth.

He describes how he did the rounds of

> all the best-reputed Stoic and Peripatetic philosophers of the time; but while I learned many pieces of logical theory from them which in the fullness of time I found to be quite useless for establishing proofs, there were very few that they had researched in any useful manner likely to lead them to the goal set before them.

Worse was to come, as the sequel shows:

> I found, additionally, that these pieces of logical theory were actually in conflict with each other, while some were even in conflict with our most basic intuitions. Indeed, as far as these teachers were concerned, I might well have fallen into a Pyrrhonian despair of knowledge, if I had not had a firm grasp of the disciplines of geometry, mathematics, and arithmetic, in which subjects I had excelled from the very first, through the schooling of my father, who had himself learned them from my grandfather and great-grandfather. I had, then, observed the incontrovertible truth manifested (and not just to myself) in predictions of eclipses, in the workings of sundials and water-clocks, and in all sorts of other calculations made in the context of architecture; and I decided that this geometrical type of proof would be the best to employ. And I had noticed that the most argumentative of dialecticians, as well as the philosophers, who were always in conflict not only with each other but with

---

4   This is one of the texts in which Galen refers to the dream that his father had, that Galen should study medicine as well as philosophy. Galen tells us this happened in his seventeenth year. In his response to my paper, Professor Nutton emphasized the importance of Galen's claim to have been trained by his father in mathematics. He drew attention to the epigraphic evidence from Pergamon for two architects of the right period who shared the same name, Nikon, as Galen's father, both of whom are associated with 'isopsephic' inscriptions in public places (where the letters are given numerical equivalents and the sum total in each line must be the same) and one of whom was responsible for an inscription describing the relations between the cube, sphere and cylinder. Tantalising as this evidence for mathematically-inclined individuals called Nikon is, Diller noted in his discussion of the issue (1936, col. 508) that the positive identification of either with Galen's father necessarily remains uncertain.

themselves, nevertheless all bestowed equal praise on the geometrical proof ... . For this reason my resolve was all the firmer to steer clear of the arguments of these people, while emulating the model provided by geometrical proof. Now those who wish to cultivate the geometrical-style proof must be advised to acquire a thorough training in it; and after that, to read my work on *Logical Demonstration*, composed in fifteen volumes.

Once again we should note the choice of examples. Eclipse prediction, for instance, requires the application of numerical parameters as much as the appeal to geometrical models. According to this text, however, geometrical proof seemed to Galen to be a sovereign remedy to resolve many of the kinds of conflicts that he observed to arise among philosophers. Just when sceptical doubts threatened to overwhelm him, he was saved by his firm grasp of mathematics. Trained himself by his father, he claims to be able to pass on a proper education in logical proof to the next generation, who are encouraged first to acquire a thorough training in geometrical-style proofs and then to study Galen's own *On Demonstration*.

But if Galen makes clear his appreciation of geometrical methods, he also recognizes that mathematics is unpopular. At *On the Usefulness of the Parts* (*UP*) X ch. 12 (II 92.23-93.10 Helmreich, trans. May), he interrupts his discussion of the eye (to which I shall be returning) with the remark

I have explained nearly everything pertaining to the eyes with the exception of one point[5] which I had intended to omit lest many of my readers be annoyed with the obscurity of the explanations and the length of the treatment. For since it necessarily involves the theory of geometry and most people pretending to some education not only are ignorant of this but also avoid those who do understand it and are annoyed by them, I thought it better to omit the matter altogether. But afterward I dreamed that I was being censured because I was unjust to the most godlike of the instruments and was behaving impiously toward the creator in leaving unexplained a great work of his providence for animals, and so I felt impelled to take up again what I had omitted and add it to the end of this book.

At the end of his discussion he returns to the same point (*UP* X ch. 14, II 109.5-9 Helmreich, trans. May).

For before I received his order (a person calling the gods themselves to witness must speak the truth), I did not intend to discuss this, not wishing to be hated by the many who would choose to suffer any ill you please rather than to have anything to do with geometry.

The end of the same chapter (*UP* X ch. 14, II 110.7-24 Helmreich, trans. May) goes even further in generalizing the problem.

---

[5]   This relates to the optic chiasma: see below, 125-6 on *UP* X ch. 13.

A god, as I have said, commanded me to tell the first use also,[6] and he himself knows that I have shrunk from its obscurity. He knows too that not only here but also in many other places in these commentaries, if it depended on me, I would omit demonstrations requiring astronomy, geometry, music, or any other logical discipline, lest my books should be held in utter detestation by physicians. For truly on countless occasions throughout my life I have had this experience: persons for a time talk pleasantly with me because of my work among the sick, in which they think me very well trained, but when they learn later on that I am also trained in mathematics, they avoid me for the most part and are no longer at all glad to be with me. Accordingly, I am always wary of touching on such subjects, and in this case it is only in obedience to the command of a divinity, as I have said, that I have used the theorems of geometry.

So Galen is torn. Geometry provides the ideal, but Galen plays down geometrical proofs because they are thought of as obscure and gain him the reputation of being a prize boor.

But now what about Galen's actual practice? It is clear that he praises the geometrical method and cites the need for training in, as well as the importance of, logical reasoning in general, but does he practise what he preaches? First there are many occasions throughout the Corpus where he usefully distinguishes between different modes of reasoning. Developing a classification that owes much to Plato and Aristotle especially, he distinguishes between epistemonic arguments, dialectical ones, rhetorical ones and sophistic ones. In one typical text, *On the Opinions of Hippocrates and Plato* (*PHP*) VIII ch. 1 (*CMG* V 4 1 2, 482.4-8, trans. De Lacy, modified), he complains that his opponents had not put together their arguments on the ruling principle of the soul (the *hêgemonikon*) in accordance with demonstrative method. 'Some of them [the arguments] were close to it – the ones Aristotle had the habit of calling dialectical. Others were further removed from it; these we divided into the rhetorical and the sophistical.'

Then we have clear indications of Galen's own ambition to provide the strictest demonstrations – on the geometrical model indeed – on certain topics, even if on some he has to admit defeat. In the final chapter of *On the Construction of the Foetus* (*Foet. Form.*) ch. 6 (IV 695.1-696.3 Kühn, trans. Singer) he first says that he sought demonstrations with regard to the demiurgic force at work in the construction of the body.

As I have said, I could never be persuaded that these [parts of the body] have come about without an extraordinarily intelligent and powerful craftsman. As to the identity of this craftsman, I had hoped to learn this from the philosophers who pronounce on the universe, and on the generation of all things; for I should have thought it a much easier matter to find out the manner in which their own bodies were made. And so I presented myself to one such person first of all, in the hope of hearing from him proofs of the

---

[6]   The first use relates to its usefulness in preventing double vision: see below, 125-6 on *UP* X ch. 13.

same sort as I had learned in geometry. But when I realized that, so far from producing geometric-style proofs, he could not even utter rhetorical probabilities, I moved to another; he too began from his own personal assumptions, proceeding to prove the opposite to the previous philosopher. I tried a third, too, and a fourth; and from none of them, as I have said, did I hear a flawless demonstration. Much grieved at this, I sought on my own resources to find a watertight argument regarding the making of animals. But I found none. I admit this fact in the present treatise; and I call upon the best philosophers engaged on this matter, if they find some clever solution, to share it with us without jealousy.

Yet if he was unable to demonstrate the construction of the body in the geometrical manner, he does claim to give epistemonic proofs on quite a number of issues, relating especially to the sources of vital activities in the living creature. The end of the same chapter in *Foet. Form.* (IV 701.7-702.4 Kühn, trans. Singer) alludes to this:

So only this do I believe myself able to state definitely about the cause of construction within animals: that it involves an enormous degree of skill and intelligence, and that after this construction the entire body is managed throughout its life by three causes of motion: that from the brain through nerves and muscles; that from the heart through the arteries; and that from the liver through the veins. I have made clear demonstrations regarding these three sources – for I did not dare rely on conjecture – in a number of treatises, especially in that dealing with the forms of the soul; but I have nowhere presumed to declare the identity of the substance of the soul. Even whether it is entirely incorporeal, whether it is something bodily, whether it is entirely invisible, or whether perishable – I have yet to find anyone who has employed geometric-style proofs on any of these questions, a point I discussed also in my treatise on the forms of the soul.

Actually in *PHP* we find a number of more nuanced statements. In book VIII and elsewhere he is absolutely confident of the quality of the proofs he can give that the ruling part of the soul is in the brain. In VIII ch. 1 (*CMG* V 4 1 2, 484.13-17, trans. De Lacy, modified), he says:

It is also a cause for shame that men who have grown old in philosophy do not recognize that only this one argument about the ruling part of the soul was formulated by the law of proof,[7] the argument in which the true added premise is that the brain is the source of the nerves, and the false one is that the heart is the source of the nerves.

He then explains, (484.34-486.9, trans. De Lacy):

Thus the true account is as short as I shall demonstrate to you; it reaches its conclusion in a few syllables, as follows: 'Where the beginning of the nerves is, there is the

---

[7] De Lacy in his translation has 'law of scientific proof' but the Greek simply has ἀποδεικτικὸς νόμος.

governing part. The beginning of the nerves is in the brain. Therefore, the governing part is there.' This one argument has thirty-nine syllables, equivalent to two and one half hexameters. A second argument is in all five lines long. 'Where the affections of the soul more visibly move the parts of the body, there the affective part of the soul is. The heart is observed to undergo a great change of motion in anger and fear. Therefore, the affective part of the soul is in the heart.' If you thus join these two arguments together, the combined total will be no more than eight hexameter lines.

However, where the third part of the soul is concerned, *PHP* VI ch. 3 (*CMG* V 4 1 2, 372.16-22, trans. De Lacy) is more cautious.

> Our purpose from the beginning has been to prove that one [part of the soul] is generated in the head, another in the heart, and the third in the liver; and in the preceding [books] that has been done for two of the parts. The desiderative remains; it requires a special proof which we shall present in this [book]. But first I preface the argument with the statement that this proof will not be from such clear evidence as before, and its premises, unlike the earlier ones, are not taken directly from the nature of the thing under investigation, but from properties peculiar to it.

Again in book VIII ch. 1, (488.34-37) he contrasts certain proofs that are described as 'sufficient' with others that are not 'epistemonic'. Yet in book IX ch. 9 (598.26-600.6, trans. De Lacy, modified), his claims are general.

> I claim to have proofs (*apodeixeis*) that the forms of the soul are more than one, that they are located in three different places, that one of them is divine, by which we reason, and the other two have to do with the feelings – with the one we are angry; with the other, which plants have too, we desire the pleasures that come through the body – and further that one of these parts is situated in the brain, one in the heart, and one in the liver. These facts admit of epistemonic demonstrations (*apodeixeis epistêmonikai*), and I made my case for them in the first six books of this treatise.

You will have spotted, for sure, that there is nothing specifically *geometrical* about many of the demonstrations claimed to be epistemonic. The actual arguments that Galen sets out for his conclusions often take the form of Modus Ponens or the first Stoic indemonstrable: if p, then q; but p; so q. Yet in book VIII especially it is geometry that Galen cites to show what an epistemonic demonstration amounts to. In VIII ch. 1, (484.17-22, trans. De Lacy, modified), he protests that he did not really need five books to discuss the governing part of the soul. There was no need even for one book, 'at least for those who have learned what epistemonic demonstration is.' Philosophers should be familiar with this, since it is more appropriate to them than to 'geometricians, arithmeticians and mathematicians, astronomers and master-builders [architects]'. 'But the philosophers have not practised it as the others have' – and he then proceeds to cite a text from Euclid's *Phaenomena* which I shall come back to shortly.

Similarly, when castigating Thessalus and his followers for not knowing what a demonstration is, in *De Methodo Medendi* (*MM*) I ch. 3 (X 29.16-30.3

Kühn) Galen blames their ignorance on their failure to study geometry, arithmetic, formal logic, analytics, or indeed logical theory of any kind. Without any training in demonstration, he continues at I ch. 4 (X 32.13-33.7 Kühn, trans. Hankinson)

> they behave like a man who tries to measure a sphere, cube, cone, cylinder or something else of that sort, without knowing any geometrical or computational theory ... . Thus anyone who asserts that the area of a right-angled triangle, in which one of the sides enclosing the right-angle is five feet long (as it might be) and the other twelve feet long, is not thirty feet but forty feet, without having any demonstration of this, would seem to be ridiculous.

Once again geometry provides his illustration, though he goes on to analyse the argument in terms of the combination of two premises, the first that the [rectangular] area enclosed by sides of five and twelve feet is sixty feet, and the second that that of the triangle in question is half that of the rectangle.

Thus far I have argued that while Galen's idea of epistemonic demonstration is a general one and not confined to mathematics, mathematical examples crop up with some regularity as illustrations of what is required. Sometimes he qualifies the demonstrations in question as *geômetrikai*,[8] sometimes as *grammikai*,[9] sometimes he runs through an actual stretch of geometrical reasoning to exemplify the mode of demonstration he is after.[10]

But now I want to press the question of Galen's understanding of mathematical arguments and of the mathematical method of proof that he invokes as his ideal. At first sight things look straightforward enough. On one crucial issue, that of the nature of the premises on which geometrical arguments are based, Galen shows himself to be fully aware that indemonstrable primary premises are needed. In the analysis of the argument in *De Methodo Medendi* I ch. 4 cited above, Galen notes (X 33.14-34.2 Kühn, trans. Hankinson) that

> each of these [premises] needs to be proved on the basis of further premises, which themselves are based on others still, until we arrive at the primary ones which derive their justification neither from others, nor from demonstration, but from themselves. It is the same, in my view, with all of the things demonstrated in medical science: all of them must be reduced to certain primary indemonstrable propositions which are self-justifying.

Galen indeed proceeds to give several impeccable examples of such indemonstrable propositions, 'which they call *axiômata*' – here evidently in the special sense of 'axioms' rather than the general one of 'propositions'. *MM* I ch. 4

---

[8]   As in *Prop. Lib.* ch. 11 (*Scr. Min.* II 117.3 and 7).
[9]   As in *Prop. Lib.* ch. 11 (*Scr. Min.* II 117.15 and 16), *Foet. Form.* IV 659.10 Kühn.
[10] As in *PHP* VIII ch. 1, and *MM* I ch. 1.

(X 34.2-16 Kühn) gives the Euclidean definition of line as 'breadthless length' (*Elements* I Def. 2) and of surface as 'that which has length and breadth alone' (*Elements* I Def. 5) even though he then runs out of steam and just gestures towards the definitions of triangle and quadrilateral and 'similarly with all the rest of them'. Moreover his examples are not confined to definitions, for he also cites two of Euclid's 'common opinions' (*koinai ennoiai*), namely that 'when two quantities are equal to a given quantity, they are equal to one another' and that 'if equal quantities are added to equal quantities, the results are equal'. He gives these two examples again, together with Common Opinion 3, that when equals are subtracted from equals, the remainders are equal, at *MM* I ch. 4 (X 36.14ff. Kühn) to illustrate one of his two subclasses of 'apparent' things, namely 'those that are grasped by the intellect on their first appearance and that are indemonstrable.'

All of this shows, it seems, an impressive grasp of axiomatic-deductive reasoning, proceeding from indemonstrable primary premisses, via valid arguments, to incontrovertible conclusions. Yet there are problems. One of the major ones has been identified by both Barnes and Hankinson. While in some of his uses in the passages I have just cited, as also in the *Institutio Logica* when he is discussing the Stoic indemonstrables,[11] Galen's 'indemonstrables' are incapable of proof, he elsewhere writes as if some of his principles are indeed evident, *enargeis*, but can nevertheless be proved. They are 'indemonstrables' (*anapodeiktoi*) only in the weaker sense of not requiring proof.

Barnes focuses on a passage from *On the Natural Faculties* (*Nat. Fac.*) II ch. 8 (*Scr.Min.* III 186.2-10, trans. Brock, modified), where Galen says:

> Now I, for my part, as I have already said, did not set before myself the task of stating what had been so well demonstrated by the ancients, since I cannot surpass these men either in my views or in my method of giving them expression. Doctrines, however, which they either stated without demonstration as being evident (*enargê*),[12] (since they never suspected that there would be sophists so degraded as to contemn the truth in these matters), or else which they actually omitted to mention at all – these I propose to discover and prove.

Now there is nothing problematic about proving certain low-level propositions from certain higher-level ones – except that taking the first to be *enargê* might be thought to be premature. But where the ultimate or primary premisses are

---

[11]   *Institutio Logica* (*Inst. Log.*) ch. 6 (15.8ff. Kalbfleisch).
[12]   Brock at this points translates 'self-evident', which may express Galen's claim. However, when he wishes, he can and sometimes does express the notion of self-evidence by adding the specification 'of itself', ἐξ ἑαυτῶν or ἐξ ἑαυτοῦ, to πιστά. See for example *MM* I ch. 4 (X 33.17 and 34.2 Kühn), *Opt. Doctr.* ch. 4 (*CMG* V 1 1, 104.10ff.), *PHP* II ch. 5 (*CMG* V 4 1 2, 142.16ff.), *Simpl.* II ch. 1 (XI 462.10ff. Kühn), *Inst. Log.* ch. 16 (39.17ff., 40.4).

concerned, trying to prove them immediately runs into the difficulties that Aristotle had long ago identified when he showed that – to avoid the twin flaws of circularity and of an infinite regress – proof must proceed from certain premisses that are indemonstrable in the strict sense of incapable of proof (*Posterior Analytics* I ch. 3, 72b5ff.). Yet, as becomes clear when he returns to the problem in *Nat. Fac.* III ch. 10 (*Scr.Min.* III 230.13-23) Galen envisages a situation where 'shameless sophists' contradict what is evident, and force Galen to put together certain arguments in their defence, defending them indeed in the manner in which the ancients themselves would, if they had still been alive.[13]

Hankinson offers a rather different analysis of Galen's position, reminding us that some principles may be clear to us, others clear 'by nature'. Galen can move from the one to the other, and can then prove the former on the basis of the latter. After further inquiry, in other words, we can get back to what is *enargês* in the strict sense of 'incapable of proof', though at an earlier stage we had assumed as evident only what was so to us.

That is certainly unobjectionable in principle as a theoretical account of how Galen can speak of proving some of his principles, but it cannot be said to have any direct support in the text of *Nat. Fac.*, nor any in a second passage that Hankinson discusses from *De Methodo Medendi* I, namely ch. 4, X 32.2ff. Kühn. There Galen criticizes the rationalists for taking disputed starting-points and failing to offer demonstrations on their basis.[14]

Rather it looks as if while, in his discussion of strict proof, Galen often distinguishes between two types of premisses that are 'evident', namely those that are clear to perception, and those that are so to the intellect, he sometimes allows a looser sense of 'evident' or 'apparent' as what is obvious, but nevertheless capable of being demonstrated. Indeed given his ambition to provide strict demonstrations well beyond the domain of mathematics itself, in medicine indeed, it is hardly

---

[13] Dealing with the faculties especially, Galen writes (trans. Brock): 'While, however, the statements which the ancients made on these points were correct, they yet omitted to defend their arguments with logical proofs; of course they never suspected that there could be sophists so shameless as to try to contradict obvious facts. More recent physicians, again, have been partly conquered by the sophistries of these fellows and have given credence to them; whilst others who attempted to argue with them appear to me to lack to a great extent the power of the ancients. For this reason I have attempted to put together my arguments in the way in which it seems to me the ancients, had any of them been still alive, would have done, in opposition to those who would overturn the finest doctrines of our art.'

[14] ἀλλὰ καὶ τὰς ἀρχὰς οἱ πλεῖστοι διαφωνουμένας λαμβάνουσιν, οὐκ ἀποδείξαντες δὲ ἐπὶ τὰ λοιπὰ κατὰ τὸν αὐτὸν τρόπον μετέρχονται, νομοθετοῦντες μᾶλλον ἢ ἀποδείκνυντες (*MM* I ch. 4, X 32.7-9 Kühn). I am grateful to Professor O'Meara for drawing my attention to the point that Galen does not here expressly say, as Hankinson's translation ('failing to demonstrate them', viz the starting-points) implies, that the starting-points themselves have to be demonstrated.

surprising that some of his principles are far less obviously self-evident than the common opinions and definitions he cites from Euclid. *MM* I ch. 4 (X 36.10ff. Kühn) is one text[15] where he contrasts what is clear to perception with what is clear to the intellect, citing the ancient philosophers for this distinction. But to illustrate the latter, after the mathematical examples I have already cited, he adds (trans. Hankinson):

> they say that 'nothing occurs causelessly' is of this type, and similarly 'everything comes to be from something existent', and that nothing comes to be from the absolutely non-existent. Equally, that nothing is annihilated into the absolutely non-existent and that it is necessary that everything must be either affirmed or denied, and many other propositions of this sort which they discuss in the logical works, and which I too have recorded in my *On Demonstration* with all the clarity of which I am capable.

The recurrent problem, as I argued in Lloyd (1996), is that once axiomatic-deductive demonstrations are attempted in such fields as physics, cosmology, or medicine, finding good-looking principles that can be claimed to be *self*-evident is extremely difficult. The problem about one of the medical examples used, namely that opposites are cures for opposites, is that this is either controversial, or vacuous – if that is, opposite is so defined as to specify what delivers the cure. Galen requires that his principles should be beyond dispute: but of course they were disputed, and his recognition of that fact surfaces when he undertakes to argue for his principles against those who 'shamelessly' denied them.

While the correct citation of a number of Euclid's definitions and common opinions makes it seem that Galen's idea of mathematical method matches Euclid's own practice, in other respects some of his examples do not follow the model of axiomatic-deductive demonstration at all closely. We may not be too concerned with some minor inaccuracies – as when Galen appears to conflate rhomboid with rhombus in his commentary on the Hippocratic treatise *On Joints*.[16] But there are

---

[15] Another such text is *On Mixture* II ch. 2, 51.14ff. Helmreich (cf 50.15ff.) where he gives what the sense of touch registers as actually hot as an example of what is evident to perception (contrast the doubts that may arise over what is potentially or *per accidens* hot, e.g. *Mixt.* III ch. 3, 98.23ff.: Galen's theory about heat is further complicated by his introduction, in the pharmacology especially, of the notion of different orders or grades of heat, e.g. *Simpl.* III ch. 10 XI 561.3ff. Kühn, ch. 13 571.13ff., V ch. 27 786.11ff.). However, he also (*Mixt.* II ch. 2, 54.4) recognizes that the sense of touch has, in a way, to be trained and may, superficially, be deceptive (cf *Simpl.* III ch. 8 XI 554.10ff. Kühn, *Adv. Lyc.* ch. 3 *CMG* V 10 3 8.15ff., ch. 6 18.17ff.). Again in *Pecc. Dig.* ch. 6 (*CMG* V 4 1 1, 63.7ff.), Galen notes that what is evident to perception and what to the intellect may appear to conflict – but that appearance will turn out to be misleading. Cf. also *Opt. Doctr.* ch. 4 (*CMG* V 1 1, 104.5ff.), *Alim. Fac.* I ch. 1 (*CMG* V 4 2, 202.14ff.), *PHP* III ch. 8 (*CMG* V 4 1 2, 232.3ff.), *Simpl.* I ch. 37 (XI 448.14ff. Kühn), *MM* I ch. 5 (X 39.7ff. Kühn).

[16] At *In Hipp. Art.* II 37 (XVIIIA 466.12ff. Kühn), Galen comments on the use of the term

several other anomalies in Galen's mathematical examples. In several cases the reasoning that Galen introduces to illustrate mathematical methods relates to what we may call applied mathematics, rather than to the geometrical proofs of the *Elements*. I shall give a couple of such cases, before I turn to the most important and extensive application of geometrical reasoning in Galen, namely in his discussions of the optic nerve.

We should first turn back to the text in *PHP* VIII ch. 1 (*CMG* V 4 1 2, 484.22-8, trans. De Lacy) where Galen gives an example from Euclid's *Phaenomena* in his exposition of geometrical proof.

> For this reason, Euclid in a single theorem, the first in his book *Phaenomena*, demonstrated in a very few lines that the earth is in the middle of the universe and stands in relation to it as a point and as the centre, and those who have mastered it accept the conclusion of the demonstration with as much confidence as they do that two times two are four; but some philosophers talk such nonsense about the size and position of the earth as to make a person ashamed of the whole profession.

Galen does not there give Euclid's proof, but it has some surprising features. Certainly the proposition to be proved is just as Galen represents it. But the proof proceeds by appealing to observations with a dioptra – of Cancer rising in the East and Capricorn setting in the West, and again of Leo rising and Arcturus setting. The claim, in Euclid, is that in both cases straight lines are formed, and this shows that these are both diameters both of the sphere of the fixed stars and of the zodiac. From that it follows first that the observer's position, at the point of intersection of the two diameters, is at the centre of the circle – and so of the sphere constituted by the fixed stars. Furthermore, granted that such an observation produces the same result wherever it is made on the surface of the earth (*Phaenomena* 12.9ff. Menge), the earth itself can be treated as having the relation of a point to that circle.

The first striking feature here is that the premisses used are empirical or observational, not the types of intellectually evident primary propositions represented by Aristotle's logical axioms or those we have in Euclid's *Elements*. Nor can we say that the observations in question are immediately obvious in the way that Galen claims that what is actually hot is evident to the sense of touch. Secondly, the result is, in any case, an idealization. The circle of the fixed stars may be so distant from the earth that the earth itself can be said to be of negligible size. But it cannot strictly be said to be of zero size, that is to say without extension, as

---

'rhomboid' in the Hippocratic text: '"Rhomboid" shapes are those with equilateral sides but are not right-angled, for thus Euclid defines the rhombus.' That is indeed a correct report of the definition of rhombus in Euclid I Def 22, but it does not acknowledge that in Euclid, rhombus is distinguished from rhomboid – the second being that figure that has opposite sides and angles equal but is neither equilateral nor right-angled.

the centre of a geometrical circle is – the objection that Archimedes brought against Aristarchus in similar circumstances.[17]

Then there are two treatises in which Galen cites Hipparchus' studies of the values of the lunar month and solar year. First in *On Critical Days* ch. 4 (IX 907.14-908.3 Kühn), Galen writes:

> That the period of the month is not exactly thirty days, but falls short of this by about half a day, was demonstrated by Hipparchus in one whole book. It is recognized even by almost all lay persons that the hollow month (as they call it) is twenty-nine days, the full one thirty. Both together must make fifty-nine days in all, if each generally falls short of thirty by half a day.

Now in this passage Galen is interested in the result, rather than in illustrating the techniques used to demonstrate it (on which he does not elaborate). Yet it is remarkable first that this is once again an empirical investigation, not a purely geometrical one, and secondly that the statement of the conclusion is anything but precise. If we compare the information we are given in Ptolemy's *Syntaxis* IV ch. 2, 270.19ff., we are there told that Hipparchus confirmed the value of the mean length of the [synodic] month, not as 'thirty days less about half a day', but (expressed as a sexagesimal fraction) as 29; 31,50,8,20 days 'approximately' (*engista*).[18]

Galen alludes once again to Hipparchus in his commentary on the Hippocratic treatise *Prognosis* (*In Hipp. Prog. Comm.* III 9, *CMG* V 9 11, 333.18-334.9). The text as we have it seems to suggest that Galen himself wrote on the length of the year, although Neugebauer suspected corruption.[19]

> The year is not only 365 days, but [one must add] a quarter of a day, and in addition about 1/100th part. Each of the months is less than thirty days, but more than twenty-nine. The period between two conjunctions of the sun and moon was called 'month' (*mên*) by the ancient Greeks, as it still is in many of the Greek cities, and anyone who wants to learn how long this period is exactly, with the proper demonstrations, has a whole book written by Hipparchus, just as there is also a treatise of our own concerning the yearly period.

The first problem here relates to the indeterminacy of the 'year' in question, and the second to the actual value that Galen gives. After Hipparchus' discovery of the precession of the equinoxes, astronomers generally worked with the tropical year (judged by the return of the sun to the same solstitial or equinoctial point) since that

---

[17]   Archimedes, *Sandreckoner* II 218.18ff. Heiberg-Stamatis.

[18]   *Syntaxis* IV ch. 2, 271.11f. Ptolemy took over this value himself. There is a complex interaction between the eclipse observations used to confirm this value, and the assumptions that those observations presuppose about the values of the solar year and lunar month.

[19]   Neugebauer (1975), I 339 n. 10. The possibility of corruption at that point does not affect the argument in my text.

was assumed to be the basic constant. The value for that which Ptolemy ascribes to Hipparchus (and which Ptolemy himself took over) is 365 and a quarter days *less* 1/300th of a day (i.e. 365; 14,48). Galen's value *may* refer rather to the sidereal year (judged by the return of the sun to the same constellation) which had been taken as basic before the discovery of precession. Even so that does not tally with the value that Ptolemy cites for Hipparchus' estimate of the lower limit of precession, for that gives a figure of 365; 15,24 for the sidereal year, not Galen's 365; 15,36.[20]

But if this text undeniably poses tricky problems of interpretation, three points are clear, first Galen makes no mention of the difference between the tropical and sidereal year and does not define which year he is speaking of, secondly that the 'demonstrations' in question are not geometrical, but depend rather on astronomical calculations, based ultimately on observational data, and thirdly that the results are approximations though no doubt believed to be both as accurate and as precise as possible.

Then in the treatise *On the Affections and Errors of the Soul* we are given a variety of examples of mathematical reasoning. Some of these mention points that do indeed belong to the axiomatic-deductive demonstrations of Euclid's *Elements*. In *Pecc. Dig.* ch. 3 (*CMG* V 4 1 1, 46.7-17, trans. Singer), Galen illustrates how the correctness of the application of a geometrical method is sometimes clear immediately from the result. Dealing first with the problem of dividing a given straight line into a prescribed number of parts, say five, seven, twenty or a hundred, he says: 'the certainty of the truth discovered in all such problems, similarly, will be manifest through things which can be clearly observed.' Other illustrations follow, namely that of circumscribing a circle round a given square (this is Euclid IV 9), circumscribing or inscribing a square in a given circle (Euclid IV 6) or drawing a circle round a given equilateral and equiangular pentagon (Euclid IV 14).

This method, he proceeds at 47.12-21 (trans. Singer)

is that employed in geometry, logic, astronomy and architecture. I use the single term 'architecture' to refer also to the design of sundials, various types of water-clock, and all kinds of mechanical devices, including also the 'pneumatic' variety. In all these subjects self-confirming proofs are available to the enquirer, as they are in astronomy. For here the facts are subject to the test of observable phenomena: an eclipse of the sun or moon,

---

[20]   Yet in Galen's *Commentary* on the treatise *On the Seventh Month Child*, for which we rely on the Arabic version (Walzer, 1934-5, cf. Neugebauer, 1949), we have another figure for Hipparchus' value for half the [sidereal] year, namely 182 days plus 15 hours plus 'a little fraction of about 1/24th of an hour'. This gives a figure of 365 days plus a quarter plus 1/288 for the year. However Neugebauer (1975), I 293 and 297, suspected an error in the last fraction caused by repeated halving and takes the correct figure to be 365 days plus a quarter plus 1/144, i.e. 365; 15,25 days.

for example, and the visible properties of fixed and moving stars, must surely count as observable phenomena.

Chapter 5 of *Pecc. Dig.* (*CMG* V 4 1 1, 54.20-55.13) continues in similar vein, with a detailed account of the construction of sun-dials, including discussion of suitable materials to use. On the one hand you need the geometrical theory of gnomons: on the other the correctness of the end-result is confirmed empirically. Galen calls this the method of analysis and synthesis, though his view here of the latter is distinctive in that it appeals to empirical data to verify the result. He proceeds with something of a paean of praise for geometry, first the discovery of the elements and then later theorems based on these, and concludes at 59.1-8, by referring to the sundial and water-clock as the most wonderful products of geometers' ingenuity.

Thus in one example after another Galen switches between the purely abstract and the empirical domain. Some of his illustrations of mathematical demonstrations are a matter of calculations based on observational data. Some of his geometrical examples concern practical procedures, the construction and use of sundials and water-clocks. It is particularly striking that whereas Euclid, *Elements* IV proves geometrically various theorems to do with the circumscription and inscription of circular and rectangular figures, Galen claims that one can verify this directly by *seeing* that the results are correct.

We have yet to consider the most sustained stretch of applied geometry in the Galenic Corpus. This is the discussion of optical problems in the last four chapters of book XI of *On the Usefulness of Parts*, which has won high praise from some (May, 1968, II 494 n. 56) though been dismissed by others (Simon, 1906, II vii-viii). Here he has precedents in, for example, the geometrical analysis of vision in Euclid's *Optics*, controversial though the reconstruction of that text has proved to be.[21] Again, his contemporary Ptolemy took the study of such problems as binocular vision further.[22] Yet Galen's work certainly goes beyond other extant studies, notably in his exploration of the optic nerves.

As usual, his discussion is convoluted, long-winded and repetitive, and he harangues his reader on the need to study geometry on several occasions within these four chapters.[23] His main arguments are, however, clear and I shall concentrate here on the particular problems on which geometry is brought to bear.

At *UP* X ch. 12 (II 94.22-95.13 Helmreich, trans. May) we have an elaborate introduction of the geometry of the cone of vision.

Let there be a circle (and I call a circle that which is everywhere equidistant from its middle), a circle seen by one of the eyes while the other remains closed; from the

---

[21]   See most recently Brownson (1981), Knorr (1994), Jones (1994), Kheirandish (1999).

[22]   See Smith (1996). There is no reference to Ptolemy's treatise on *Optics* in Galen's own discussions of vision.

[23]   See for example *UP* X ch. 12, II 97.4ff. Helmreich, and compare also the texts from *UP* cited above 113-14.

mid-point of the circle (which is also called its centre) think of a straight path to the pupil of the eye that is seeing it, a path not bending in any direction or deviating from its straight course; think rather of that straight line as you would of a thin hair or the filament of a cobweb accurately stretched from the pupil to the centre of the circle. Again, from the pupil to the line which bounds the circle and is also called its circumference imagine a series of very many other lines extending like thin cobwebs. Call the figure bounded by all these straight lines and by the circle a cone, and think of the pupil as its apex and the circle as its base.

Galen proceeds to explain how any obstruction blocks vision (95.21ff.), cites mathematicians who say that objects that are seen are seen in straight lines (96.12ff.) and explains how the position of objects seen by the right eye differs from that when seen by the left (97.12ff.). He suggests a test to confirm that when the pupil of either eye is pressed, objects may appear double, and then at 97.22ff. he constructs the first of his geometrical diagrams to illustrate how the field of vision of each eye differs: 'Hence neither pupil will see the object in the place where the other sees it, and both together will not see it where either sees it separately' (99.14-16, trans. May). His geometrical demonstration is confirmed, so he claims, 99.16ff., by a number of tests, looking at a pillar first with one eye, then with the other, then with both.

Galen does not have much to say about aspects of the psychology of perception, where the brain compensates in its interpretation of what each eye sees,[24] but the use of geometry is unexceptionable, and, as noted, it is certainly not unprecedented. Even so he is faced with a problem of strict consistency. In this chapter the pupil is treated as a point, at the apex of the cone of vision, whereas in chapter 15, the pupil is recognized to be a circular aperture allowing access to the elliptical lens.

But then in the next chapter, *UP* X ch. 13, Galen turns to the problem of how double vision is avoided, discussing in particular the route taken by the optic nerves within the brain. To avoid double vision the eyes have to be on the same plane, and this is secured by the meeting of the nerves in the optic chiasma. At II 104.20-105.13 Helmreich (trans. May), he writes:

> For if two straight lines meet at a certain, common point as their apex, they are evidently in one plane, even if they happen to be produced from that point an infinite distance in different directions. And [other] straight lines that join at any point these two straight lines when they have been produced indefinitely lie in the same plane with the two, because every triangle lies entirely in one plane. Now if there is anyone who does not understand what I have said, he clearly does not know even the elements of geometry. It would be a long task if I were to write demonstrations of such things, and indeed a person would not understand these either unless he had studied a great deal beforehand. In the eleventh book of his *Elements*, Euclid has certainly demonstrated the very thing of which I have just been speaking; it is the second theorem in that book and the proposition is stated as follows: 'If two straight lines intersect one another, they are in

---

[24] This point was urged against Galen by Siegel (1970), 107ff., 111ff.

one plane, and every triangle is in one plane.' You must, then, learn the demonstration from Euclid and when you have learned it, come back to me and I will show you in an animal these two straight lines, the channels from the brain (*encephalon*).

We might question just how much geometry a reader would have to have mastered in order to appreciate the very elementary point that Euclid makes in *Elements* XI 2. XI 1 shows that it cannot be the case that two different sections of a single straight line are in different planes, and XI 2 shows on that basis that two intersecting lines are in the same plane, from which it follows that every triangle is (though that proof elicited negative comments from Heath who criticised it on the grounds of lack of generality, Heath, 1926, III 275). On the assumption that the optic nerves meet at the chiasma, it follows that *represented diagrammatically* the nerves lie on the same plane. Yet there are two obvious problems. First the nerves are not two-dimensional lines, but three-dimensional bodies. Galen insists, indeed, that the optic nerves have lumina and transmit *pneuma*. Secondly the optic nerves are anything but straight. Indeed at the eye Galen himself acknowledges that they form a bulb round the eye. Each of them 'curves round it [the eye] circularly like a net [the retina] as far as the crystalline humour [the lens] and surrounds and holds within it the vitreous humour, so that the pupil lies in a straight line with the whole root of the eye where the nerve begins to be resolved' (*UP* X ch. 13, II 105.13-19 Helmreich, trans. May: compare also his report on his dissections of the eye and optic nerves in *On Anatomical Procedures* X chs 1-3, Duckworth, 1962, 27-43). As to their paths back from the chiasma to the posterior part of the *encephalon* (their ultimate origin) their 'straightness' is, once again, a matter of what is – very approximately – straight.

In the next chapter Galen sees off rival views of the function of the optic chiasma,[25] but returns once again to a geometrical analysis in *UP* X ch. 15 (II 111.9ff. Helmreich), where he shows why it is better that the lens should be flattened, rather than spherical in shape. This is to allow a greater proportion of its surface to be reached by rays entering the circular aperture of the pupil. The reconstruction of the diagram Galen has in mind is problematic, for in most versions the pupil is separated at some distance from the lens, and the assumption of the interpreters is that the rays of light cross over between the back of the pupil and the elliptical lens.[26] Whether or not that is the correct interpretation of Galen's diagram, in any event he will get his result, that a greater area of the lens will be

---

[25] This chapter is interesting in that Galen has to argue both that the optic chiasma unites the nerves, and that their ultimate sources lie in the *encephalon*. Their double origin there is not allowed to tell against the doctrine that the primary sense-organ (τὸ πρῶτον αἰσθητικόν) is single, namely the *encephalon* itself (II 107.18ff. Helmreich). We also have a clear reference at 109.13ff. to the *pneuma* the optic nerves contain.

[26] Compare the diagrams in Kühn (1821-33), III 839-40, Helmreich (1904), 112, and May (1968), I 494. May in any case suggests that the order of the letters identifying the points on the diagram at 112.15 is not what the interpretation she offers leads one to expect.

exposed to the pupil if the lens is flattened rather than perfectly spherical. Yet the problem that then arises – that Galen does not tackle – is how the rays of light impinging on the lens are collected and focussed, enabling the optic nerves to transmit their signals to the brain.

Galen's attempt, in these four chapters, to give a single, coherent, mathematically-based theory of vision is ambitious but must be thought to be at best only partially successful. The pupil is now treated as a point, now as a circular aperture; the optic nerves are treated now as lines, straight ones indeed, now as three-dimensional bodies. The unity of vision is secured by the optic chiasma, but might be thought to be threatened by the continuation of each of the optic nerves to one side of the back of the brain. Above all we may have doubts about the marriage between the pneuma-based account of vision and the purely geometrical analysis offered not just of what happens outside the eye, but also of aspects of what occurs within the brain. To be sure, the defence might be offered that any mathematical analysis will involve simplifications or idealizations. Yet in principle that analysis should preserve the essential features of the physical situation and should be translatable back into it.

*

Let me now take stock of the heterogeneous material we have reviewed. Galen's admiration for 'mathematical method' is evident in one text after another. He prides himself on his mathematical training and knowledge and he cajoles his readers with orders to train themselves similarly to be able to follow his expositions. Yet in practice many of these are quite elementary – and need to be excused with the argument that many of his readers are ignorant of mathematics and doctors in particular detest it.

Mathematics provides Galen with his ideal largely because it yields examples not just of valid reasoning, but of certain conclusions.[27] If it had just been validity that Galen was after, logic would have done equally well. What mathematics adds is that it can deliver incontestable results – providing powerful weapons against sceptics and shameless sophists of various types. Yet Galen's understanding of mathematical demonstration is a catholic one.[28] Sometimes it is clear that what he

---

[27] The ideal in *Pecc. Dig.* ch. 1 (*CMG* V 4 1 1, 43.3ff.), is, as we saw, the person free from error, ἀναμάρτητος. MM XIV ch. 9, K X 972.11ff., is one text that describes the aim as instruction that is incontrovertible, ἀναμφισβήτητος.

[28] It was argued in discussion that his idea of mathematical demonstration might be perfectly sound and conform to Euclid's and/or Aristotle's, even while some of Galen's exemplifications may be sloppy. I believe, however, that we can and must use the latter in order to arrive at a verdict on how clear Galen's understanding of mathematical proof was. In particular, the notion of an appeal to an empirical procedure to verify a mathematical relationship departs from anything we can find in Euclid. The further valuable suggestion was made that Galen's actual performance, in this area, might vary with the audiences to which the treatises in question were addressed. I have noted that

has in mind is indeed the axiomatic-deductive modes of reasoning of the type we find in Euclid's *Elements*. There, with the notable exception of the parallel postulate, which some later commentators, such as Ptolemy and Proclus, claimed – ill-advisedly – should be a theorem proved within the system, Euclid's Definitions, Common Opinions and Postulates were indeed accepted as self-evident, and it was this, combined with the validity of the arguments on their basis, that secured the incontrovertibility of his results. But at several points Galen goes beyond – or rather departs from – that model.

First, many of his examples show that he does not always have axiomatic-deductive reasoning in mind when he cites mathematics. Some instances relate to calculations or arguments on the basis of empirical data, some of which involve tricky technical observations and some of which give approximate conclusions. In his discussion of optics, both the consistency of his geometrical arguments, and their relation to the physical situation they are to illuminate, are problematic. Most strikingly, in some cases Galen suggests that the results of geometrical reasoning can be verified by observation. That corresponds perhaps well enough to procedures that the manufacturers of sun-dials and water-clocks may have used to check the accuracy of their instruments. But it certainly runs counter to Greek mathematical practice when Galen uses observation to verify purely geometrical conclusions.

Secondly, and more fundamentally, his notion of what is 'evident', *enargês*, is stretched to include not just what is so to the intellect, but also what is so to perception. His primary principles include empirical propositions – as indeed they must if he is to apply his model to medicine. Yet what is evident to perception never of course attains the *a priori* incontestability of the equality axiom. Galen indeed alludes to some of the problems of empirical manifestness in his talk of the need to train the sense of touch to recognize correctly what is actually hot, and elsewhere he certainly shows an awareness of the possible pitfalls that are presented by the multiple ambiguities of that term and the problems of its application to what is merely potentially hot or to what is inferred to be hot. Yet that does not deter him from claiming his empirical principles to be 'evident' – and thus the secure foundation for arguments on their basis.

I conclude first that we do not have to be radical sceptics or shameless sophists to be dubious about the status of the starting-points of Galen's medical reasonings, and secondly that these doubts extend also to some of his applications of mathematical models in that domain.[29]

---

he himself remarks that doctors detest mathematics. But that did not stop him using mathematical examples and arguments on plenty of occasions where his readership certainly *included* medical practitioners among others, as is surely the case with *MM*, *PHP* and *UP* in particular.

[29] I am most grateful to my respondent, Professor Nutton, and to all those who raised questions at the Colloquium or in subsequent correspondence, and especially to Christopher Gill, Jim Hankinson, Lindsay Judson, André Laks, Jim Lennox, Dominic O'Meara, Peter Singer and Philip van der Eijk.

References

I cite the texts of Galen by the *Corpus Medicorum Graecorum* (*CMG*) editions, for preference, failing them by the Teubner editions (e.g. *Scripta Minora, Scr. Min.*), or failing either by the edition of Kühn, 1821-33. I use May's translation of *UP*, De Lacy's of *PHP*, Hankinson's of *MM*, Brock's of *Nat. Fac.*, Singer's of *Pecc. Dig., Ord. Libr., Libr. Prop., Foet. Form.*, with the modifications that I note: otherwise the translations are my own.

Barnes, J.B. (1991), 'Galen on Logic and Therapy', in F. Kudlien and R.J. Durling (eds), *Galen's Method of Healing*, Brill, Leiden, 50-102.

Berryman, S. (1998), 'Euclid and the Sceptic: A Paper on Vision, Doubt, Geometry, Light and Drunkenness', *Phronesis* 43, 176-96.

Brock, A.J. (1916), *Galen On the Natural Faculties*, Heinemann, London/G.P. Putnam, New York.

Brownson, C.D. (1981), 'Euclid's Optics and Its Compatibility with Linear Perspective', *Archive for History of Exact Sciences* 24, 165-94.

De Lacy, P. (1978-84), *Galen On the Doctrines of Hippocrates and Plato*, 3 vols, Akademie-Verlag, Berlin.

Diller, H. (1936), 'Nikon (18)', *Pauly-Wissowa Real-Encyclopädie*, Vol XVII,1 (Halbband 33), J.B. Metzler, Stuttgart, cols. 507-508.

Donini, P.-L. (1992), 'Galeno e la filosofia', in W. Haase (ed.), *Aufstieg und Niedergang der römischen Welt*, Band 36.5, De Gruyter, Berlin, 3484-3504.

Duckworth, W.L.H. (1962), *Galen On Anatomical Procedures, the Later Books*, trans. W.L.H. Duckworth, edd. M.C. Lyons and B. Towers, Cambridge University Press, Cambridge.

Frede, M. (1987), 'On Galen's Epistemology', in M. Frede, *Essays in Ancient Philosophy*, University of Minnesota Press, Minneapolis, 279-98.

Hankinson, R.J. (1991a), 'Galen on the Foundations of Science', in J.A. López Férez (ed.), *Galeno: Obra, Pensamiento e influencia*, Universidad Nacional de Educación a Distancia, Madrid, 15-29.

Hankinson, R.J. (1991b), *Galen On the Therapeutic Method Books I and II*, Clarendon Press, Oxford.

Hankinson, R.J. (1992), 'Galen's Philosophical Eclecticism', in W. Haase (ed.), *Aufstieg und Niedergang der römischen Welt*, Band 36.5, de Gruyter, Berlin, 3505-22.

Heath, T.L. (1926), *The Thirteeen Books of Euclid's Elements*, 3 vols, 2nd ed. (1st ed. 1908), Cambridge University Press, Cambridge.

Helmreich, G. (1907-9), *Galen De Usu Partium*, 2 vols, Teubner, Leipzig.

Jones, A. (1994), 'Peripatetic and Euclidean Theories of the Visual Ray', *Physis* 31, 47-76.

Kheirandish, E. (1999), *The Arabic Version of Euclid's Optics*, 2 vols (Studies in the History of Mathematics and Physical Sciences, 16), Springer, New York.

Kieffer, J.S. (1964), *Galen's Institutio Logica*, Johns Hopkins Press, Baltimore.

Knorr, W.R. (1994), 'Pseudo-Euclidean Reflections in Ancient Optics: A Re-Examination of Textual Issues Pertaining to the Euclidean *Optica* and *Catoptrica*', *Physis* 31, 1-45.

Kühn, K.G. (1821-33), *Claudii Galeni Opera Omnia*, 22 vols, Knobloch, Leipzig.

Lloyd, G.E.R. (1996), 'Theories and Practices of Demonstration in Galen', in M. Frede and G. Striker (eds), *Rationality in Greek Thought*, Clarendon Press, Oxford, 255-77.

May, M.T. (1968), *Galen On the Usefulness of the Parts of the Body*, 2 vols, Cornell University Press, Ithaca, New York.

Neugebauer, O. (1949), 'Astronomical Fragments in Galen's Treatise On Seven-Month Children', *Rivista degli Studi Orientali* 24, 92-4.

Neugebauer, O. (1975), *A History of Ancient Mathematical Astronomy*, 3 vols, Springer-Verlag, Berlin.

Siegel, R.E. (1970), *Galen On Sense-Perception*, Karger, Basel.

Simon, M. (1906), *Sieben Bücher Anatomie des Galen*, 2 vols, J.C. Hinrichs, Leipzig.

Singer, P. (1997), *Galen: Selected Works*, Oxford University Press, Oxford.

Smith, A. Mark (1996), 'Ptolemy's Theory of Perception', *Transactions of the American Philosophical Society* 86,2.

Tieleman, T. (2002), 'Galen on the Seat of the Intellect: Anatomical Experiment and Philosophical Tradition', in C.J. Tuplin and T.E. Rihll (eds), *Science and Mathematics in Ancient Greek Culture*, Oxford University Press, Oxford, 256-73.

Toomer, G.J. (1985), 'Galen on the Astronomers and Astrologers', *Archive for History of Exact Sciences* 82, 193-206.

Walzer, R. (1934-5), 'Galens Schrift "über die Siebenmonatskinder"', *Rivista degli Studi Orientali* 15, 323-57.

Chapter Seven

The Music of Philosophy in Late Antiquity

Dominic J. O'Meara

The ambiguous title of this paper is intended to suggest two themes which I would like to develop: (I) music as it was conceived by, and of particular interest to, philosophers in Late Antiquity, in particular the Neoplatonic philosophers of the fourth, fifth and sixth centuries (Iamblichus, Syrianus, Proclus, Damascius, Olympiodorus); and (II) the impact of music, as these philosophers conceived of it, on the way in which they approached other areas of inquiry.

As regards the first theme, it will be seen that the term 'music', as it will be used here, has a very limited and particular sense: it refers to what might be called 'harmonics', i.e. that part of mathematical science which examines the quantifiable ratios represented in musical intervals. This way of seeing music, which I will call the 'Pythagorean' view of music, was to assume more and more importance as Neoplatonic philosophers, beginning in particular with Iamblichus in the early fourth century, came to give mathematics a central, pivotal role in philosophy, as part of their increasing interest in the Pythagorean origins and components of Platonic philosophy. The Pythagorizing of Platonism in Late Antiquity would result in more emphasis being given to the mathematical sciences, which included, along with arithmetic, geometry and astronomy, 'Pythagorean' music. The Pythagorizing of Platonism also led to a tendency to 'mathematize' the various branches of philosophy. Thus it can be shown[1] that arithmetical and geometrical conceptions and methods were influential in the metaphysics and physics of late ancient Neoplatonists. We can in consequence ask if music, too, as it was understood by the Neoplatonists, influenced them in the way they approached their other philosophical inquiries? This question forms the second theme of my paper.

Although some of the texts to which I will refer, in particular Augustine's *De musica* and Boethius' *De institutione musica*, have exerted enormous influence in history and are relatively well-known, with the exception of some work published in particular by Stephen Gersh (1992, 1996), little has been done in examining the

---

[1]   See O'Meara (1989).

Greek background to Augustine and Boethius, as I have indicated it above: the Greek Neoplatonic interpretation and philosophical appropriation of music. As the subject is very large and can become rather complex, I will attempt in this paper merely to provide a general framework, pointing to some questions and making some suggestions.

I

How was music, as one of the four mathematical sciences, understood in the Neoplatonic schools of Late Antiquity? We might begin our answer to this question by recalling Boethius' influential distinction between three kinds of music: 'cosmic music', 'human music', and music as found in instruments (*De inst. mus.* I, 2). 'Cosmic music' is what must be supposed to arise from the mathematical structures and cycles of the heavenly bodies, of the seasons and of the elements constituting the world, whereas 'human music' has to do with the structures composing the human soul, the human body and the relation between soul and body. Both cosmic and human music, *we* might feel, actually belong to physics and biology, to the study of the organization of the cosmos and of human nature. It is music in the *third* sense, music arising from man-made instruments, that is the object of the mathematical science of which Boethius wishes to treat in his *De institutione musica*.

  The notions of cosmic and human music evoke Pythagoreanism, and we can suppose that the third kind of music that will be presented by Boethius in his book is also Pythagorean in approach, to the extent at least that Boethius is believed to draw his information and inspiration largely from a no longer extant introduction to music written by a second-century propagandist of Pythagoreanism, Nicomachus of Gerasa.[2] To have some idea of the emphasis Nicomachus would have put on music as Pythagorean, we can read his *Manual of Harmonics* in which Pythagoras appears as the 'very first' (πάμπρωτος) discoverer of the essentials of 'harmonics'.[3] Now 'harmonics' is described by Porphyry as the first part of music, according to the Pythagoreans.[4] Music also includes rhythmics, metrics, what relates to instruments, to poetry and delivery. However, harmonics is the first part of music, Porphyry tells us, 'in order, having an elementary function, and contemplative of first principles'.[5] The reference to the 'elementary function' of harmonics in music may have to do with the didactic virtues of harmonics as both an elementary and

---

[2] On Boethius' use of Nicomachus, cf. Guillaumin's introduction to his edition of Boethius *Inst. arith.* (= Boethius, 1995), XXX-XXXI.

[3] *Man.* chs. 5-6.

[4] Porphyry, *In Ptol. harm.* 5.21-6 (I take it that the third person plural here refers to the Pythagoreans).

[5] 5.26-7.

fundamental basis for the study of music. At any rate the priority, in terms of theoretical knowledge, of harmonics in the list of the parts of music given by Porphyry is clear. If music has to do with what is expressed in instruments, it is the harmonics expressed in these instruments that is of primary interest in a 'Pythagorean' approach.

The same point can be made by means of the contrast Damascius draws between Pythagorean and Aristoxenian music. Developing a distinction made in Plato's *Philebus*, Damascius compares 'music that uses sense-perception as its criterion, and the truly scientific method, e.g. musical theory based on the harmonic ratio, the latter practised by the Pythagoreans, the former by the school of Aristoxenus'.[6] This contrast is by no means new. It is already made by Ptolemy, for example, and, before him, by Ptolemais of Cyrene in extracts from the *Pythagorean Elements of Music* attributed to her which Porphyry quotes.[7] As opposed, then, to an Aristotelian, empirical study of instrumental music such as that proposed by Aristoxenus and his followers, the 'Pythagorean' approach preferred by the late Antique Neoplatonist takes an interest in music as expressed by instruments to the extent that it is based on harmonic ratios: these ratios are the primary and fundamental object of music as a mathematical, theoretical science.

Let us try to describe now in more detail the primary object of musical science, harmonic ratios, as understood by the Neoplatonist philosopher. I have already referred to Nicomachus as an important source for Boethius' manual of music. Nicomachus had been made a key part of the curriculum of the Neoplatonic schools by Iamblichus, who found in him a Pythagorizer after his own heart and an author of useful manuals which Iamblichus integrated and adapted in his 10-volume work *On Pythagoreanism*. He used Nicomachus' *Introduction to arithmetic* in vol. IV of *On Pythagoreanism* (= *In Nicomachi arithmeticam introductionem*) and, I would suggest, in vol. IX, the lost introduction to music by Nicomachus also used by Boethius. Vol. IX of Iamblichus' *On Pythagoreanism* is no longer extant, but we may be able to reach some idea of its contents by reading Boethius' *De inst. mus.* and by allowing for the adaptations that would have been made both by Iamblichus and by Boethius.

Nicomachus is already an important presence earlier in Iamblichus' *On Pythagoreanism*, for example in vol. III (= *De communi mathematica scientia*), where Iamblichus deals with mathematical science in general and, in this context, following Nicomachus, describes the object of music, as distinguished from the objects of the other mathematical sciences.[8] The differentiation of the object of music begins from a distinction, among beings in general and in the universe in

---

[6] Damascius, *In Phileb.* 225 (transl. Westerink); cf. Plato, *Phileb.* 56a, *Rep.* 531b2-c4; Plotinus, *Enn*, 6.3, 16.20-24.

[7] Ptolemy, *Harm.* I.2; Porphyry, *In Ptol. harm.*, 24.1-6, 25.9-26.4 (translated in Barker, 1989, 240-42).

[8] Cf. Gersh (1996), 87-8.

particular, between the nature of the discrete and that of the continuous. The discrete is numerical plurality ($\pi\lambda\hat{\eta}\theta o\varsigma$), which tends to numerical infinity, whereas the continuous is magnitude ($\mu\acute{\epsilon}\gamma\epsilon\theta o\varsigma$), which can be infinitely divided. Since the infinite is unknowable, divine providence has produced two sciences which limit the infinites of the discrete and of magnitude and have made them knowable: arithmetic as the science of finite plurality or number, and geometry as the science of finite magnitude.[9] Within this division between kinds of objects and their corresponding sciences, Nicomachus, followed by the Neoplatonists, introduces two subdivisions: of plurality into plurality *per se* and plurality in relation to another; and of magnitude into magnitude at rest and magnitude in movement. These subdivisions yield the objects characterizing the remaining mathematical sciences, music and astronomy. Thus, whereas arithmetic deals with plurality (number) in itself, music concerns number in relation. And whereas geometry deals with magnitude at rest, astronomy concerns magnitude in movement. From this we can conclude that the 'Pythagorean' definition of the subject-matter of musical science, as taken over by Iamblichus and Proclus from Nicomachus, amounts to seeing music as a sort of extension, or subsidiary, of arithmetic: as arithmetic studies numbers, so music studies the relations or ratios ($\sigma\chi\acute{\epsilon}\sigma\epsilon\iota\varsigma$, $\lambda\acute{o}\gamma o\iota$) between numbers. The suggestion of subsidiarity is made by Iamblichus, in relation to astronomy, which has a position in relation to geometry parallel to that of music in relation to arithmetic.[10]

The Nicomachean division of the four mathematical sciences will be puzzling, if we take it to be a kind of dichotomous classification in terms of genera and species, in which two main genera (the discrete and the continuous) are subdivided further, thus yielding four species of objects to which correspond the four mathematical sciences. For the principles distinguishing the species seem unrelated: why is one genus, that of the discrete, divided by the distinction *per se* / in relation to another, whereas the other genus, that of magnitude, is divided by the distinction in rest / in movement? However, as is made clear in the following chapter of Nicomachus, the division of the mathematical sciences does not represent a classification in terms of genus and species, but an ordered series based on priority in which the posterior members of the series (music and astronomy) presuppose, but are not presupposed by, the prior members of the series (arithmetic and geometry) and in which arithmetic is the first science presupposed by all of the other sciences.[11] Thus the distinctions yielding the sub-classes (*per se* / in relation to another, at rest / in movement) represent in fact orders of priority in which what is *per se* is prior to

[9] Nicomachus, *Intro. arith*. I.3; Iamblichus, *De comm. math. sc*. 7, 28.17-31.4; Proclus, *In Eucl*. 35.17-36.7; Boethius, *De inst. mus*. II.3; Gersh (1996), 87-8.

[10] Iamblichus, *De comm. math. sc*. 31.1.

[11] Nicomachus, *Intro. arith*. I.4, 9.9-11.23; Iamblichus, *De comm. math. sc*. 4, 14.23-15.2. Ordered series of prior and posterior terms are an important feature of Neoplatonic philosophy, on which cf. Lloyd (1990), 76-8.

what relates to another, and what is at rest is prior to what is in movement.[12] Thus arithmetic and music are not co-ordinate species, but arithmetic, by virtue of its objects, is prior to and presupposed by music, just as astronomy is posterior (and subsidiary) to geometry. We need only find an order of priority subordinating geometry to arithmetic (I will indicate shortly how this may be done) in order to see the complete Nicomachean classification as a series based on priority: arithmetic, the first member of the series, is followed by geometry, which presupposes arithmetic, and these two members of the series are followed in turn by the sciences which presuppose them, music, which is posterior to arithmetic, and astronomy, which is posterior to geometry.

Pythagorean music deals then with relations between numbers or finite pluralities. Pluralities of what? Iamblichus refers to music as articulating the relations between sounds and the quantity of excess and deficiency in these relations.[13] In order to explain this claim, we might recall Nicomachus' definition (*Manual*, ch. 12) of relation ($\sigma\chi\acute{\epsilon}\sigma\iota\varsigma$) as 'the ratio ($\lambda\acute{o}\gamma o\varsigma$) measuring the distance in each interval' between sounds; his distinction (ch. 2) between continuous speech and discrete human sounds, the object of music, in which sounds are separated, unconfused ($\dot{\alpha}\sigma\acute{u}\gamma\chi\upsilon\tau o\nu$), articulated quantities; and his demonstration (ch. 4) that the intervals between sounds are a function of differences in quantity and number (length of sounded strings, size of holes in wind-instruments, etc.). However, I do not think that this means, for Iamblichus, that the object of study in Pythagorean music is *sounds*, as they are articulated in measurable intervals expressing numerical ratios. To put the matter in another way, we might ask the question: what is the precise ontological status of the numerical relations that are the object of Pythagorean music?

Iamblichus deals with this question in *On Pythagoreanism* vol. III to the extent that it concerns mathematical science in general, without specific reference to the objects of music.[14] However, the position he takes can be assumed to apply to the objects of music. He refuses to ascribe either ontological priority or posteriority to the objects of mathematical science in relation to the nature of soul. This means that the objects of mathematical science exist neither prior to the constitution of soul, nor posterior to it. Since the material universe and the sounds that it includes are produced after the soul and by soul, it follows that the objects of music, numerical relations, exist prior to the constitution of the world and of its sounds. Iamblichus, however, does not identify the nature of soul with that of the objects of mathematical knowledge: in some way, which is left unexplained, soul and the objects of mathematical science are of equal ontological rank.

---

[12] Nicomachus, *Intro. arith*. 11.1-2 and 13-14.
[13] Iamblichus, *De comm. math. sc.* 30.23-5.
[14] *De comm. math. sc.* ch. 10. For a translation and detailed commentary on this text, cf. Dörrie and Baltes (2002), 50-53 and 228-44.

The unclear relation between soul and mathematical objects can be understood better if we appeal to a theory concerning mathematical objects which may go back to Iamblichus and is clearly formulated a little later by Syrianus and Proclus.[15] According to this theory, mathematical objects are *concepts* which are articulated by discursive reason in the form of numerical plurality (arithmetic) and the projection of this plurality in extension, the imaginative space of geometry. Mathematical objects are discursive conceptual projections of higher truths, present to soul as above discursive reason and as innate in the nature of soul, what later Neoplatonists call 'substantial reasons' (οὐσιώδεις λόγοι). Thus mathematical objects exist in soul, but are not identical with soul: they are the way soul elaborates a discursive scientific knowledge of its own constitution. This can be described quite easily in the case of the objects of music: since soul, in Plato's *Timaeus*, is a combination of components 'bound' as a structure by particular harmonic intervals, soul, in exploring in music such numerical relations, is in fact developing a discursive knowledge of her own inner constitution. Syrianus asks rhetorically: 'What then: is there no contemplator of the harmonic ratios which the god gave soul before the ordering of the visible world?'.[16] The contemplator is soul herself and she does this by projecting in musical science the structures that compose her. Referring to the *Timaeus*, Proclus tells us: 'let us say that it is by virtue of her [the soul's] otherness, i.e. the plurality and diversity of the ratios in her, when she has been constituted and has noted that she is both one and many, that the understanding (διάνοια) projects numbers and the knowledge of numbers which is arithmetic: and by virtue of the unity of plurality in her and the community of bond that binds her together, she projects music... . Again, her activities being firmly rooted in her constitution, she produces geometry out of her own nature...'.[17]

If I may summarize briefly this rather long account of the objects that are of concern to 'Pythagorean' music, as a science adopted and interpreted by Neoplatonic philosophers, we may say that this music deals with *concepts* that are discursive, scientifically developed projections of truths about numerical relationships, which truths pre-exist in soul as innate and constitutive of her very nature. Such numerical ratios may find expression in audible sounds and in instruments. Such sounds may remind us of a musical knowledge innate in us,[18] but they are not the objects of Pythagorean music. This music, is, as Proclus says in the similar case of geometry,[19] a way for us of looking at ourselves, a form of self-knowledge, an approach to the structure of our soul.

---

[15] Cf. Sheppard (1997); O'Meara (1989), 166-9; O'Meara (2001); Dörrie and Baltes (2002), 239-41.
[16] Syrianus, *In met.* 25.8-10.
[17] Proclus, *In Eucl.* 36.17-37.3; cf. *In Tim.* II 136.5-20.
[18] See Porphyry, *In Ptol. harm.* 25.26-9; Boethius, *De inst. mus.* I.9.
[19] Proclus, *In Eucl.* 141.4-142.2.

To describe the Neoplatonic conception of Pythagorean music, I would like to refer, not only to the way in which this music's objects are conceived, but also, much more briefly, to the method(s) which might also characterize it. Returning to Iamblichus, we find in *On Pythagoreanism* vol. III an account of mathematical method in general, an account which may be taken to include music. Mathematical method involves procedures (division, definition, syllogistic argument) which are also found in logic and which can be described as following the best practices of reasoning as exemplified in logic.[20] Proclus finds a rigorous application of these methods in Euclid's geometry and tends to describe as 'geometrical' any argument or demonstration that represents the best of method in discursive reasoning.[21] An attempt to apply Euclidean method in music can be found in the short demonstration that Proclus adds to the little treatise of Pythagorean music that he inserts in his *Commentary on the Timaeus.*[22] In this demonstration, he proves in Euclidean fashion the theorem that 'if in a disjunct proportion[23] one of two mean terms is the arithmetic mean between the extremes, then the other mean term is the harmonic mean between the extremes'. A Euclidean demonstration of musical truths is already to be found in particular in the *Sectio canonis* attributed to Euclid and which is quoted by Porphyry in commenting on Ptolemy's *Harmonics* and also used by Boethius in his *De inst. mus.*

I would like to conclude the first part of my paper with some indications concerning the content of Pythagorean music, in particular as regards some key ideas that would have been of particular interest to Neoplatonic philosophers in their assimilation of what they considered to be Pythagorean music. Their sources of information for Pythagorean music would have included, not only the work of Nicomachus used by Iamblichus, but also texts attributed (rightly or wrongly) to such Pythagoreans as Philolaus, Archytas, and, as we have seen, Ptolemais of Cyrene. To judge from Porphyry's commentary on Ptolemy's *Harmonics*, other materials were also of interest, not only Ptolemy's work, but also texts of Aristoxenus (also cited by Proclus) and the *Sectio canonis*. Until the necessary research has been done, the question must remain open as to whether or not the Neoplatonic philosophers made any new theoretical contributions to the body of Pythagorean music that they found in these sources. At any rate the following ideas in Pythagorean music, among others, were of particular interest to them.

Pythagorean music, we have seen, deals with relations, or ratios, between numbers. These relations include the following, according to Iamblichus:[24] 'the

---

[20] See O'Meara (1989), 47.

[21] See O'Meara (1989), 171.

[22] Proclus, *In Tim.* II 173.11ff. Proclus also planned to add to his commentary an appendix on mathematical theorems which would probably have included harmonics (cf. *In Tim.*, III 76.24-9).

[23] On disjunct proportions cf. Nicomachus, *Intro. arith.* II.21, 121.15; Boethius, *De inst. mus.* II.13; Münxelhaus (1976), 84-6.

[24] *De comm. math. sc.* 30.13-14.

equal and unequal, the multiple, the epimoric, the epimeric, and suchlike'. This list corresponds to the series of relations explained, in the same order, by Nicomachus, who is followed by Iamblichus in the following book of *On Pythagoreanism*.[25] The various kinds of relations are described as follows. 'Equality' of relation between numbers is given when there is no excess or deficiency of one number in relation to another, whereas 'inequality' exists where there is such excess or deficiency. There are various kinds of inequality, including multiple, epimoric and epimeric relations. A *multiple* relation is when one number is a multiple of another (n:nx; e.g. 1:2). An *epimoric* relation occurs when one number includes another number together with a fraction of that number (n:n+n/x). The most important epimoric relations are the *hemiolic* (n:n+n/2; e.g. 2:3) and the *epitritic* (n:n+n/3; e.g. 3:4). An *epimeric* relation exists when a number includes another number together with several fractions of that number. Further types of relation are produced by combining the first types. Without going into the details of this, we should note at least that the list of kinds of relations, as forms of inequality, represents a progression in inequality, or rather increasing degrees of a falling away from equality (thus: double, one and a half, one and a third).[26] In showing how we can derive the various forms of inequality, represented by the various kinds of relation, from equality, Boethius claims: 'As unity is the origin of plurality and number, so equality is the origin of ratios'.[27] Equality is the equivalent, in music, of the one in the science prior to it, arithmetic. And as all numbers derive from the one, so the series of kinds of relations or ratios, representing increasing degrees of inequality, derive from equality.

The relations or ratios measuring intervals in music can be concordant (σύμφωνος) or discordant (διάφωνος). Porphyry quotes various definitions of concord given in various authors and suggests also that the Pythagoreans had various ways of referring to it.[28] One of these, naming concord as a unity (ἑνότης), corresponds to the definition Nicomachus gives of concord: 'Systems [i.e. combinations of one or more intervals] are concordant when the notes which bound them are different in magnitude, but when struck or sounded simultaneously, mingle with one another in such a way that the sound they produce is single in form (ἑνοειδή) and becomes as it were one sound. They are discordant when the sound from the two of them is heard as divided and unblended'.[29] The Nicomachean

---

[25] Nicomachus, *Intro. arith.* I, 17ff.; Iamblichus, *In Nic. arith. intro.* 35.11ff. Verity Harte has suggested to me that such a series may be what is being referred to in Plato, *Phileb.* 25a7-b1.

[26] See the arguments in Ptolemy, *Harm.* I.7; Augustine, *De mus.* I.ix.15; Boethius, *De inst. mus.* II.7.

[27] Boethius, *De inst. mus.* II.7 (transl. Bower); cf. Nicomachus, *Intro. arith.* I 23.6ff.; II 1.1.

[28] Porphyry, *In Ptol. harm.* 95.30-32; 96.

[29] Nicomachus, *Man.* ch. 12, 262.1-6 (transl. Barker); cf. Nicomachus, *Intro. arith.*, 115.2-3; Iamblichus, *In Nic. arith. intro.* 119.20 (ἑνοειδῶς); Boethius, *De inst. mus.* I.28. Compare Plato, *Phileb.* 17c11-d7 (above n. 25).

concept of concord sees it, then, as a unity in plurality, as diverse sounds which, while both mixing and remaining diverse, sound together *as if one*, in unison.[30] The word for this 'one-like' character of concord (ἐνοειδής) first occurs, I believe, in Nicomachus' music and would subsequently become a fundamental term in Neoplatonic metaphysics.

If concordant ratios are ratios that are unified, and equality, the source of musical ratios, is equivalent to the principle of unity in arithmetic, then we can conclude that the types of relations or ratios distinguished in Pythagorean music, to the extent that they are forms of inequality proximate to equality, represent degrees of concord.[31] And indeed the numerical relation closest to equality, the multiple relation, is described as the highest concord, the 'most complete' (κατακορεστάτη), the 'concord of concords'.[32] The first multiple relation (1:2) sounds as the octave. Next in the progressive departure from equality come epimoric relations of which the first are the hemiolic and epitritic: these, also, are recognized as concords, the hemiolic (2:3) sounding as the fifth, the epitritic (3:4) sounding as the fourth. These are the principal kinds of concord (or harmony) recognized by the Pythagoreans, according to the sources used by the Neoplatonists. However octave, fifth and fourth constitute an order of priority, a series (1:2; 2:3; 3:4) in which the octave is the first and highest member. The octave represents the nearest numerical relations come to unity, the closest diverse elements can come together to becoming one.

II

With these elements of Pythagorean music in hand, we may begin the inquiry I would like to introduce, in the second part of this paper, concerning the use and impact of Pythagorean music in late Antique Neoplatonic philosophy. As in Plato, music has, for the Neoplatonist, an important place in philosophical education. As Calcidius indicates: 'Music orders the soul rationally, calling her back to her former nature and making her at last into what she was when god at first made her'.[33] This educational purpose is the inspiration of Augustine's *De musica*[34] and is described

---

[30] Cf. Plato, *Rep.* 617b6, quoted by Plotinus in *Enn.* 4.3 12.24. Plotinus may be referring to the Pythagorean (Nicomachean?) concept of concord in *Enn.* 1.3 1.26 (τὸ μὴ ἕν); cf. *Enn.* 1.6 2.20.

[31] Cf. Boethius, *De inst. mus.* I.32; II.18. Cf. Plato, *Phileb.* 25d11-e2 (and above n. 25); Gersh (1996), 119-20.

[32] Nicomachus, *Man.* ch. 5, 244.19-21; ch. 9, 252.12; Porphyry, *In Ptol. harm.* 163.4; Iamblichus, *In Nicom. arith. intro.* 120.9-10; Damascius, *In Phaed.* I 368.10.

[33] Calcidius, *In Tim.* 267, 273.2-3; cf. Plato, *Tim.* 90c2-d7.

[34] Which deals however mostly with the part of music that comes after harmonics, i.e. rhythmics. An attempt to argue for an Augustinian spiritual education through music (from which however Platonist metaphysics is removed) can be found in Davenson (1942).

also by Aristides Quintilianus (III, 27), who refers to music, in the context of a Platonic vision of the descent of soul in the body,[35] as in the service of philosophy, assisting the soul in her return from this world to a transcendent life.

Late Antique Neoplatonists saw this return of the soul to her transcendent divine origins as a divinization, or assimilation of the soul to divine life. Indeed this divinization is the goal of their philosophy and their philosophy, in general and in its various branches, was seen as method or way for the soul to attain this goal. Thus the various sciences constituting the philosophical curriculum, the practical sciences (ethics, politics) and the theoretical sciences (physics, mathematics and metaphysics), represented stages in a progressive scale aimed at the transformation and divinization of the soul in which soul, beginning with the acquisition of lower forms of moral perfection or virtue (the ethical and political virtues, cultivated on the level of the study of the practical sciences) gained access to higher degrees of virtue and assimilation to divine life (the purificatory virtues and the theoretical virtues developed in the theoretical sciences).[36]

In taking account of this elaborate edificatory system, we might ask where music might fit in this scheme and how it might fulfil the function assigned to it in the scheme. Boethius suggests that, while sharing with the other mathematical sciences a theoretical function, music also has a moral role.[37] Fitting this to the Neoplatonic scale of virtues and sciences, it would seem to follow that music has, with the other mathematical sciences, a role fairly high up in the scale, in the cultivation of the theoretical virtues through theoretical science, but that it also has an edificatory function lower down in the scale, at the start of the education of the soul, on the level of the practical virtues and sciences. I would like to describe in more detail these two levels at which music can have a function in philosophical education, levels which might be taken as corresponding roughly (i) to the educational role given to music in Plato's *Republic* Books II-III, on the one hand, and (ii) to the role assigned to mathematical science in the image of the line at the end of book VI, on the other. I start with the lower level (i), music as part of moral education, the beginning level represented by the ethical and political virtues. As this subject is discussed by Anne Sheppard,[38] I will limit myself to making some brief remarks.

(i) Plato's appeal in *Republic* II-III for the use of music as an edificatory method is recalled by Olympiodorus in his commentary on the *Gorgias*. Olympiodorus compares the kind of music in question, which he describes as 'divine', with a 'popular' or degenerate type of music. Divine music acts on the passions, mastering them and ordering the soul.[39] Olympiodorus has in mind in particular the tripartite

---

[35]　Another chapter in Aristides Quintilianus on a Platonic descent of soul in the body (II,17) is discussed in detail by Festugière (1954).

[36]　Cf. O'Meara (2003), chs. 3-5.

[37]　Boethius, *De inst. mus.* I.1.179.

[38]　In her article 'Music Therapy in Neoplatonism', published in the present volume (in which she refers in particular to an important text in Proclus, *In Remp.* I 59.20-60.6).

[39]　Olympiodorus, *In Gorg.* p. 41.1-20. Cf. Plato, *Tim.* 47c6-e2; Aristotle, *Politics* VIII,

soul of the *Republic*, soul composed of reason, spirit and desire, in which the soul is brought into order when reason rules spirit and desire. Music can act on the irrational parts of the soul, since it can have an influence on spirit and on desire.[40] This suggests, I think, that the moral edification brought about by music that Olympiodorus has in mind is not so much that represented by the 'political virtues', in the late Neoplatonic scale of virtues, as that corresponding to what Neoplatonists described as the 'ethical virtues', which consist in a moral habituation preliminary to the cultivation of practical reason developed in the 'political virtues'.[41] Music then can play a role in the moral habituation of a soul preparatory to its access to the first stage of a philosophical education properly speaking, that represented by the practical sciences and virtues. As an example of this moralizing effect of music, Olympiodorus tells the story of how Pythagoras used music to cure a youth of his erotic passion.[42] A century earlier than Olympiodorus, also in Alexandria, Hypatia cured a pupil afflicted with the same passion, of which she was the object. But, Damascius tells us,[43] she did not use music: she had recourse to a more drastic remedy, a form of visual shock-therapy.

(ii) His passions sorted out, Hypatia's young admirer could begin his philosophical education in the practical sciences and virtues, progressing then to the higher levels of perfection represented by the theoretical sciences and virtues, where music might be met again, but this time as one of the mathematical sciences forming part of the theoretical sciences. Here the mathematical sciences, including music, act as a means for human reason to make the transition from theoretical knowledge of the world (physics) to the highest level of theoretical knowledge and virtue, that reached in metaphysics ('theology' or 'dialectic' as this science was then called), in which the soul reaches a grasp of the transcendent divine principles of her own nature and of the world.

The bridging function of mathematics, facilitating the passage from materiality to the knowledge of immaterial being had been described by Plato in his image of the line (*Rep.* VI, 511ad). Plotinus summarizes this idea as follows: 'He must be given mathematical studies to train him in philosophical thought and accustom him to firm confidence in the existence of the immaterial'.[44] This passage in Plotinus was used by Iamblichus in *On Pythagoreanism* III, was quoted again by Proclus and is often used later by the Alexandrian Neoplatonists.[45] It describes the training

---

5-7; Plutarch, *De Iside* 80, 384a (the Pythagoreans).

[40] Olympiodorus, *In Gorg.* 41.3-4.

[41] For a summary of the theory of 'ethical virtue', as distinguished from 'political virtue', see O'Meara (2003), 46-8.

[42] This story is often told in late Neoplatonic texts from Alexandria; cf. the *app. crit.* (*ad loc.*) of Olympiodorus and Boethius, *De inst. mus.* I 1.185. See Sheppard's paper in this volume.

[43] Damascius, *Vit. Is.* 43A.

[44] Plotinus, *Enn.* 1.3 3.5-7 (transl. Armstrong).

[45] Iamblichus, *De comm. math. sc.* 55.15-19; Proclus, *In Eucl.* p. 21.20-24; cf. the *app.*

in pure reason Neoplatonists found in mathematics, a study involving, they believed, the rational development of a knowledge of transcendent principles, thus preparing the soul for access to yet higher levels of knowledge. In the case of music, 'Pythagorean' music as these philosophers understood it, we can see that this music was a foretaste of arithmetic: it could lead back to arithmetic (the study of number *per se*), which in turn, as the highest of the mathematical sciences, would prepare the student for the transition to metaphysics.

The mediating, pivotal function of mathematics in the scale of sciences is expressed in the idea that mathematics anticipates, foreshadows, the science above it, metaphysics, as if a image of it, just as mathematics represents itself a kind of paradigm or model of the sciences below it in the scale of sciences. This idea is developed by Iamblichus in two chapters (15 and 30) of *On Pythagoreanism* vol. III (*De comm. math. sc.*) and by Proclus in his *In Eucl.* Iamblichus' chapters concern, as usual, the mathematical sciences in general, but we might ask if anything might be said concerning music in particular as an image of metaphysics and model of physics and of the lower, practical sciences. In ch. 15, Iamblichus uses expressions which could allude to music with reference to metaphysics, physics and ethics. However, these expressions (εὐταξία, ἀναλογία, equality, ὁμολογία, the λόγοι of virtues),[46] if capable of being linked to musical theory, are not necessarily and exclusively linked to music, and Iamblichus' indications remain, in general, rather sketchy. Later in the work *On Pythagoreanism*, in volumes V-VII (which are no longer extant), Iamblichus dealt with *arithmetic* in relation to physics, ethics and metaphysics and it is possible, due to the close link between arithmetic and music, to find in some fragments remaining from these books, as we will see, indications relating music to these other sciences.

If, however we look first at Proclus' parallel treatment of the matter in his *In Eucl.*, we find more specific information. Proclus explains the importance of mathematics for physics by referring to the account of the making of the universe in Plato's *Timaeus*, an account in which musical ratios play a crucial role. This allows us to take it that his references to 'good order' (εὐταξία), proportion, equality may be taken to concern music.[47] And, when he comes to mathematics as paradigmatic for ethics, Proclus seems to have music specifically in mind where he refers to the 'harmonious life', naming musical concords (among other mathematical paradigms) in relation to the principles of the virtues.[48] This suggests that we might do well to concentrate on the importance of music as a theoretical science for ethical science and for physics. I will discuss in particular music's value for ethical science and conclude my paper with some comments about music's relevance for physics.

---

    crit. (*ad loc.*) of Plotinus (1951-1973); Julian the Emperor, *Or.* IV.5 248b.

[46]   *De comm. math. sc.* 55.13 and 24-5; 56.7-8.

[47]   Proclus, *In Eucl.* 22.17-24.

[48]   Proclus, *In Eucl.* 24.4-14.

Going back to Iamblichus' work *On Pythagoreanism*, if we look at the fragments that have survived, as I have argued,[49] from vol. VI, *On Arithmetic in Ethical Matters*, we can find some clues concerning the importance that musical theory might have for ethics. Iamblichus claims that the first principle of ethics is 'measure'. Other principles are 'limit' and the 'perfect' (or 'complete'). 'Completion ($\tau\epsilon\lambda\epsilon\iota\acute{o}\tau\eta\varsigma$)', Iamblichus tells us, 'unitarily ($\dot{\epsilon}\nu o\epsilon\iota\delta\hat{\omega}\varsigma$) brings to fulfilment the best measure of life'.[50] This language suggests that a complete, fulfilled, happy life is based on measure and involves a unification of a diversity of components, on the model, perhaps, of the unitary effect achieved in musical concord. This, I think, is the suggestion being made in the fragment that follows: 'There is further as a model of good character ($\tauo\hat{u}$ $\sigma\pi ou\delta\alpha\acute{\iota}ou$) the mean which binds together the difference in numbers, making all harmonious ($\pi\rho o\sigma\acute{\eta}\gamma o\rho\alpha$), producing all proportions, and making the soul into something well-adjusted ($\epsilon\dot{u}\acute{\alpha}\rho\mu o\sigma\tau o\nu$)'.[51] Analogies or proportions, which are combinations of ratios, can be arithmetic, geometric or harmonic. But Iamblichus may be thinking more particularly of the Pythagorean concept of concord. A little further on in the fragments, Iamblichus compares particular numbers with particular virtues. Wisdom is compared with the monad, justice with the number 4 or 5 and moderation ($\sigma\omega\phi\rho o\sigma\acute{u}\nu\eta$) with the number 9, since moderation is the cause of 'symmetry'.[52] The symmetry in question may be that paradigmatically represented by the concord of the octave, since the identification of the virtue of moderation with the octave is made by Proclus in a passage of his commentary on Plato's *Republic* to which I would like now to turn.

The context of this passage is Plato's reference in the *Republic* to the virtue of moderation as being a concord ($\sigma u\mu\phi\omega\nu\acute{\iota}\alpha$).[53] Plato does not actually identify this concord as that of the octave,[54] but this is what Proclus takes him to mean. This concord includes and unifies all of the different components of the moral life. What this means is that the three parts of the soul, reason, spirit and desire, function together as one, thanks to the virtue of moderation which embraces them all. Proclus describes the relations between the several parts of the soul in terms of the intervals of the fourth (desire as related to spirit) and the fifth (spirit as related to reason). This expresses for him both the closer (natural) proximity of spirit to desire (both are irrational in nature), as in the interval of a fourth (e.g. 3:4), and the closer (moral) relation of spirit to reason (spirit obeys reason), as in the interval of a fifth (e.g. 2:3). As a concord, the fifth precedes the fourth, and both taken

---

[49] O'Meara (1989); the text is printed and translated on pp. 223-7.
[50] O'Meara (1989), p. 222.4-9.
[51] p. 224.12-15.
[52] p. 224.31-52. Cf. Aristides Quintilianus III.23.
[53] Plato, *Rep.* 430e, 431e; cf. 443d; Olympiodorus, *In Gorg.* 5.1-4. See Long (1991) for a study of the use by early Stoics of Pythagorean/Platonic harmonics with reference to the virtues.
[54] Cf. Winnington-Ingram's note in Festugière's transl. of Proclus, *In Remp.* II, p. 194.

together compose the highest concord, the octave.[55] Wisdom is the virtue of reason as the highest, ruling part of the soul; moderation and courage characterize spirit in its alliance with reason in controlling desire, moderation being found again in desire, but starting in reason. Spanning all parts of the soul, moderation is thus what unifies the soul's 'intervals' and the secondary concords (fifth and fourth) that they constitute, making *as if one* the life of the complex diversified whole that is the soul.[56] In explaining these harmonies of the virtuous soul, Proclus refers to the Pythagoreans and, as we can see, goes quite far in making use of their theory of musical concord. The effect of this, I think, is a particular emphasis on the *one-likeness* of the good life led by the whole made up of different parts that is the soul. This emphasis means also that the virtue of moderation emerges as of particular importance: it corresponds to the highest concord, the unity that the moral life can attain. But what of the fourth cardinal virtue, the virtue which is presupposed, according to Plato's *Republic*, by the other virtues, justice?

In one version of his lectures on Plato's *Phaedo*, Damascius provides us with a little more information on Proclus' comparison between musical intervals and the virtues. He tells us that wisdom is a concord between the knower and the object of knowledge, and that justice, too, is a concord: 'Justice is discriminating concord, whereas moderation is integrating concord; justice seeks its own in such a way as to keep each thing distinct (ἀσύγχυτον), yet common to all. Moderation, then, is concord between the controlling and the controlled, justice between the rulers and the ruled.'[57] The point seems to be that justice and moderation are equal and complementary virtues, each expressing a different aspect of the Pythagorean concept of concord according to Nicomachus:[58] the aspect of distinction between functions which are not confused, justice, and the aspect of the unified order that is achieved, moderation. It is the same concord, in short, whose aspects find expression in the concepts of justice and moderation. Justice and moderation, as virtues concerning the whole structure of soul's life, contrast, it seems, with the two other cardinal virtues which have to do with subordinate intervals in or between a part or parts of the whole.

Damascius indicates that he does not agree with all of what he reports from Proclus.[59] This disagreement is more extensive in another version of his lectures on the *Phaedo*.[60] There, he makes the point[61] that wisdom is to be seen, not as a purely cognitive activity, but as a practical virtue involving desire, and is rather a concord

[55] As for example in the series 6, 8, 9, 12, where 8 and 9 are fourths and fifths in relation to the octave 6:12. Cf. Nicomachus, *Man.* ch. 6; *Sectio canonis*, prop. 6; Iamblichus, *In Nic. arith. intro.* 120.7ff.
[56] Proclus, *In Remp.* I 211.26-213.27.
[57] Damascius, *In Phaed.* II 55.
[58] Above, 136, 139.
[59] Damascius, *In Phaed.* II 55.9-11.
[60] Damascius, *In Phaed.* I 372.
[61] Made in more detail in II 55.

of what benefits and is benefited. He also rejects the contrast between justice and moderation, as virtues of the whole ('octaves'), and wisdom and courage, as virtues of parts (lesser concords): rather, wisdom and courage are also octaves, extending throughout the whole of the soul. If it is true, Damascius concedes, that wisdom applies more to reason, and courage more to spirit, it is also the case that moderation also is more proper to desire, 'imposing a certain restraint on its shamelessness and looseness', as in the case, we might add, of Pythagoras' wanton youth and Hypatia's amorous student. Finally, Damascius claims that, just as all virtues are present in all of the soul, so also in each part of the soul are to be found concord and harmonic ratio, bringing into harmony the many contrary desires in each part.

Damascius, we might conclude, goes very far in throwing into confusion Proclus' correlations between virtues and musical intervals. Proclus' distinction between the octave(s) that are justice and moderation and the secondary concords that are wisdom and courage disappears: all four virtues appear to be octaves. And within each part of the soul emerge further complexities, further wholes composed of parts: they, too, require unification through structures of concordance. Whatever we may think of this disagreement between Damascius and Proclus, and whether or not we might feel that there is something arbitrary in these combinations of music and ethics, the important point, I think, is that in approaching ethical concepts, the late Neoplatonists could find in music a theory of relations, of structure and in particular of unification, which influenced the way in which they saw the moral life, a life whose paradigms, they believed, were to be found in a higher theoretical science, in music.

I would like to conclude with just a few words about the relation between Pythagorean music and physics. We could compare music and physics along lines similar to those we have followed in relating music to ethics. However our enquiry would become very extensive. The reason for this is the fact that in his account of the making of the world in the *Timaeus*, Plato describes the making of the world-soul in terms of a very involved and quite obscure theory of harmonic intervals. The soul, in turn, orders the world, which is in consequence an expression of soul, a structure also representing harmonic relations, constituting what Augustine calls the *carmen universitatis*.[62] The extraordinary complexities and richness of Plato's harmonical accounts of the constitution of the soul and of the world mean that the Neoplatonist commentators on Plato's *Timaeus* were led to have recourse to the literature of Pythagorean music at their disposal in order to explain Plato's text. Thus Proclus' incomplete but nevertheless enormous commentary on the *Timaeus*, based principally on the commentaries (now lost) of Iamblichus and Syrianus, is to a considerable extent devoted to presenting Pythagorean music in connection with explaining the production of soul and of the world. This entails, for our inquiry, a task not yet attempted and which cannot be

---

[62] Augustine, *De mus.* VI.xi.29.

attempted now: the reconstruction in detail of Pythagorean music as known and integrated by Neoplatonism, and the exploitation of this reconstruction in determining how the Neoplatonists' version of Pythagorean music is used in, and affects, their accounts of the nature of soul and of the ordering of the world. We are very far at the moment from being able to see the results of such an inquiry.[63] However, I believe we can at least expect that Pythagorean music will have the function of a paradigmatic science for physics, a science of relations providing, along with the other mathematical sciences, models of concepts of use in sorting out the organization of soul and of the world.[64]

References

(i) *Texts*

Aristides Quintilianus (1963), *De musica*, ed. R. Winnington-Ingram, Teubner, Leipzig.

Augustine (1947), *De musica*, ed. and transl. G. Finaert and F. Thonnard, Desclée de Brouwer, Paris.

Boethius (1867), *De institutione arithmetica*, *De institutione musica*, ed. G. Friedlein, Teubner, Leipzig.

Boethius (1995), *Institution arithmétique*, ed. and transl. J.-Y. Guillaumin, Les Belles Lettres, Paris.

Calcidius (1975), *Commentarium in Timaeum*, ed. J.H. Waszink, Warburg Institute, London and Brill, Leiden.

Damascius (1977), *In Phaedonem*, ed. and transl. L.G. Westerink, *The Greek Commentaries on Plato's Phaedo*, vol. 2, North-Holland, Amsterdam.

Damascius (1959), *In Philebum*, ed. and transl. L.G. Westerink, North-Holland, Amsterdam.

Damascius (1999), *Vita Isidori*, ed. and transl. P. Athanassiadi, *Damascius. The Philosophical History*, Apamea Cultural Association, Athens.

Iamblichus (1891), *De communi mathematica scientia*, ed. N. Festa, Teubner, Leipzig.

Iamblichus (1894), *In Nicomachi Arithmeticam introductionem*, ed. H. Pistelli, Teubner, Leipzig.

Nicomachus (1866), *Introductio arithmetica*, ed. R. Hoche, Teubner, Leipzig.

Nicomachus (1895), *Manuale harmonicum*, ed. K. von Jan, *Musici scriptores graeci*, Teubner, Leipzig.

Olympiodorus (1970), *In Platonis Gorgiam commentaria*, ed. L.G. Westerink, Teubner, Leipzig.

Philoponus (1999), *Ad Nicomachi Introductionem arithmeticam*, ed. G. Giardina, CUECM, Catania. (Symbolon, 20).

Plotinus (1951-73), *Enneads*, ed. P. Henry and H.R. Schwyzer, and, Desclée de Brouwer, Paris, and L'Édition Universelle, Brussels (editio maior).

Porphyry (1932), *In Ptolemaei Harmonica commentarium*, ed. I. Düring, Elander, Göteborg.

---

[63]   For a recent study in this area, see Lernould (2000).

[64]   I am indebted to the participants in the colloquium for their questions and help, in particular Anne Sheppard, Verity Harte and Peter Adamson.

Proclus (1903), *In Platonis Timaeum*, ed. E. Diehl, Teubner, Leipzig.
Proclus (1899), *In Platonis Rempublicam*, ed. W. Kroll, Teubner, Leipzig.
Ptolemy (1930), *Harmonica*, ed. I. Düring,Elander, Göteborg.
Syrianus (1902), *In Metaphysica commentaria*, ed. W. Kroll, Reimer, Berlin.

(ii) *Translations and Studies*

Barker, A. (1989), *Greek Musical Writings Vol. II Harmonic and Acoustic Theory*, Cambridge University Press, Cambridge (includes transl. of Nicomachus, *Man.*; Ptolemy, *Harm.*; Aristides Quintilianus).
Bower, C. (1989), *Fundamentals of Music*, Yale University Press, New Haven (transl. of Boethius *De inst. mus.*)
Burkert, W. (1972), *Lore and Science in Ancient Pythagoreanism*, transl. E.L. Minar, Harvard University Press, Cambridge, Mass.
Davenson, H. (1942) (H.-I. Marrou), *Traité de la musique selon l'esprit de saint Augustin*, Baconnière, Neuchatel.
Dörrie, H. and Baltes, M. (2002), *Der Platonismus in der Antike*, vol. VI.1, Frommann-Holzboog, Stuttgart.
D'Ooge, M.L., Robbins, F., Karpinski, L. (1926), *Nicomachus of Gerasa: Introduction to Arithmetic*, Macmillan, New York (transl. and commentary).
Festugière, A.J. (1954), 'L'Ame et la musique, d'après Aristide Quintilien', in his *Etudes de philosophie grecque*, Vrin, Paris, 1971, 463-86.
Festugière, A.J. (1966-1968), *Proclus: Commentaire sur le Timée*, Vrin, Paris (transl.).
Festugière, A.J. (1970), *Proclus: Commentaire sur la République*, Vrin, Paris (transl.).
Gersh, S. (1992), 'Porphyry's Commentary on the "Harmonics" of Ptolemy and Neoplatonic Musical Theory', in S. Gersh and C. Kannengiesser (eds), *Platonism in Late Antiquity*, University of Notre Dame Press, Notre Dame, 141-55.
Gersh, S. (1996), *Concord in Discourse. Harmonics and Semiotics in Late Classical and Early Medieval Platonism*, Mouton de Gruyter, Berlin.
Lernould, A. (2000), 'Mathématiques et physique chez Proclus: L'interprétation proclienne de la notion de 'lien' en *Timée* 31b-32c' in G. Bechtle and D. O'Meara (eds), *La philosophie des mathématiques de l'Antiquité tardive*, Éditions universitaires, Fribourg, 129-47.
Lloyd, A.C. (1990), *The Anatomy of Neoplatonism*, Clarendon Press, Oxford.
Long, A.A. (1991), 'The Harmonics of Stoic Virtue', in *Oxford Studies in Ancient Philosophy*, Supplementary volume, *Aristotle and the Later Tradition*, Clarendon Press, Oxford, 97-116.
Münxelhaus, B. (1976), *Pythagoras musicus. Zur Rezeption der pythagoreischen Musiktheorie als quadrivialer Wissenschaft im lateinischen Mittelalter*, Verlag für systematische Musikwissenschaft, Bonn.
O'Meara, D. (1989), *Pythagoras Revived. Mathematics and Philosophy in Late Antiquity*, Clarendon Press, Oxford.
O'Meara, D. (2001), 'Intentional Objects in Later Neoplatonism', in D. Perler (ed.), *Ancient and Medieval Theories of Intentionality*, Brill, Leiden, 115-25.
O'Meara, D. (2003), *Platonopolis. Platonic Political Philosophy in Late Antiquity*, Clarendon Press, Oxford.
Sheppard, A. (1997), '*Phantasia* and Mathematical Projection in Iamblichus', *Syllecta Classica* 8, 113-20.

Chapter Eight

Music Therapy in Neoplatonism[1]

Anne Sheppard

I

Dominic O'Meara's chapter in this volume, 'The Music of Philosophy in Late Antiquity', examines the Neoplatonic treatment of 'Pythagorean' music, concentrating on 'harmonics', i.e. music as one of the mathematical sciences. Although the Neoplatonists were able to find a Platonic basis for this approach to music, as O'Meara shows, it may nevertheless seem far removed from well-known Platonic texts such as *Republic* 3 where *mousikê* brings together music and poetry rather than music and mathematics. However, the Neoplatonists also saw music as having an educational and therapeutic role. O'Meara mentions this, citing a passage from Olympiodorus' commentary on the *Gorgias*,[2] but he then turns to the Neoplatonists' use of music as a mathematical paradigm of ethics, rather than exploring further their view of the effect of music on the passions. In fact, as I shall argue, the Neoplatonists integrated the traditional Greek view of music's effect on the passions into their system and associated this too with Pythagoras.

'Pythagorean' music, in O'Meara's sense, and music as therapy are brought together in a passage from the fifth essay of Proclus' commentary on the *Republic*.[3] Here, in an essay in which he is considering a series of problems arising from Plato's discussion of poetry, Proclus claims that, according to Plato, there are four types of *mousikê*. The first, and greatest, is philosophy, following *Phaedo* 61a; the second is the inspired poetry described at *Phaedrus* 245a. The third is presented by Proclus as follows:

λέγει δὲ ἄρα καὶ τὸ τρίτον μουσικῆς εἶδος, οὐκέτι τοῦτο καθάπερ τὸ προρρηθὲν ἐνθεαστικόν, ἀναγωγὸν δὲ ὅμως ἀπὸ τῶν φαινομένων ἁρμονιῶν εἰς τὸ ἀφανὲς τῆς θείας ἁρμονίας κάλλος· φιλόκαλος γὰρ καὶ ὁ τοιοῦτος μουσικός, ὥσπερ καὶ ὁ ἐρωτικός, εἰ καὶ ὁ μὲν δι' ὄψεως, ὁ δὲ δι' ἀκοῆς ἀναμιμνήσκεται τοῦ καλοῦ.

---

[1] This paper is a revised and expanded version of my response to Dominic O'Meara's paper at the colloquium which gave rise to this volume.
[2] Olympiodorus, *In Gorg.* 40.30-41.24. Cf. O'Meara in this volume, 140-1 and n. 39.
[3] *In Remp.* I 56.20-60.13.

Then he also talks about the third kind of *mousikê*: this one is no longer inspired, like the one mentioned before, but nevertheless it leads up from perceptible harmonies to the imperceptible beauty of the divine harmony. For this kind of *mousikos* too loves beauty, just like the lover, although the latter is reminded of beauty by means of sight while the former is reminded by means of hearing.

Proclus had described the first type of *mousikos* as a lover as well as a philosopher, one who tunes his soul taking the divine harmony as a model. It looks from this passage as though the third type of *mousikos*, who is also a lover, is at the same level as the philosopher: notice in particular how Proclus describes such a person as going from perceptible to imperceptible harmonies – the imperceptible harmonies cannot be heard but are accessible to reasoning. Then Proclus comes to the fourth type of *mousikê*:

λέγει δὴ οὖν καὶ ἄλλην ἐπὶ ταύταις μουσικήν, τὴν παιδευτικὴν τῶν ἠθῶν διά τε ἁρμονιῶν τῶν εἰς ἀρετὴν καὶ ῥυθμῶν, ἀνευρίσκουσαν τίνες μὲν ἁρμονίαι καὶ ῥυθμοὶ παιδεύειν δύνανται τὰ πάθη τῶν ψυχῶν καὶ πλάττειν ἤθεσι βελτίστοις ἐν πάσαις πράξεσι καὶ περιστάσεσιν, τίνες δὲ ἐναντίοι τούτοις ἐκμελεῖς αὐτὰς ἀποτελοῦσιν ἐπιτείνουσαι ἢ χαλῶσαι καὶ εἰς ἀναρμοστίαν ἄγουσαι καὶ ἀρρυθμίαν.

Finally he talks about yet another kind of *mousikê* in addition to these, one which educates the character by means of modes[4] and rhythms which lead to virtue, discovering which modes and rhythms can educate the passions of the soul and mould them with excellent character traits in all actions and circumstances, and which ones, opposite to these, put souls out of tune by tightening or loosening them and leading them to disharmony and lack of rhythm.

This type of *mousikê* educates the passions and Proclus goes on to relate it explicitly to the discussion of music in Plato, *Republic* 3.

Of these four types of *mousikê*, only two are what we would call 'music' and these two correspond to the two levels at which, according to O'Meara, music has a function in Neoplatonic philosophical education.[5] Proclus is following not just Plato but classical Greek tradition in general in classing both poetry and music as *mousikê*, although the claim that philosophy too is *mousikê*, indeed the greatest *mousikê*, is of course Platonic. It is also worth noting that Proclus' third type of *mousikê* is the only one for which he does not appeal to any 'proof text' in Plato. This is hardly surprising if, as I suppose, this third type is the 'Pythagorean' music discussed in O'Meara's paper.

---

[4] Since Proclus has Plato's discussion of different musical modes very much in mind, I translate ἁρμονίαι here as 'modes' rather than 'harmonies'.

[5] See O'Meara's paper in this volume, 140-1.

II

Although, as O'Meara notes at the end of his paper, there is more work to be done by way of reconstructing this 'Pythagorean' music, my concern here is rather with Proclus' fourth type of music, educational or therapeutic music. Greek thinkers had long recognized the powerful effect of music on the emotions; discussion of this idea before Plato is associated with the name of Damon and allusions to it can also be found in Aristophanes.[6] In *Republic* 3 398c-400 Plato's Socrates discusses which musical modes, instruments and rhythms should be allowed in the ideal state. It is assumed that some modes, instruments and rhythms will be more effective than others in training the characters of the state's future guardians. This passage of the *Republic* was discussed critically by Aristotle in *Politics* 8 1342a28-b17. Aristotle criticizes Socrates for accepting the Phrygian mode while rejecting the *aulos* among musical instruments, arguing that both are orgiastic and arouse the emotions or passions (*pathê*). The Dorian mode, on the other hand, is a mean among modes and well-suited to education.[7]

Both Plato and Aristotle thought that it was possible to train the emotions and that habituation had an important role to play in moral education. Their discussions of the effect of music on the emotions occur in the context of education. The notion of music as therapy, as some kind of cure, comes to the fore with Aristotle's pupil, Theophrastus. The surviving evidence for Theophrastus' views on music includes both remarks on the psychological effects of music and some claims that music can actually cure bodily afflictions, such as sciatica.[8] The following statement comes almost at the end of a long fragment of Theophrastus preserved in Porphyry's commentary on Ptolemy's *Harmonics*:

μία δὲ φύσις τῆς μουσικῆς· κίνησις τῆς ψυχῆς ἡ κατ᾽ ἀπόλυσιν γινομένη τῶν διὰ τὰ πάθη κακῶν.

The nature of music is one. It is the movement of the soul that occurs in correspondence with its release from the evils due to the emotions.[9]

Somewhere in the period between Theophrastus and the Neoplatonists, the idea that music can be used for the therapy of the passions became associated with Pythagoreanism. Plutarch refers to 'the Pythagoreans' as using the sound of the lyre to charm and cure the emotional and irrational part of the soul, while Sextus Empiricus tells a story about Pythagoras' use of the *aulos* to sober up some

---

[6]   See Barker (1989), 457-8 n. 1.
[7]   See also Plato, *Laws* 653c-673a.
[8]   See Theophrastus frs. 719-725 (music and the soul) and fr. 726A-C (music and the body).
[9]   Translation from Theophrastus fr. 716, ll. 130-31; cf. Barker (1989), 118.

drunken youths.[10]

Book 2 of Aristides Quintilianus' work on music deals at length with the effect of music on the emotions. The idea that music can be therapeutic is particularly discussed in 2.5 and also appears at the end of 2.7. Aristides also considers Plato, *Republic* 399ab in 1.9. Aristides Quintilianus was probably writing some time in the third century AD. It has been argued that he used Porphyry's commentary on Ptolemy's *Harmonics* and that his work shows the influence of Neoplatonism in various ways.[11] Whether this is right or not, he does seem to be familiar with some of the ideas current in the Platonism of late antiquity. We may at least treat him as evidence that the notion of music as therapy was part of the late antique intellectual background and we should not be surprised to find it taken up and developed by the Neoplatonist philosophers.

Iamblichus offers a brief but interesting discussion of music in *De mysteriis* 3.9. Throughout *De mysteriis* 3 Iamblichus argues that supernatural phenomena are not to be explained in human terms, and so in chapter 9, when he comes to discuss divine possession (*enthousiasmos*) in the context of religious rites involving music, he argues against two common ideas about music. The first of these is τὸ μὲν οὖν κινητικόν τι καὶ παθητικὸν εἶναι τὴν μουσικήν, καὶ τὸ τῶν αὐλῶν ἐμποιεῖν ἢ ἰατρεύειν τὰ πάθη τῆς παρατροπῆς ('that music is moving and sensuous, and that the sound of pipes causes or heals disordered passions'.[12]) Iamblichus declares that therapy of this kind is a product of human skill and nothing to do with the divine. He then goes on to argue that such possession is due rather to the kinship between musical harmony and the divine harmony of the universe. However he is concerned to differentiate his own view from another view which represents both the body and the soul as sharing in the experience of the music; this other view uses the terms *aperasis, apokatharsis* and *iatreia* ('purging, purification and cure') and holds that the soul itself consists of harmony and rhythm.

Iamblichus in the *De mysteriis* is of course responding to Porphyry's *Letter to Anebo*, and 3.9, like many chapters of the work, begins with a quotation from Porphyry which Iamblichus wishes to rebut. I suggest that he found both the idea that music can be a kind of therapy and the connection between harmony in the soul and the divine harmony in Porphyry. We have already seen that Porphyry included Theophrastus' remarks on music as therapy in his commentary on Ptolemy's *Harmonics*. Iamblichus' reasons for denying the relevance of therapeutic music to religious rites are clear enough. He has more difficulty in distinguishing his own understanding of the relationship between the human soul and divine harmony from Porphyry's. From our perspective both of them subscribe to the theory of

---

[10] Plutarch, *De Iside* 80, 384a (cf. O'Meara's paper in this volume, 140-1 n.39); Sextus Empiricus, *Adv. Math.* 6.8 (cf. Barker, 1989, 493-4 n.209).

[11] See Mathiesen (1983), 10-13.

[12] Translation from Clarke, Dillon and Hershbell (2003), 139. See also the brief discussion in Clarke (2001), 78.

'Pythagorean' music as described by O'Meara; but, if Iamblichus is to be believed, they offered different explanations of how the human soul is able to respond to the divine harmony.

If I am right, the distinction between a mathematical kind of 'Pythagorean' music and a therapeutic kind was already present in Porphyry. Iamblichus in the *De mysteriis* is concerned neither with education nor with healing but with religious rites, and so reworks the Neoplatonic view of music for his own purposes.

The effect of music on the emotions is also discussed in another passage from the fifth essay of Proclus' *Commentary on the Republic*, I 60.14-63.15. Here Proclus is expounding Plato, *Republic* 3 398c-400, and asks what kinds of modes (*harmoniai*) and rhythms Plato considers useful in education. Proclus tries to answer Aristotle's criticism of this passage, mentioned above, and argues that it is the Dorian mode which is suitable for education while the Phrygian, admitted by Plato but regarded by Aristotle as orgiastic, is appropriate to sacred rites. He appeals to other passages of Plato (*Laches* 188d and *Minos* 318b)[13] in support of this interpretation. The result is a typical piece of late Neoplatonic exegesis, assuming unity in Plato's own thought and seeking to reconcile Plato and Aristotle. The Neoplatonic interest in religious ritual, so evident in Iamblichus, is useful to Proclus here since it allows him to distinguish between the Dorian and the Phrygian modes, as Aristotle did, while claiming that both have beneficial effects on the emotions.

This paper started with a passage of Olympiodorus, discussed by O'Meara, which mentions the effect of music on the emotions.[14] As O'Meara notes, Olympiodorus tells a story about Pythagoras using music to cure a young man of his erotic passion. This story is in fact simply a variation on the material I have already discussed from Plutarch and Sextus Empiricus.[15] Its tralatician nature is betrayed by a certain confusion in Olympiodorus' account as to whether the instrument used was a lyre or an *aulos*.[16] Just before he tells this story Olympiodorus mentions the use of a trumpet in rousing to war and of *auloi* or a lyre in rousing to pleasure. Both the mention of the trumpet and the Pythagoras story are found in a passage of Ammonius, Proclus' pupil and Olympiodorus' teacher, and the trumpet is mentioned again in a similar passage of the late Alexandrian commentator, David, immediately after a reference to Olympiodorus.[17] Ammonius alludes to 'theatrical melodies' (*theatrika melê*) and David to 'theatrical instruments' (*theatrika organa*) as having a relaxing effect on the soul; this is perhaps another way of referring to the effects of the *aulos* and the lyre.

---

[13]　The Neoplatonists accepted the *Minos* as genuinely Platonic.

[14]　See 149 above, with n. 2.

[15]　See 151-2 above.

[16]　The lyre is mentioned at 41.8, but by 41.11 Olympiodorus is referring to 'the *aulos* or the lyre'.

[17]　See Ammonius *In Isagogen* 13.21-31 and David *In Isagogen* 64.32-65.9.

Another late Alexandrian commentator, Elias, offers much the same material with a striking addition.[18] He too tells the story of Pythagoras' use of music as therapy; he too mentions *theatrika mele* as relaxing and the use of the trumpet in war. Like David he also alludes to animals persuaded to go out to pasture by the music of the *syrinx*. Although Elias says μέχρι τῆς σήμερον ἔχομεν ἐπάσματα μουσικά ('we have musical incantations down to the present day'), the parallels not only with Ammonius, Olympiodorus and David but also with the earlier material I have discussed in this paper suggest that all this talk of the effects of music is traditional, handed down from one commentator to another, with little reference to personal experience or the realities of life in late antiquity. The Elias passage concludes with two stories about the power of music. One is again highly traditional, the Homeric story of the bard left with Clytemnestra by Agamemnon.[19] The second is as follows:

καὶ Συνέσιος δὲ ὁ φιλόσοφος ὁ γενόμενος ὕστερον Κυρήνης ἐπίσκοπος βαρβάρων ἐπιστάντων τῇ Κυρήνῃ διά τινων μελῶν ἔτρεψε τούτους, καὶ φεύγοντες ἔκοπτον ἀλλήλους μηδενὸς διώκοντος.

And Synesius the philosopher, who later became bishop of Cyrene, routed the barbarians, when they attacked Cyrene, by means of certain tunes and as they fled they struck each other although no-one was pursuing them.

I have been unable to discover any other source for this remarkable story. Although Synesius' own *Letters* contain a number of allusions to his role in defending Cyrene against barbarian attacks[20] nothing is said, either there or in any other source known to me, about his use of music in such a defence.

Since more than a hundred years separate Synesius from Elias, the story could hardly be described as a contemporary reference. It is nevertheless very unusual for a Neoplatonic commentator to allude in this way to an event involving a real person in a past which, if not exactly recent, is not yet remote. The lapse of time may indeed explain how music has made its way into the story: Synesius' defence of Cyrene against the barbarians had presumably become something of a legend and Synesius himself has been credited with powers like those of Pythagoras. We may wonder whether Elias' presumed Christianity made him particularly interested in using a story about a Christian bishop who was also a Neoplatonist philosopher.

O'Meara's paper indicates the importance of 'Pythagorean' music for the

---

[18] Elias, *In Isagogen* 31.8-25.

[19] See *Odyssey* 3.267ff. Since Homer says that Clytemnestra only gave in to Aegisthus after the bard had been abandoned on a desolate island, his virtue and *sôphrosunê* are emphasized in the critical tradition, as it appears in the scholia, Strabo and Athenaeus. This is picked up by Proclus who at *In Remp.* I 194.18-27 describes him as making Clytemnestra's irrational soul *sôphrôn* by means of educational songs. See Sheppard (1980), 169.

[20] See, for example, *Letters* 104, 130, 132 and 133.

Neoplatonists as part of mathematical science. We saw at the beginning of my paper that O'Meara's suggestion that the Neoplatonists also believed that music had a function at a lower, less scientific level is confirmed by Proclus' classification of levels of *mousikê* in the fifth essay of the *Commentary on the Republic*. I have tried to show that alongside the ample material on 'Pythagorean' music in Neoplatonic texts there is also a good deal of evidence for an interest in the effect of music on the emotions. Here, as so often elsewhere, the Neoplatonists were building on earlier tradition. The Neoplatonists consider the effect of music on the emotions from several different points of view: sometimes, particularly when engaged in exegesis of Plato's *Republic* or *Gorgias*, they think in terms of music's role in moral education; at other times they pick up on the tradition, found from Theophrastus onwards, that music can function as therapy; in Iamblichus in particular we find an interest in the role of music in religious ritual.

The notion of music as therapy is associated with the name of Pythagoras from Plutarch and Sextus Empiricus down to David and Elias. Although I have referred to the type of music discussed by O'Meara as 'Pythagorean' throughout much of this paper, I have deliberately put the term 'Pythagorean' in quotation marks. The Neoplatonists regarded therapeutic music as also included in Pythagorean theory. Perhaps we should describe the two levels of music under discussion as scientific and therapeutic music, or even – since according to the Neoplatonists it is the rational soul which responds to 'scientific' music, the irrational soul to 'therapeutic' music – as rational and irrational music, rather than as 'Pythagorean' music and music of some other kind. A full account of Neoplatonic views of music would need to cover both the scientific and the therapeutic kind. Music is, after all, a complex phenomenon: regarded nowadays as one of the arts, it is nevertheless susceptible both to scientific analysis and to philosophical study. It should come as no surprise that the Neoplatonic view of music reflects that complexity.

References

Ammonius (1891), *In Porphyrii Isagogen*, ed. A. Busse (*Commentaria in Aristotelem Graeca* 4.3), Reimer, Berlin.
Aristides Quintilianus (1963), *De musica*, ed. R.P. Winnington-Ingram, Teubner, Leipzig.
Barker, A. (1989), *Greek Musical Writings Vol. II Harmonic and Acoustic Theory*, Cambridge University Press, Cambridge.
Clarke, E.C. (2001), *Iamblichus' De Mysteriis: a manifesto of the miraculous*, Ashgate, Aldershot.
David (1900), *In Porphyrii Isagogen*, ed. A. Busse (*Commentaria in Aristotelem Graeca* 18.2), Reimer, Berlin.
Elias (1900), *In Porphyrii Isagogen*, ed. A. Busse (*Commentaria in Aristotelem Graeca* 18.1), Reimer, Berlin.
Iamblichus (2003), *On the Mysteries*, eds E.C. Clarke, J.M. Dillon and J.P. Hershbell, Society of Biblical Literature, Atlanta (also Brill, Leiden, 2004).
Mathiesen, T.J. (1983), *Aristides Quintilianus*, On Music, In Three Books. *Translated with*

Introduction, Commentary and Annotations, Yale University Press, New Haven.

Olympiodorus (1970), *In Platonis Gorgiam*, ed. L.G. Westerink, Teubner, Leipzig.

Proclus (1899), *In Platonis Rempublicam*, ed. W. Kroll, Teubner, Leipzig.

Sheppard, A.D.R. (1980), *Studies on the 5th and 6th essays of Proclus' Commentary on the Republic*, Vandenhoeck and Ruprecht, Göttingen.

Theophrastus (1992), *Sources for his Life, Writings, Thought and Influence*, eds W.W. Fortenbaugh, P.M. Huby, R.W. Sharples (Greek and Latin) and D. Gutas (Arabic), vol. II, Brill, Leiden.

Index of Works and Passages Cited from Ancient Authors

General Index

For entries marked * the Index of Works and Passages Cited should also be consulted.

Abas 78
Academy 73 n. 3, 80, 95-6, 102
    Academic Sceptics 111
acid 91-2, 94
acoustics 82
Acron 73
adhesion 98
Aegimius of Elis 78
Aëtius 85
affections, feelings 96, 116 *and see*
    emotions, passions
Agamemnon 153
ageing 63
Aias 78
air 18
Alcamenes of Abydos 78
Alcmaeon of Croton 78, 80, 84, 98
* Alexander of Aphrodisias 73 n. 4, 83
Alexandria, Alexandrian 83, 89
algebra 31
* Ammonius 153
analogy 37, 45, 46-7 n. 72
analysis 81, 102, 124
anatomy 4, 17, 66 n. 19, 68 n. 21, 76-7,
    79-81, 87-90, 98-9
Anaxagoras 14 n. 24, 84
Anaximander 19-20
Anaximenes 19-20
anger 116
animals 55-71, 99, 113, 115 *and see*
    zooology
* Anonymus Londiniensis 73, 77 n. 14, 79,
    93-5, 100-102
Antiphon 9, 35 n. 38
appearances 4, 98 *and see* phenomena
approximate, approximation 123, 128
Aquinas 39 n. 49
Aratus 28 n. 16
Archestratus of Gela 101 n. 66
architects, architecture 110, 112, 116, 123
Archytas 137

argument 19, 111, 115-17, 128
Aristarchus 122
* Aristophanes 150
Aristotelian, Aristotelianism 87, 102 *and*
    see Lyceum, Peripatetics
* Aristotle 1-5, 6 n. 12, 20, 23-71, 73-4, 77 n.
    14, 78-83, 85-7, 93-4, 99, 101-102,
    114, 119, 121, 127 n. 28, 152
    authenticity of works 82
Aristoxenus 133, 137
arithmetic, numbers 31-2, 34, 37-41, 45-8,
    56, 60 n. 13, 67, 112, 116-17, 131,
    134-6, 138-9, 142
arteries 17, 89, 115
Asclepiades 50, 85
astronomy 2, 5, 9-10, 17-18, 25, 28 n. 16,
    29, 38, 41, 44 n. 68, 48, 50, 61,
    110, 114, 116, 122-3, 134-5
Athenaeus 89, 92, 153 n. 19
* Augustine 132
axiom, axiomatic 23-4, 27, 28 n. 16, 29 n.
    18, 31-2, 34, 39-42, 44 n. 67, 45-6,
    52, 111, 117-18, 120-121,123,128

Babylon, Babylonians 10
bandages 76, 87-8
bile 91, 94
biochemistry 50
biology 46 n. 72, 50, 55-71, 81-2, 88-90, 132
bitter (taste) 91-92, 94, 96
blood 7 n. 72, 17-18, 59, 61, 65-6, 91, 94-5,
    97, 101
* Boethius 132-3
Bologna 66 n. 19
bone 61, 64, 67 n. 20
botany 75 n. 10, 78, 88 *and see* plants
boundaries, disciplinary 65, 69-70
brain 67, 83, 101, 115-16, 125, 127
breath 74-5, 94 *and see pneuma*
bruises 76
Bryson 9, 34-7, 51

Printed in the United States
by Baker & Taylor Publisher Services